Development Economics in the Twenty-First Century

T0298390

Development Economics has been identified as a homogeneous body of theory since the 1950s, concerned both with the study of development issues and with the shaping of more effective policies for less advanced economies.

Development Economics in the Twenty-First Century brings together an international contributor team in order to explore the origins and evolution of development economics. This book highlights the different elements of 'high development theory' through a precise reconstruction of the different theoretical approaches that developed between the 1950s and the 1970s. These include the theory of balanced and unbalanced growth theory, the debate on international trade, the concept of dualism, dependency theory, structuralism, and the analysis of poverty and institutions. The chapters highlight the relevance and usefulness of these analyses for the contemporary theoretical debate on development issues.

Comparative perspectives are explored and analysed, including those of Keynes, Hirschman, Krugman and Stiglitz. The chapters situate development economics within current debates among economists and historians of economic thought, providing a platform for future research. This book is suitable for researchers and students with an interest in development economics, the history of economic development and the economics of developing countries.

Claudia Sunna is Researcher of Political Economics at University of Salento, Lecce, Italy.

Davide Gualerzi is Associate Professor at the Department of Economic Sciences, School of Political Sciences, University of Padua, Italy.

Perspectives in Economic and Social History
Series Editors: Andrew August
Jari Eloranta

Forthcoming Titles

Development Economics in the Twenty-First Century

**Edited by Claudia Sunna
and Davide Gualerzi**

Routledge
Taylor & Francis Group

LONDON AND NEW YORK

First published 2016 by Routledge

2 Park Square, Milton Park, Abingdon, Oxfordshire OX14 4RN

52 Vanderbilt Avenue, New York, NY 10017

Routledge is an imprint of the Taylor & Francis Group, an informa business

First issued in paperback 2020

British Library Cataloguing in Publication Data
A catalogue record for this book is available from the British Library

Library of Congress Cataloging in Publication Data
Development economics in the twenty-first century / edited by Claudia Sunna and Davide Gualerzi.
pages cm
1. Development economics—History—21st century. I. Sunna, Claudia. II. Gualerzi, Davide, 1952-
HD75.D48724 2015
338.9—dc23
2015021672

ISBN: 978-1-84893-538-9 (hbk)
ISBN: 978-0-367-66857-0 (pbk)

Typeset in Times New Roman
by Swales & Willis Ltd, Exeter, Devon, UK

Contents

Contributors

Mauro Boianovsky is Professor of Economics at the University of Brasilia, Brazil. His main research interests are in the history of economic thought, especially history of macroeconomics, monetary economics, growth economics and development economics. His publications include articles in *History of Political Economy*, *European Journal of the History of Economic Thought*, *Structural Change and Economic Dynamics*, *Review of Political Economy*, *Cambridge Journal of Economics* and other journals. He has also published chapters in edited volumes, written the book *Transforming Modern Macroeconomics: Exploring Disequilibrium Microfoundations, 1956–2003* (Cambridge University Press, 2013) and edited the collection *Business Cycle Theory* (vols. 5–8, Pickering & Chatto, 2005).

Alan B. Cibils is Professor and Researcher at the National University of General Sarmiento in Buenos Aires, Argentina, where he also chairs the Political Economy Department. His research interests include monetary theory and policy, financial systems and economic development. He holds a PhD in Economics from the American University in Washington, DC, and is the author of numerous articles, book chapters and working papers.

Francesco Farina is Professor of Economics at the University of Siena, Italy, where he held the Jean Monnet Chair in European Macroeconomics. He teaches International Economic Policy and Development Economics at the University of Siena, International Economics at the LUISS, Rome and Fiscal Policy in the PhD Programme of the Department of Economics and Law of the University of Roma-Sapienza. He is the author of books and articles published in international journals, dealing with monetary economics, macroeconomic policies, social choice and behavioural economics. He is Director of the Inter-University Centre of Research on the Welfare State (Bocconi-Milan, Rome-Sapienza and Siena).

Davide Gualerzi has a PhD in Economics from the New School for Social Research, New York, USA and is Associate Professor at the Department of Economic and Managerial Sciences 'Marco Fanno', University of Padua, Italy. He taught at the University of Pisa and was Assistant Professor of Economics at Bard College, Annandale-On-Hudson, New York. His research interests are in the fields of macroeconomics, theory of economic development, history of economic analysis, and urban and regional development. His latest book is *The Coming of Age of Information Technologies and the Path of Transformational Growth: A Long Run Perspective on the Late 2000s Recession* (Routledge, 2010).

Alejandro Nadal is Professor at the Centre for Economic Studies of El Colegio de México. He received his PhD in Economics from the University of Paris (Nanterre) in 1981. His publications cover a wide variety of subjects, from technical change and resource management, to macroeconomics and general equilibrium theory. His most recent book is *Rethinking Macroeconomics for Sustainability* (Zed Books, 2011). He is Co-Chair of the Theme on the Environment, Macroeconomics, Trade and Investment (TEMTI) of CEESP-IUCN. He is Co-editor of the online academic journal *Economic Thought* of the World Economics Association. Professor Nadal publishes a weekly column in *La Jornada*, one of Mexico's national newspapers.

Cosimo Perrotta is Professor of the History of Economic Thought, University of Salento, Italy and was Council Chair of the European Society for the History of Economic Thought between 2002 and 2006. He has published articles and essays in *History of Political Economy*, *European Journal of the History of Economic Thought*, *History of Economic Ideas* and many other journals. His books include *Consumption as an Investment* (Routledge, 2004) and *L'arretratezza del Mezzogiorno*, with Claudia Sunna and others (Bruno Mondadori, 2012).

Matthew Smith is Senior Lecturer in Economics at the University of Sydney, Australia. His main research interests are in the modern revival and development of classical economics and in the theories of demand-led growth by reference to the history of economic development. He has published *Thomas Tooke and the Monetary Thought of Classical Economics* (Routledge, 2011) and several articles in academic journals and collected volumes.

Claudia Sunna has a PhD in History of Economic Thought and is Researcher in Economics at University of Salento, Italy. She coordinates the research group of the same University for a Gender Sustainability Index. Her research interests include development and population theory in historical perspective, and labour and gender studies. Her publications include *L'arretratezza del Mezzogiorno*, with Cosimo Perrotta and others (Bruno Mondadori, 2012), *Globalization and Economic Crisis*, edited with Cosimo Perrotta (Siba ESE, 2013), 'Albert O. Hirschman sobre América Latina: teoría y política del desarrollo económico' (*Puente@Europa*, 2013) and 'Raúl Prebisch and the Keynesian theory in Latin America' (Routledge, 2014).

Foreword

This is a book which must be read because it tells a story which is not so easy to be found in modern textbooks on development economics. Everyone mentions the 'founding fathers' and their contributions: Rosenstein-Rodan's big-push, Rostow's stages, Hirschman's unbalanced growth, Lewis's dualism, Myrdal's poverty trap, but this book is a unique attempt to examine and to compare the views on economic development of these authors. The book adopts an historical point of view, but it also emphasizes the analytical implications of these theories. History of economic ideas, going back to Smith and Ricardo, is also being used for a better understanding of these views on development. Throughout the various chapters it emerges that all these authors shared some opinions on what development is and on the conditions for economic growth.

Let us point out just four of the major messages which the different chapters bring to us and which should be of an outermost value in modern development views.

First, economic development is not a pure quantitative fact, but it implies transformation and discontinuity with previous social structures and may be even institutions.

Second, non-economic elements and conditions cannot be separated from economic growth; think of Rostow's pre-conditions for take-off and of the notion of 'social overhead capital' by Rosenstein Rodan.

Third, all these authors aim to explain how to trigger economic development in Less Developed Countries, LDCs, thus they investigate the causes of growth of the national economy and the state is an important player. The object of investigation are the forces which affect long-run economic development. Given the conditions of the international capitalist economy some of them are skeptical about the growth possibilities of LDCs and foresee a situation of chronic poverty and 'dependency'.

Fourth, even if all their main interest is the growth of national wealth these writers are well aware that economies are not an homogenous entity, but are made up of sectors, which can be very much different, all the more so in developing countries. Therefore development economics must analyse the differences between advanced and backward sectors, agriculture and manufacturing, the countryside and the cities, the formal and the informal sectors. In various degrees most of these economists can be considered to share a structuralist view, according to which no development strategy can ignore the initial productive structure of a country. Development and better economic performances require major changes in the structure and in the productive capacity of the countries.

The book tells us the story of 'structuralist school' which originated in Latin America in the late forties and early fifties thanks to the contributions of Prebisch, Singer and Furtado. Authors such as Hirschman, Myrdal, Rostow and Rosenstein-Rodan do not belong to that school, but they share the view the in order to develop economies have to undergo major changes in their productive structure.

Thanks to its historical/analytical point of view we find in the book the discussions of the role of phenomena such as externalities and increasing returns, the role of the primary sector and of commodity production *vis à vis* that of manufacturing, capital accumulation and its impact on technical progress, the working of the labour markets. All these aspects are examined with respect to their analytical implications for economic growth. The contributors to the book lead the reader who is mainly acquainted with mainstream neoclassical growth theories to discover that international trade is not necessarily beneficial to growth and that differential productivity growth is a major force in the process of transformation and development.

We find some remarkable examples of rather unknown episodes; such as Julius Boeke 1953 dualistic model on Indonesia, Furtado's analysis of a 'Dutch disease' type of phenomenon in

Venezuela in the early 1950s, Rostow's notion of 'reactive nationalism' which he puts among the pre-conditions for take-off.

The first four chapters of the book delve more on the contributions of the 'founding fathers', while the last four chapters present somee modern reassessments. Therefore the book is not just an occasion to praise the visions on economic development of the fifties, it also explains the reason of the change which took place during the eighties and led to the dominance of the 'market efficiency hypothesis' and to the policies named as Washington Consensus. The book takes us to some modern reappraisals of these earlier contributions. We find the neo-structuralist and the post-keynesian approaches, but also the modern vies on the 'dependency' of southern economies from the northern ones and from the new emerging countries in Asia.

The contributors to the book highlights earlier visions in view of modern contentions and present some very interesting policy considerations. The book focuses on contributions to development theories coming from Latin America, where in the fifties many authors asked for industrialization and the abandonment of a model which assigned to Latin America the role of 'granary' of the world, supplying the 'North' with primary commodities. But since the late eighties this same model has become extremely fashionable again fashion and today many economists consider the commodity-export-based development as the winning strategy for Latin American countries, with Asia in place of the 'North' and soya replacing corn and beef. As Cibils notices this a case of 'return to the future' based on the bonanza deriving from the rising commodity prices since 2000. A bonanza which has recently stopped.

Dear reader this is not a textbook, nor a monographic work on the structuralist approach and on dualistic development models, but it is an essential reading for those who are interested in understanding the real mechanisms of economic development. The 'resurgence' of the high development theories of the fifties and sixties and their actualization is a necessary phase in the reconstruction of development economics. All the contributors to this book helps us, the readers, to take the needed steps in this direction.

Gianni Vaggi
University of Pavia, July 2015

Introduction

The rise and decline of development economics in the history of economic thought

Davide Gualerzi and Claudia Sunna

'Why this old stuff?': an example by Davide Gualerzi

During one of my lectures a couple of years ago, as I was exposing the theory of cumulative causation based on Myrdal's *Economic Theory and Underdeveloped Regions*,[1] I could not help noticing the uneasiness of one of the students. I thought the topic was most important and that I was doing a decent job at presenting the, not so easy, fundamental ideas presented by Myrdal. After a while the student finally asked the question: 'Why are you telling us about a book that was written in the fifties? What does it have to do with today's development?'.

The student was one of the good ones in the class, although maybe excessively self-reliant – at least he did say what might be in the mind of others. But I was surprised and disappointed. I attempted to explain why Myrdal was indeed important for the study of development and of regional differences. I must have been somewhat effective because he did come to class more regularly. I should add that somebody more competent – and with much better background in economics – did whisper to his ear and to my pleasure: 'but this is a classic!'.

Now there may be plenty of reasons for my student's comment. This little anecdote however does point to the main problem this collection wants to address. The body of theory known as development economics has largely lost its importance in research and teaching. One main reason might be that it is hard to connect it up with today problems of development, dominated by the question of globalization and emerging economies, and therefore with the current discourse on development. As far as the scientific community is concerned it seems that, to use Krugman's words, the development theory of Hirschman and Myrdal became to economists 'not so much wrong as incomprehensible'.[2]

A changing world economy

Truly the analysis of development, backwardness and catching-up confronts today a profoundly changed world economy. The penetration of technology and modern production techniques into what used to be called, in a Cold War milieu, the 'Third World', has now run a long course. Furthermore, we have seen phenomena of development that have drastically changed the simplified counter-position of development and underdevelopment, therefore redefining the entire question of centers and peripheries of the world economy. In the 1980s we saw the rise of the 'four tigers' (Hong-Kong, Taiwan, Singapore and especially South Korea). Then, from the 1990s onwards, the attention shifted to the emerging economies and in particular toward the new giants in Asia and Latin America. Today the so-called BRIC(S) highlight the formidable challenge posed by the development of a heterogeneous 'periphery' and the understanding of the changing world order. These phenomena have dramatically modified the perspective on development and have at the same time shaped today's research agenda.

It is precisely the need for a theoretical framework with a historical perspective that can rescue the analysis of development from the simple application of the principles of mainstream economic theory. That drives the interest for an approach mostly forgotten in the recent literature.

The debate during the past decade on globalization and the emerging economies has renewed interest in the study of development and underdevelopment. Oddly enough, this renewal has only rarely looked back at the work of the founding thinkers of development theory and to what we refer as development economics. We have seen for example a discussion of globalization taking place in a sort of a history of economic thought vacuum. Similarly the analysis of emerging economies has shown little sign of digging into the roots of development theory and, more recently, the big revival of the institutional approach to development issues, *à la* Acemoglu and Robinson, has shown little interest at any historical analysis of development economics.[3] This happens at a time in which the economic crisis of the advanced countries adds to the discussion on the worldwide development trends. This makes even more compelling examining how old and new approaches can account for the new hierarchies in the world economy.[4]

There are indeed new questions and the new problems in development. It so happens that today's concerns appear almost divorced from the questions asked in the 1950s and the 1960s. This owes a lot to the dramatic changes in the political and institutional framework, entering the phase after de-colonization and the end of the Socialist bloc. If one looks at Myrdal's description of the world economic order in 1957 and to his identifications of three main areas in the world economy, that is to say the developed countries, the Socialist economies and the 'Third World', the change in overall picture is rather clear. A second reason for the distance between what is discussed today and the early development theory is the rise, from the 1980s, of the Washington consensus out of the international institutions designed, after the Bretton Woods agreements of 1944, to stabilize the post WWII international economic order and to advise the Less Developed Countries (LDCs).

This collection of essays aims at re-establishing a sort of continuity in the study of development, by examining the foundations laid out by what Krugman has labeled 'high development theory' of the 1950s–1970s. An essential aspect of this examination is reconstructing the debate on the rise and decline of development economics. This is important to see what remains vital of that approach and how that can guide today's analysis of development and underdevelopment.

The roots of development economics: the seminal contributions

Development economics has its roots in a series of seminal contributions. Although hard to classify as a school of economic thought, they are nevertheless identifiable for their pioneering effort to define an approach to the study of underdeveloped economies. Despite the differences between their methods of enquiry and their different approaches, development economists first defined the new field of investigation shaping the conception of the development problem. This is very important considering that this approach is largely forgotten today.

The history of economic development naturally provided an empirical basis to identify the main social, political and economic elements they considered to be conducive to promoting growth. In addition, after a long period of neglect, there was an advancement in the theory of economic growth, largely in the footsteps of Harrod and Domar. On the one hand, we have the post-Keynesian growth theory, with the contributions by Kaldor and Robinson at Cambridge University; on the other hand, the developments along traditional neo-classical lines by Solow and Swan, which became the dominant theory.[5]

Many of the early development theorists were émigrés from Europe, fleeing political persecution. German speaking economists largely contributed to the establishment of this new field of study in Great Britain and the United States. Very important contributions were those in Latin America, which are however less known.

The pioneers of the discipline were focusing on the question of backwardness and lack of industrialization in the underdeveloped regions and areas of Europe. The classic article by Rosenstein-Rodan (1943) was written to address the problem of development in Eastern and South Eastern Europe.[6] Besides Rosenstein-Rodan the most known émigrés are probably Alexandre Gerschenkron, Albert Hirschman, Kurt Mandelbaum and Hans Singer. Institutional centers for the development of the new discipline in Great Britain were mainly London and Oxford, where Mandelbaum and Rosenstein-Rodan were teaching. Together with a few others, like Gunnar Myrdal, these were the founders of the newly born discipline. Very important contributions were those in Latin America, and in this case the first prominent figure was Raúl Prebisch.

High development theory was largely set aside after the 1970s. The exception is, to some extent, Latin America. The Latin American school has indeed shown a remarkable resilience. Especially the work done at United Nations Economic Commission for Latin America (CEPAL in Spanish and Portuguese) contributed to maintain alive the insights of high development theory, inspiring a view of development where government, industrial policy and planning have an essential role to play.[7] It is open to question, however, how influential outside, but also within Latin America, the approach is on current research and development policies design. This might depend on the lack of a sustained effort to update and make relevant to today's development problem the insights of the theory.

In line with the general purpose of bringing back into today's debate the fundamental insights of early development economics the volume examines the seminal contributions and their relationship to the analysis of development problems of today. The main purpose is revitalizing the original approach and, in this way, contributing to a more adequate theoretical perspective capable of accounting for the question of emerging economies. In other words contributing to a rethinking of development and development economics. This effort is already present in the recent literature.[8] The collection takes a particular route, that of looking at the foundations of the discussion on development. This appears necessary for further research, and in particular for addressing questions now prominent in the debate of development, such as the role of institutions, and what might be the role of the public sector and of government. These issues were clearly part of the concerns of the early development theorists.

Their ideas appear to be largely forgotten and that affects negatively the study and teaching of development today. Why was the approach abandoned? Clarifying this point is a preliminary step to understand the sense of developing economics in the history of economic thought.

The rise and decline of development economics

We need to recall the historical phase in which the sub-discipline of development economics arose. In the literature there are different, and to some extent complementary, explanations for this rise. According to Hirschman, development economics originated from the orthodoxy of Anglo-Saxon economics as a consequence of the 'Keynesian Revolution'. Keynes had demonstrated that traditional economics was applicable only in the context of full employment of resources, while his approach was apt to respond to the difficulties faced by industrialized countries during 1930s. As a consequence 'the ice of monoeconomics had been broken and the idea that there might be yet another economics had instant credibility'.[9] The newly born discipline had the task to formulate new approaches and categories to cope with the problems of underdevelopment left untouched by the traditional approach.

In Myrdal explanation historical circumstances are the main reason for the intellectual formation of development economics. He argues that after World War II, the convergence of three historical and political events led social scientists to intensify their scientific efforts towards underdeveloped countries. These events were first of all decolonization, secondly the demand for development programs expressed by the newly independent countries and finally the Cold War. The internal affairs of underdeveloped countries became relevant to the conflicting great powers their interest motivated by military or more general strategic purposes.[10] The overall effect was a general widening of welfare state policies from developed countries toward underdeveloped countries. An effect that Myrdal tried to classify as the 'welfare world'.[11]

Beginning with the 1980s the destiny of the early development economics is mostly seen as strictly related to the fortune of the Keynesian consensus. With the decline and, at times, even the discredit of the Keynesian consensus, the whole discipline of development economics was considered moribund.

On top of that Hirschman argues there were the attacks to the legitimacy of development economics, coming from both mainstream Neoclassical and Marxist theory. The Neoclassical economists claimed that development economics had rejected the validity of the principle of efficient allocation of resources. The Marxists emphasized the fact that development economics was ineffective because was not as radical as required in underdeveloped countries. Caught between these two fires, development economics declined as a respected field of theoretical investigation. The decline was further fueled by the un-effectiveness of the policies implemented in the 1950s and 1960s based on the ideas of development theorists.[12]

The various sources of disappointment with development economics are well summarized by Hirschman himself. The sub-discipline, as he calls it, came into being as a result 'of an a priori unlikely conjunction of distinct ideological currents'. Although extraordinarily productive at one point, that created problems subsequently:

> because of its heterogeneous ideological makeup, the new science was shot through with tensions that would prove disruptive at the first opportunity. Secondly, because of the circumstances under which it arose, development economics became overloaded with unreasonable hopes and ambitions that soon had to be clipped back.[13]

Krugman's assessment of the decline of development economics is instead noticeable because it is all 'internal' to the theory. He argues that:

> development theorists were unable to formulate their ideas with the precision required by an increasingly model-oriented economic mainstream and were thus left behind. Although I believe this to be the main explanation of what went wrong, it is also true that the practical failures and empirical evidence had something to do with the decline of development economics.[14]

Krugman regards the essence of 'high development theory' as to what he calls the Rosenstein-Rodan's 'big push' argument. Upstream is the large investment necessary to establish modern industry, downstream the effects of higher wages. Modern, large-scale industry has higher productivity and that allows for higher wages. That has beneficial effects on market size. On the other hand modern methods of production, which are potentially more productive, call for a large market. Three consequences follow: (1) a large investment in one industry might be unprofitable in isolation, therefore the need for a coordinated investment in many industries (i.e. the essence of the big push), (2) essential to the story are the increasing returns that originate from the self-reinforcement coming from the interaction between economies of scale and the size of the market, (3) the development model rests on some form of dualism manifested in the contrast between the modern sector and the traditional one. The first one pays higher wages and draws workers from the second one. The fundamental idea underlying high development theory is then the virtuous circle driven by external economies in which modernization breeds modernization. Some countries remain stuck in a low level trap and that is 'a powerful case for government activism as a way of breaking out of this trap'.[15]

As for the reasons why development economics was largely abandoned Krugman, rather than the historical and political circumstances, focuses on the changes occurring in economic theory and in particular on the shift in the method of economic analysis.

Krugman argues that by the late 1950s mainstream economics was becoming increasingly hostile to the fundamental ideas of development economics. Economies of scale 'were very difficult to introduce into the increasingly formal models of mainstream economic theory'.[16] Indeed, high development theory rested on something that nobody knew exactly how to put into formal models. But model building increasingly became the standard in the profession. The new generations of economists could not make sense of that body of theory and simply ended up ignoring it. Model building became the standard of the profession, and in the process the development theory of Hirschman and Myrdal was mostly set aside.

As the title of the 1995 paper suggests, Krugman argues that the main ideas of high development theory are making a come back. Modeling of those ideas is possible due to the advances in economic theory, and much of his work. He wants to argue that central elements such as externalities in development and increasing returns are no longer a challenge to economic thinking as they were in the years of the first rise of development economics.

In his reply to Krugman Stiglitz observed that the lack of formal models cannot tell the story of fall of development economics. Increasing returns, imperfect competition and technological change, were studied, for instance by Kaldor and Arrow. Many formal models were constructed and published. That applies to the modeling of externalities also. Thus, 'the lack of such models simply cannot account for the temporary demise of high development theory- if that had happened. Conversely, had Rosenstein-Rodan (1943) succeeded in formalizing his ideas, I doubt that those ideas would have been any more palatable'.[17] There was no decline in the 'supply' of theoretical analysis but rather a weakening of the 'demand' for ideas. It was then the change in intellectual and political context the crucial point.[18]

Ultimately, according to Stiglitz, development economics did not suffer a real decline. It is alive and well in the theoretical work of many researchers on questions such as those of externalities. As in the case of Krugman, Stiglitz also see his work contributing to maintain on the due course the analysis of development. This would open an interesting discussion on whether the interest of many economists on themes important for development is in itself a contribution to the analysis of underdeveloped countries, or whether it would require a theoretical framework indeed focused on the development process and on the circumstances that surrounded it.

Stiglitz underlines that, at the end of the twentieth century, a rising attention was given to the institutional aspects of development, to the problems of sustainable development, and finally to the problems of measurement of economic development. What was really changed was the level of interest toward these subjects that permeates both the scientific community and the international organizations devoted to the promotion of economic development (World Bank, International Monetary Fund, UNDP).

The change of intellectual and political context pointed out by Stiglitz as the fundamental reason for the decline of development economics is in fact argued in more depth by other scholars. The point is that intellectual development was intertwined with the historical and political context of the period that goes from the end of WWII to the 1960s. Heinz W. Arndt, himself an émigré at Oxford, has argued that international political factors had an important role in shaping the approach to development – among them, the end of the colonial powers and the rise of national independence movements. The presence of the Soviet Union and the spread of its influence gave the so-called Third World countries a certain degree of bargaining power.[19] This echoes the point of view expressed by Myrdal since the 1970s.

Regarding development economics Jomo speaks of 'historical amnesia', which to some extent spared the analysis of development, linked as it is to the history of the transition to the 'post-colonial' era. This is why, he argues, to preserve the meaning of the original theory stylized abstraction should be combined with an attention to the historical context in which the theory was first developed.[20]

During the 1980s, the political perspective changed towards what was later firmly established as the Washington Consensus.[21] We can observe the parallel with the discredit of the Keynesian consensus as mentioned above and occurring in the same years. The claim to a superior understanding, the 'one size fits all' approach, was based, Stiglitz argues, on an erroneous notion of the way markets operate. Increasingly development has been shaped by this newly emerged 'global governance', in fact a policy orientation best suited to well-defined interests.[22]

Historiography of development economics and history

The question of the actual (according to Krugman) or supposed (according to Stiglitz) decline of development economics has raised a range of approaches from the historical point of view. As seen above, Hirschman decrees the end of development economics in the early eighties but his reflection is not accepted unanimously. Jan Tinbergen in 1984 sustains that 'an accumulation of experience on a subject [development] whose urgency is still increasing seems . . . inconsistent with the concept of decline'.[23] Likewise, again in 1984, according to Lewis, 'Development Economics is not at its most spectacular, but it is alive and well'.[24]

The question of the actual decline of development economics, in our view, is not simply a problem of views between supporters and detractors. At the core of this question there is the very definition of what development is and what the sources of economic growth are.

It is undeniable that the eighties were a watershed for development economics. In those years it came to fruition the neoclassical critique which has its origins in the sixties, that is, in the same period of the rise of development economics. The reference goes to Hla Myint and Peter Bauer.

According to Myint the justification given to the need for a specific discipline to study the problems of development is based on two orders of reasons. First it is claimed that the mainstream economic theory is unrealistic and therefore, to study the real problems of development in the LDCs, there is the need for an alternative approach. Secondly, the issues dealt by orthodox economic theory are not relevant to the study of the less developed economies because, for example, are referred to the problems of optimal allocation of resources, or to the issue of how to maintain full employment, or on how to analyze growth problems in mature economies.[25]

Given this premise, Myint argues that the criticism of the lack of realism of economic theory could be applied to development economics too and to 'the planning policies in the underdeveloped countries'. Since developing countries are not homogeneous from the economic and institutional perspective 'it is highly unlikely that any single standard model of development planning will be appropriate for all of them'.[26]

In the same way, according to Bauer, there is a 'spurious consensus' inside development economics based on: the emphasis on poverty and on the vicious circle generated by poverty, population growth, restricted domestic markets, subsistence agriculture, insignificance of industry, luxury consumption of higher classes of societies and unproductive use of their income. But, he follows:

> the consensus is, surprisingly, even more pronounced on issues of policy than on matters which are ostensibly descriptive or analytical. The salient aspects of the consensus on policy are: insistence on comprehensive central planning (a large measure of state control of economic activity outside subsistence farming); on compulsory savings . . . ; and on large-scale foreign aid. . . . The major elements are manifestly invalid, being inconsistent with empirical evidence, elementary logic, or well established propositions of economics.[27]

The debate within development economics in the years of 'high development theory' is centred on the overlap between development theory and development policy. In other words, according to Myint, development economics lacks that general nature and relevance that would have a theoretical approach applicable to all LDCs, and, according to Bauer, the normative approach of development economics is blatantly inconsistent with the fundamentals of economic theory.

The neoclassical criticism toward development economics, as noted above and as prophesied by Hirschman in 1981, reaches its peak in the eighties with the work of Ian Little and Deepak Lal.[28]

According to Little there is no a need to analyze the issue of economic development with a theoretical apparatus different from that of neoclassical economics.

Moreover, the 'planning approach' of development economists was a failure compared to the objectives that they had fixed and therefore must be completely abandoned.[29]

In Lal's work his approach is decidedly more 'militant'. *The Poverty of Development Economics* is essentially a pamphlet against the 'dirigiste' intervention of development economists in the LDCs and it stresses, once again, that the cause of the failure of development economics is closely related to 'the alleged irrelevance of orthodox economics'.[30]

To sum up, according to the neoclassical critics, development economics has focused exclusively on the normative analysis of the development processes and has not created any general analytical framework on which to build an effective theory of economic development. In the second place, development economists have assumed that market failures in LDCs could be overcome only through state intervention in the economy and that is of course considered the main limitation of the approach: it underestimates 'government failures' and the negative effects of government policies.

After the triumph of the neoclassical critique, we have observed a reversal from macroeconomics to microeconomics in the study of economic development. We moved from the emphasis on state intervention to the benefits arising from the operation of the free market, from a historical vision integrated in policy intervention in the long run to the unique recipe of economic policy derived from the sum of short-term microeconomic theories.[31] On this last point, as put it by Little, 'the long run is an integral of short runs'.[32]

From this evolution of ideas the Washington Consensus emerged. As pointed out above it was a clear set of policies that includes: a strategy of market liberalization and export promotion; the stabilization of the macroeconomic aggregates; the privatization of state enterprises and a set of rules to facilitate the functioning of the price system and, therefore, of the markets. This set of policies was later supplemented, but never modified, with the study of the 'residual' elements of the aggregate production function, i.e. human capital and institutions/social capital.

After the rise of the neoclassical theory of development what remains undetermined is the very definition of growth in the sense of what are the determining processes and the key ingredients.[33] In other words, despite the elaboration of these questions, there is still little explanation of the sources of economic growth. Especially the recent economic crisis highlights that this question is dramatically unresolved. As an example of the state of the art it is sufficient to look at the words of the report editors of the World Bank 2010 *Commission on Growth and Development*, Michael Spence and Danny Leipziger:

> while we felt that the benefits of growth were not fully appreciated, we recognized that the causes of growth were not fully understood . . . our understanding of economic growth is less definitive than commonly thought even though advice sometimes has been given to developing countries with greater confidence than perhaps the state of our knowledge would justify.[34]

This admission is almost amazing for anyone with a passing knowledge of classical economic thought or who has simply read the works of Rostow, Lewis, Hirschman, Prebisch, Furtado and so on. We can only imagine the impact that this excessive confidence might have had on development policies since the eighties.

The lack of a clear vision of what factor or factors are crucial to encourage the process of growth might be the result of the progressive 'dematerialization' of the sources of growth. Development and growth theory has gone from the consideration of capital accumulation to the emphasis on investment in human capital and to the question of social capital as a fundamental cause of the development processes.

This last step has involved a close analysis of the theme of the 'right' institutions needed to foster development.[35] In economic theory this has been translated in a set of 'necessary' rules and institutions, often imposed through commercial treaties or with conditional loans, such as the protection of intellectual property rights, liberalized financial institutions, independent Central Banks, democracy and an efficient bureaucracy. This happened even if, as remarked by Chang, advanced countries did not have this institutional framework before becoming developed.[36]

The policy-biased approach of high development theory has found no viable substitute after the neoclassical counterrevolution. The goal of finding effective policies to support the development of LDCs has over time become increasingly difficult if not impossible.

As for the decline of development economics, we think that Krugman's explanation focused on the difference of method between the 'old' development economics and the modelling approach of modern economic theory is, in a sense, missing the point. It is not the method used by development economists that is incomprehensible to the growth theorists. What is substantially different is the vision of the development process and in particular the importance of a historical view of the development processes. In development economics the very object of study cannot be understood and analyzed outside of a historical perspective.

Development economists such as Paul Rosenstein-Rodan, Ragnar Nurkse, Simon Kuznets, Arthur Lewis, Walter Rostow and Celso Furtado were concerned with the 'big picture' questions in explaining growth and development and were in varying degrees also economic historians.[37]

Moreover, as pointed out by Lewis in a contribution on 'The State of Development Theory' in 1984, 'the relation between incentives and institutions is one of the oldest parts of Development Economics'. The forefathers of development economics were well aware that in the LDCs there was a mixed combination of traditional and modern institutions but 'they did not expect to reach conclusions in this area from principles only. Their writings about such matters are as much historical as economic analysis'.[38] From that particular approach emerged many mixed historic-economic categories such unbalanced growth, dual economy, disguised unemployment, structural inflation, dependency, growth poles and low-level equilibrium trap. At the same time, however, it was clear that the validity and enforceability of these categories changed with the historical moment and with the place in which they were used: 'their conclusions recognize that the same question requires different answers at different time . . . and cannot therefore be answered without reference to circumstances'.[39]

For the modern microeconomic approach to development issues, the search for applicable models at all latitudes is still based on the regularities of human behaviour and to the choice response to price incentives. This approach has removed from the analysis everything that could not be included in the analytical model, either because it was not measurable or not strictly defined as 'economic', since it may be derived from sociology or anthropology.

Even if the modern development analysis is often based on empirical observation and is provided with a plenty of data and case studies, as noted by Meier, 'economists still need to put forward a relevant theoretical framework to bring some logical order to the data' and to establish some significant conjuncture with policy making.[40]

The 'big picture' and the vision of the season of high development theory are still missing.

The contributions in the volume

The debate on the rise and fall of development economics is the background against which one should look at the essays in the volume.

Early development economics was the result of a systematic thinking about progress: it rested on an original intellectual process intertwined with particular historical circumstances. Similarly today the changes in the world economic order require a new original intellectual development and a historical perspective on theoretical advances. That is suggested also by the widespread failure of market-oriented policies to determine sustained growth and generalized welfare increases in many of the developing economies. On the other hand the success of the emerging economies seem to have occurred running against the Washington consensus recommendations.

These are the conditions, theoretical and historical, for a reconsideration of the development theories that flourished in the post-WWII era. While many aspects of those writings are still relevant today, the international economy has substantially changed; policy prescriptions and objectives of the 1950s and 1960s might not be applicable today.

Without any claim of an exhaustive exposition the chapters in the book deal with the content of the pioneering contributions, the debate they generated, and the relevance for the contemporary analysis on development. Chapters 1, 2, 3 and 4 deal with the seminal contributions such as those of Rosenstein-Rodan's 'big push' and Walt Rostow's 'take-off' in the framework of historical growth modelling, Hirschman's analysis of the development process through imbalances and backward and forward linkages, the debate around the theory of trade and the dual development models. Chapters 5 and 6 examine a series of contributions following the two lines of investigation still vital especially in Latin America, the first concerning structuralism and neo structuralism, the second on the relevance of dependency analysis. The two issue-oriented chapters at the end of the volume, dealing with poverty and macroeconomics for development, complete the modern perspective on the issue of development. We would like to think that the collection contributes to advance a much needed intellectual development stimulating further research along the lines set out by the early development theorists.

Notes

1 G. Myrdal, *Economic theory and under-developed regions* (London: Duckworth, 1957).
2 P. Krugman, 'The Fall and Rise of Development Economics' (2005), at http://web.mit. edu/krugman/www/dishpan.html, [accessed 20 January 2015], p. 1.
3 See D. Acemoglu and J. A. Robinson, Why Nations Fail: *The Origins of Power, Prosperity, and Poverty* (New York: Crown Publisher, 2012). The authors, besides attaching a classical development flavour to the title of their book, analyze the institutional framework of the development process without acknowledging anyone of the founding father of this approach, i.e. A.O. Hirschman, G. Myrdal, W.A. Lewis, P.N. Rosenstein-Rodan, W.W. Rostow, and so on.
4 See H. B. Chenery, 'Introduction to Part II', in H.B. Chenery and T.N. Srinivasan (eds), *Handbook of Development Economics*, Vol. 1 (Amsterdam: North Holland, 1988), pp. 197–202 (p. 197).
5 See the contributions in P. Aghion and S. N. Durlauf (eds), *Handbook of Economic Growth*, Vol. 1a (Amsterdam: North Holland, 2005).
6 P. N. Rosenstein Rodan, 'Problems of Industrialization of Eastern and South Eastern Europe' *The Economic Journal*, 53: 210/211, (1943), pp. 202–11.
7 J. Mattar, 'Panorama de la gestión pública en América Latina. En la Hora de la Higualdad' (Santiago: CEPAL, 2011).
8 See for instance H. J. Chang (ed.), *Rethinking Development Economics* (London: Anthem Press, 2003).
9 A. O. Hirschman, 'The Rise and Decline of Development Economics', in *Essays in Trespassing, Economics to Politics and Beyond* (Cambridge: Cambridge University Press, 1981), pp. 1–24, on p. 6.
10 G. Myrdal, 'The World Poverty Problem', in *Against the Stream.: Critical Essays in Economics* (New York: Vintage Books [1968] 1975), pp. 65–100.
11 G. Myrdal, 'Place of Values in Social Policy', in *Against the Stream. Critical Essays in Economics* (New York: Vintage Books, 1975), pp. 33–51, on pp. 46–51.
12 Hirschman, 'The Rise and Decline of Development Economics'.
13 Ibid., p. 2.
14 P. Krugman, 'Toward a Counter-Revolution in Development Theory', in *Proceedings of the World Bank Annual Conference on Development Economics* (Washington DC: World Bank, 1993) pp. 15–38.
15 P. Krugman, 'The Fall and Rise, p. 2.
16 Ibid., p. 3.
17 J. Stiglitz, Comment on 'Toward a Counter-Revolution in Development Theory' by P. Krugman, in *Proceedings of the World Bank Annual Conference on Development Economics* (Washington DC: World Bank, 1993), pp. 39–50, on p. 41.
18 According to Stiglitz 'a far more plausible explanation for the seeming demise of high development theory is that the same currents that led to the dominance of free market ideology in the United Kingdom and the United States were reflected – at least in the United States – in the dominance of those ideas in certain intellectual circles. In short, it was as much the market demand for ideas as the supply of models that was crucial' (ibid., p. 42).

19 H. W. Arndt, *Economic Development. The History of an Idea* (London: The University of Chicago Press, 1987).

20 K. S. Jomo (ed.), *Pioneers of Development Economics: Great Economists on Development* (London, Zed Books, 2005), on p. vii. On the transition from the Washington Consensus to the post-Washington Consensus see B. Fine, C. Lapavitsas and J. Pincus (eds), *Development Economics in the Twentieth-first Century: Beyond the Post-Washington Consensus* (London: Routledge, 2001).

21 That can be described as a set of policy prescriptions cemented in an ideology, advocated by the IMF and the World Bank, and the US Treasury. For a reconstruction of the transition from the Keynesian Consensus to the Washington Consensus see H. W. Singer, 'Editorial: The Golden Age of the Keynesian Consensus – The Pendulum Swings Back', *World Development*, 25: 3, (1997), pp. 293–95.

22 The IMF and the World Bank emerged from the Bretton Woods agreements in the aftermath of the Second World War. These institutions have embraced what Stiglitz labels 'market fundamentalism'. 'Keynes would be rolling over in his grave were he to see what has happened to his child', J. Stiglitz, *Globalization and its discontents* (New York–London: Norton, 2002), on p. 13.

23 J. Tinbergen, 'Optimal Development Policies: Lessons from Experience', *World Economy*, 7: 1, (1984), pp. 112–17, on p. 116.

24 W. A Lewis, 'The State of Development Theory', *The American Economic Review*, 74: 1, (1984b), pp. 1–10, (p. 10).

25 H. Myint, 'Economic Theory and the Underdeveloped Countries', *The Journal of Political Economy*, 73: 5, (1965), pp. 477–91.

26 Ibid., p. 478.

27 P. T. Bauer, 'The Spurious Consensus and its Background' in P.T. Bauer, *Dissent on Development: Studies and Debates in Development Economics* (Cambridge, MA: Harvard University Press, [1969] 1972), pp. 306–42, on p. 309.

28 I. M. D. Little, *Economic Development: Theory, Policy and International Relations* (New York: Basic Books, 1982); D. Lal, *The Poverty of "Development Economics'* (London: Institute of Economic Affairs, 1983).

29 I. M. D. Little, *Economic Development*, ch. 2.

30 D. Lal, *The Poverty of 'Development Economics'*, ch. 1.

31 See G. M. Meier, 'The Old Generation of Development Economists and the New', in G. M. Meier and J. E. Stiglitz (eds), *Frontiers of Development Economics: The Future in Perspective* (Oxford: Oxford University Press, 2001), pp. 13–23.

32 I. M. D. Little, *Economic Development*, p. 17.

33 See G. M. Meier, 'The Old Generation', pp. 25–26.

34 M. Spence and D. Leipziger (eds), *Globalization and Growth: Implications for a Post-Crisis World* (Washington DC: World Bank, 2010), on p. xii.

35 D. C. North, *Institutions, Institutional Change, and Economic performance* (Cambridge: Cambridge University Press, 1990).

36 H. J. Chang, *Kicking Away the Ladder: Development Strategy in Historical Perspective* (London: Anthem Press, 2003), on ch. 3.

37 Other significant contributors to development economics from an historic perspective are Albert O Hirschman, Raúl Prebisch, Hans Singer, Theodore Shultz, Moses Abramovitz, Jacob Schmookler and Alexander Gershenkron.

38 W. A Lewis, 'The State of Development Theory', p. 7.

39 Ibid.

40 G. M. Meier, *Biography of a Subject: An Evolution of Development Economics* (Oxford: Oxford University Press, 2005), on p. 198.

1 Historical growth modelling

Rostow's 'take-off' and Rosenstein-Rodan's 'big push'

Matthew Smith

1.1 Introduction

Of the development economists of the 1950s and 1960s Walter Rostow (1916–2003) stands out as one who built an historical-based model in order to identify the stages of development of economic systems and, in particular, to identify the main factors which can explain the transformation of an undeveloped country to a developed country. In Rostow's 'stages of economic growth' model there are five evolutionary stages of possible economic development, as based on his study of the historical patterns of development of the advanced nations up to 1960. The critical stage, and indeed, the most contentious, in Rostow's model, is the 'take-off' stage, which characterizes the period when an economy experiences a transformation *decisive* in putting it on the path to sustained growth and development and becoming an economically advanced nation. This 'take-off' notion has subsequently been employed by some economic historians and development economists. In connection to this model Rostow endeavoured to develop a theoretical apparatus – 'a system' – for interpreting economic history and identifying the main forces in society which explained the take-off of economies. This attempt by Rostow to bring together theory and history to explain economic growth is itself of great interest.

Another to develop a model in post-war development economics was Paul Rosenstein-Rodan (1902–1985) with his 'big push' model. Different from the historical-based model of Rostow, this model was instead developed by Rosenstein-Rodan from theoretical principles to rationalize a policy of large-scale co-ordinated investment that would provide the momentum – a 'big push' – to the development of undeveloped regions.

There is an affinity between these two models in the sense that Rosenstein-Rodan's big push can be seen as an economic strategy to achieve Rostow's take-off. Indeed, consistent with Rosenstein-Rodan's model, Rostow argued that the crucial take-off stage of economic development involved a marked acceleration in the growth of investment which embodied rapid technical progress.[1]

This chapter will critically examine the models of these two development economists and appraise their contemporary significance to explaining growth and proposing policies which promote economic development. In section 1.2 we examine Rostow's historically-based 'stages of economic growth' model. Then, in section

1.3, we examine the theoretical apparatus developed by Rostow, principally to explain the take-off growth stage. In section 1.4 we consider Rosenstein-Rodan's 'big push' model and his grand policy to promote economic development. Our conclusion in section 1.5 critically appraises these two models, showing that their insights can be better appreciated by reference to a coherent theoretical framework provided by the demand-led approach to explaining growth.

1.2 Rostow's 'stages of economic growth' model

The 'stages of economic growth' model began with the notion of the 'take-off' first articulated by Rostow in *The Process of Economic Growth*, published in 1952: 'The process of take-off may be defined as an increase in the volume and productivity of investment in a society, such that a sustained increase in per capita real income results'.[2]

This notion was considerably elaborated by Rostow in terms of the history of economic development in the article, 'The Take-off into Sustained Growth', published in the *Economic Journal* in 1956. In this article Rostow formulated a three-stages model of the growth process, consisting of 'preconditions for take-off', 'the take-off', and 'when growth becomes normal and relatively automatic'.[3] It was in the article 'The Stages of Economic Growth', published in *The Economic History Review* in 1959, that Rostow first articulated his 'stages of economic growth' model, consisting of five historical stages of development.[4] The most comprehensive account of the model was then subsequently given in his book, *The Stages of Economic Growth: A non-Communist Manifesto*, first published in 1960.[5] This book included a global geo-political outlook, a repudiation of Marx and Marxism and a rationalization of the emergence of communism in the twentieth century with reference to the Cold War. In this connection Rostow was quite explicit that a major motive for promoting global economic development was to staunch the spread of communism. Indeed, Rostow proposed his model – understood in conjunction with his theoretical apparatus – as a superior alternative to that which he attributed to Marx and the 'Marxists'.[6] But, as indicated above, Rostow's model was fundamentally developed out of a desire to explain the growth process from an historical perspective. Hence, in the opening sentence of his book Rostow writes. 'This book presents an economic historian's way of generalizing the sweep of modern history. The form of this generalization is a set of stages-of-growth'.[7]

The five stages of Rostow's model consists of (1) 'the traditional society', (2) 'preconditions for take-off', (3) 'the take-off', (4) 'the drive to maturity' and (5) 'the age of high mass consumption'. According to Rostow each country can be categorized as being in one of these stages of economic development and in which only the most advanced countries have historically evolved through all five stages. Hence, the advanced nations, led by the United States and including Britain, France, Germany and Japan, are considered to have reached the fifth stage of growth; whereas, for example, Turkey, Argentina, China and India, were judged to be only in the take-off stage.[8] On the basis of this model Rostow estimated timelines for when countries in his study evolved through each of the historical stages of development from the take-off stage onwards. Thus, for example, Rostow estimated that for Britain, the first nation to take-off, the take-off occurred in the period 1783–1802, the drive to maturity occurred in the period 1803–1850 and the economy entered the stage of mass consumption from the early 1930s.[9] Each of the five evolutionary stages in Rostow's model are defined by certain economic, social and political characteristics considered important to comprehending the general pattern of development in modern history.

1.2.1 Traditional society

The most economically backward stage, 'the traditional society', is defined by Rostow as 'one in whose structure is developed within limited production functions, based on pre-Newtonian science and technology, and on pre-Newtonian attitudes towards the physical world' where 'Newton is here used as a symbol for that watershed in history when men came widely to believe that the external world was subject to few knowable laws, and was systematically capable of productive manipulation'.[10] This stage is characterized by technological backwardness with an incapacity for systematic technological progress thereby placing a limit 'on the level of attainable output per head'.[11] For Rostow the economy is overwhelmingly based on agriculture. It is a society characterized by a 'hierarchical social structure' in which there is limited social and economic mobility and in which 'family and clan connexions played a large role in social organization'.[12]

Whilst Rostow does not use the term feudalism to describe this historical stage he writes that it is often characterized by 'central political rule' but in which the 'centre of gravity of political power generally lay in the regions, in the hands of those who owned or controlled the land'.[13] In the contemporary 'post-Newtonian' world the traditional society is one in which there is the possibility for technological progress but it remains 'untouched or unmoved by man's new capability for regularly manipulating his environment to his economic advantages'.[14] Nevertheless, the meaning of 'the traditional society' in Rostow's model is obscure, essentially capturing all those economically backward societies which have yet to evolve into the next historical stage of establishing the preconditions for take-off.

1.2.2 The pre-conditions for take-off

The second stage of growth in Rostow's model is one in the process of transition from tradition society to the take-off stage in which the preconditions for take-off are developed. It is a period characterized by society exploiting 'the fruits of modern science, to fend off diminishing returns' and in which 'the insights of modern science' are 'translated into new production functions in both agriculture and industry'.[15] The historical reference for this 'preconditions of take-off' stage appear to be 'Western Europe of the late seventeenth and early eighteenth centuries' which he associates with modernity and the enlightenment.[16]

From history Rostow identified two kinds of cases of the pre-conditions stage experienced by countries. The first and more general kind were those countries in which 'the creation of the preconditions for take-off required fundamental changes in well-established traditional society: changes which touched and substantially altered the social structure and political system as well as techniques of production'. This case is consistent with the historical economic development of the nations of 'most of Europe', the 'greater part of Asia, the Middle East and Africa'.[17] Rostow makes it clear that his characterization of the pre-condition for take-off mainly relate to this general case. The second kind of nations are those which he called 'born free', being all English-speaking countries and former colonies of Britain who inherited social and political institutions and cultural attitudes from the mother country, assisted by possessing abundant natural resources. These include the United States, Australia, Canada and New Zealand. Because these nations 'never became so deeply caught up in the structure, politics and values of the traditional society' there was less resistance to modernization.

The significance of this distinction in Rostow's thinking is that in the general case often an important motivating force to development is the fear of a nation in the stage of 'traditional society' being overtaken and dominated by more advanced nations. Thus he writes:

> As a matter of historical fact a reactive nationalism – reacting against intrusion from advanced nations – has been a most important and powerful motive force in the transition from traditional to modern societies, at least as important as the profit motive.[18]

For historical examples of this pattern, Rostow refers to the cases of Germany, Russia, Japan and China. Whilst Rostow focuses on the role of nationalism in economic development, he appreciates that a common feature of all these nations is that liberal democratic institutions were weak and their central governments autocratic.[19]

According to Rostow a 'decisive' factor in the pre-conditions to take-off is the political development of 'an effective centralized national state – on the basis of coalitions touched with a new nationalism'.[20] This is brought about by the emergence of a new elite who 'supersede' the 'old land-based elite' and whose interest lies with economic and social modernization, and especially in connection with promoting technical progress.[21] It is associated with a growing appreciation 'that economic progress is a necessary condition for some other purpose, judged to be good: be it national dignity, private profit, the general welfare, or a better life for the children'.[22] Besides the development of the institution of national government, this stage is characterized by the development of financial institutions for 'mobilizing capital', the development of transport and communications infrastructure, a widening in the 'scope of commerce' in the internal economy and externally, and the emergence of 'enterprising men' in the 'private economy, in government, or both – willing to mobilize savings and to take risks in pursuit of profit or modernization'.[23]

Rostow believed that in this stage the period of socio-political, economic and technical development necessary to establish the pre-conditions for take-off varied historically between nations. Until a transformation of society has progressed to a point where certain structural pre-conditions are in place, take-off cannot occur.

Firstly, there requires to be 'a build-up of social overhead capital, notably in transport' in order to create a 'national market', to productively exploit 'natural resources' and to enable the 'national government effectively to rule' to provide a 'setting of peaceful order'. This would require a national government 'capable and willing to take a degree of responsibility for the build-up of social overhead capital (including its finance)'.[24] Indeed, Rostow believed that because of 'the long period of gestation and pay-off, the lumpiness, and the indirect routes of pay-off' involved with building social overhead capital governments played 'an extremely important role in the precondition period'.[25]

Secondly, there must have begun a 'technological revolution in agriculture' to ensure a sufficient increase in agricultural productivity to meet the increased demand for food which arises from a 'disproportionate rise in urban populations'.[26] This will require 'a willingness of the agricultural community to accept new techniques and to respond to the possibilities of the widened commercial markets'.[27] In this connection Rostow contended that agricultural exports were important in generating foreign exchange needed to purchase foreign-produced capital goods as well as other imports, especially food. In addition, the expansion in agriculture and rural income will provide a significant source of demand for manufacturing industry, mainly for inputs to production. Furthermore, Rostow believed that at a time when agriculture still dominated the economy, rising rural incomes played an important role, through taxes and private saving, in financing 'social overhead capital' and 'loanable funds to the modern sector'. He cites nineteenth-century land reforms by 'Japan, Russia and many other nations' as 'an effort to increase the supply of capital available for social overhead and other essential modernizing processes'.[28]

Thirdly, a new generation of 'enterprising men' in the private sector and government must emerge to bring about the necessary modernization of the social and economic structure. This is clearly connected to the required institutional changes discussed above. In order to 'get the rate of investment up' Rostow argued that 'men in the society must be able to manipulate and apply . . . modern science and useful cost-reducing inventions' and 'some other men in the society must be prepared to undergo the strain and risks of leadership in bringing the flow of inventions productively into the capital stock'. Others 'must be prepared to lend their money long-term, at high risk, to back the innovating entrepreneurs' of 'modern industry'.[29] In addition, Rostow refers to the need for a trained workforce adaptable to 'an economic system whose methods are subject to regular change, and one which also increasingly confines the individual in large, disciplined organizations allocating to him specialized narrow, recurrent tasks'.[30]

Lastly, for Rostow the structural pre-conditions above, involving the creation of new markets and availability of new inputs to industry, enabled the initial and then sustained expansion of strategic 'enclaves of modern industrial activity' that characterized the decisive take-off stage. This supposes that in the pre-conditions stage these 'enclaves' of modern industry, which become the leading sectoral drivers in Rostow's take-off, are already established. Hence, in the case of Britain, the first nation to take-off, Rostow writes that it 'alone was in a position to weave together cotton manufacture, coal and iron technology, the steam engine, and ample foreign trade to pull it off'.[31]

1.2.3 The take-off

The third stage of 'take-off' is conceived by Rostow to be the decisive transformation in the historical development of a nation in which it gets onto a path of self-sustaining economic growth. He explained it as follows:

> The take-off is defined as the interval during which the rate of investment increases in such a way that real output *per capita* rises and this initial increase carries with it radical changes in production techniques and the disposition of income flows which perpetuates the new scale of investment and perpetuate thereby the rising trend in *per capita* output.[32]

The take-off is therefore seen to be a period in which there is considerable technical progress, embodied in, and driven by, a substantial increase in the rate of investment, which provides the impetus to a continuous self-perpetuating process of growth. Once the self-perpetuating process is achieved '[g]rowth becomes its normal condition. Compound interest becomes built, as it were, into its habits and institutional structure'.[33]

In attempting to provide a more precise definition of the take-off stage, Rostow set out three basic conditions:

1   A rise in the rate of productive investment from, say, 5 per cent, or less to over 10 per cent of national income, or net national product (NNP).
2   The development of one or more substantial manufacturing sectors, with a high rate of growth
3   The existence or quick emergence of a political, social and institutional framework which exploits the impulses to expansion in the modern sector and the potential external economy effects of the take-off and gives to growth an on-going character.[34]

In elaborating on the first condition Rostow endeavours to provide quantitative reasoning based on the assumptions that the marginal capital-output ratio for an economy 'in its early stages of economic development' is 3.5:1 and the population grows at 1–1.5 per cent per annum. On this basis, in order for the rate of net national product (NNP) per capita to be sustained (i.e. at zero growth) investment (saving) needs to be 'something between 3.5 and 5.25 per cent' of NNP. Therefore for NNP per capita to grow at the rate of 2 per cent investment (saving) must increase to 'something between 10.5 and 12.5 per cent of NNP'. On these assumptions Rostow contends that a 'transition from relatively stagnant to substantial, regular rise in NNP per capita, under typical population conditions, requires that the proportion of national product invested should move from somewhere in the vicinity of 5 per cent to something in the vicinity of 10 per cent'.[35] Putting aside measurement problems, this argument assumes no technical progress in the take-off, which is likely to reduce the capita-output ratio and thereby the required (measured) investment as a proportion of NNP to achieve a growth rate of 2 per cent of NNP per capita. Instead, Rostow indicated that there would be variations in the required investment rate for take-off according to differences in the population growth rates, the capita-output ratio and the amount of infrastructure, especially for transport, needed in the pre-take-off and take-off stages, of nations.[36] A major problem in empirically verifying this condition is the paucity of historical investment data, especially for nations in the pre-take-off stage. Nevertheless, Rostow appeals to available historical data of investment/NNP ratios for countries which, but for the exceptions of Sweden and Canada, are at various stages of undevelopment.[37] Elsewhere, Rostow (1963) maintains that:

> a careful scrutiny of both contemporary and historical data – where they exist – including the data for Great Britain, Germany, Sweden and Japan in this volume are consistent with this view: the investment rate is likely to rise during take-off; the extent of the rise will vary with specific factors, notably the scale of social overhead capital.[38]

He emphasizes though that 'a rise in the investment rate is not the sole relevant criterion for take-off'.[39]

With regard to the second condition, a feature of Rostow's explanation of the take-off is the central role played by what he calls 'leading sectors' or 'primary growth sectors' that provide the impetus to the overall expansion in modern manufacturing industry. These sectors are those which offer the best 'possibilities for innovation or for the exploitation of newly profitable or hitherto unexplored resources' such as to 'yield a high growth rate and set in motion expansionary forces elsewhere in the economy'.[40] The most historically important leading sector for take-off identified by Rostow is the railways: 'it was decisive in the United States, France, Germany, Canada, and Russia; it has played an extremely important part in the Swedish, Japanese and other cases'.[41] According to Rostow railways provided a major impetus to industry by stimulating the coal, iron and engineering industries, by lowering the costs of transport and widening the geographical market for products and by facilitating a 'rapidly enlarging export sector' which also enables the economy to obtain foreign capital for development. In the case of Britain's take-off however, Rostow identified the cotton-textile industry as the key leading sector, generating 'demand for coal, iron and machinery' as well as for working capital and cheap transport which, in turn, promoted wider industry investment and technological progress.[42] By reason of its export earnings the industry also enabled greater imports necessary to industrial expansion. For

Rostow though, historically the leading sectors have varied 'from cotton textiles, through heavy industry complexes based on railroads and military end products to timber, pulp, dairy products and finally a wide variety of consumers' goods'.[43]

In Rostow's model the take-off is a dynamic process led by rapid investment growth and technical innovation in the primary growth sectors which, through cost-reductions and inter-sectoral industry demand, generate an expansion in 'supplementary growth sectors' (e.g. coal, iron and engineering) which, in turn, promotes further investment and innovation that spreads to all sectors, including 'derived growth sectors' such as food production and housing which grow more steadily with 'total real income'. Hence, associated with the rapid expansion of manufacturing industry, is ongoing structural change and progressive urban development.[44]

The third condition of Rostow essentially consists of political, social and institutional changes that brings about widespread entrepreneurship for ongoing technical innovation in response to commercial opportunities and leadership in industry and government to provide 'social overhead capital' as required and create the capital market to finance the rapid expansion of investment.[45] With regard to the latter, Rostow is referring not just to the development of the financial system, but relatedly to the ability to access foreign capital funds and to the redistribution of income (profits) from the traditional agricultural sector to modern sector in order to enable the greater 'plough-back of profits in rapidly expanding particular sectors' of manufacturing industry.[46]

The take-off periods for major economies estimated by Rostow are, in chronological order, as follows:[47]

Great Britain	1783–1802
France	1830–1860
United States	1843–1860
Germany	1850–1873
Japan	1878–1900
Russia	1890–1914

This indicates that Rostow believed the take-off typically took 20–30 years.

1.2.4 The drive to maturity stage

In Rostow's model the take-off leads to the drive to maturity stage, being a 'long interval of sustained if fluctuating progress, as the now regularly growing economy drives to extend modern technology over the whole front of its economic activity'.[48] In this stage growth is seen to be self-perpetuating in which the rate of investment is between 10 to 20 per cent of national income and output per capita grows at a steady positive rate. It is characterized by the spread of the most advanced technology from a 'relatively narrow complex of industry' to other new industries associated with a continuous expansion of manufacturing industry. This is associated with ongoing structural change 'with new leading sectors gathering momentum to supplant the older leading sectors of the take-off'.[49] Hence, in the case of Germany, Great Britain, France and the United States, Rostow contended that there was a transition in the last quarter of the nineteenth century from growth dominated by railways along with coal, iron and heavy engineering industries to that dominated by steel, shipping, chemical, electricity and machine tools industries.[50] The structural pattern of this development will vary between nations according to not just 'the pool of technology', but also to 'the nature of resource endowments', to 'the character of the take-off, and the forces its sets in motion' and to 'the policies of governments'.[51] According to Rostow the drive to maturity, a state at which 'society has effectively applied the range of (then) modern technology to the bulk of its resources', typically took 60 years after the take-off stage had begun. His estimates for the historical dates at which major countries reached this state of maturity are 1850 for Great Britain, 1900 for the United States, 1910 for Germany and France, 1940 for Japan and 1950 for Russia.[52]

1.2.5 The age of high mass-consumption

After maturity the next stage of development in Rostow's model is the age of high mass consumption in which 'leading sectors shift towards durable consumer's goods and services'.[53] It marks a stage of development in which living standards rise for the mass population and in which consumer goods and service industries are the fastest growing. Rostow identified the automobile as symbolic of this age; one in which 'various electric-powered household gadgets were gradually diffused'.[54] This stage is characterized by the greater allocation of resources to social welfare and security, by urbanization and, socially, by a greater 'individualist-utilitarian creed'.[55] In Rostow's model the first nation to enter this stage is, not surprisingly, the United States from the early 1920s, followed by Canada in the mid-1920s, Britain in the early 1930s, by Australia in the late 1930s, then, after the Second World War, by France and Germany, and Japan in the mid-1950s.[56]

1.3 Explaining the 'take-off' growth process

What is interesting about Rostow as an economic historian explaining the growth process is the attempt in his book of 1952, *The Process of Economic Growth*, to formulate a theoretical apparatus (or 'system') to do so.[57] This 'system' is employed by Rostow to interpret the historical patterns of economic development and so to identify the forces which he considers important to explaining growth. It clearly informs his stages of economic growth model. Moreover, in formulating this system, Rostow is influenced by his study of economic history. In this connection he takes an approach to explaining growth and development which endeavours to marry history with economic theory. No doubt Rostow considered economic theory to be important to his historical analysis.[58]

In the early 1950s growth theory in economic science was enjoying a renewed interest following the development of the Harrod and Domar models and the Keynesian inspired trade cycle theories.[59] Nevertheless, only after the mid-1950s there was a significant progress in growth theory, with the Solow-Swan model and with post-Keynesian contributions by the Cambridge School in England. According to Rostow:

> The most vital and fully articulated bodies of modern economic thought have been developed within Marshallian short-period assumptions; that is, the social and political framework of the economy, the state of the arts, and the levels of fixed capacity are assumed to be given and, usually, fixed . . . these are intolerable assumptions for the historian.[60]

Hence, for Rostow, Book IV of Alfred Marshalls's *Principles of Economics* (1890) 'constitutes perhaps the most extensive and rigorous statement of the factors governing changes in the rate of growth and productivity of the factors of production that exist in the literature'.[61]

At the heart of Rostow's theoretical apparatus is a pseudo aggregate production function in which output is 'determined by the scale and productivity of the working force and capital' where 'for the purposes of this analysis' capital comprises 'land and other natural resources as well as scientific, technical and organizational knowledge'.[62] It essentially consists of identifying the major social, political, economic and related institutional forces which influence and determine the rate of change of the 'two complex variables', which could be described as the productive powers of the labour force combined with the capital stock (including all material inputs) employed in aggregate production. In Rostow's apparatus this is articulated by way of six 'propensities': (1) 'the propensity to develop fundamental science (physical and social)'; (2) 'the propensity to apply science to economic ends'; (3) 'the propensity to accept innovations'; (4) 'the propensity to seek material advance'; (5) 'the propensity to consume'; and (6) 'the propensity to have children'.[63] While Rostow admits that these propensities are not conducive to quantitative measurement, they can be conceptually defined in terms of their responses to other variables in the sense, for example, that the propensity to have children will tend to increase with real income and/or the greater religious domination of society.[64] Fundamentally, these propensities are 'conceived to be a function of the value system of society' as founded in the social and institutional structure of society.[65] Indeed, Rostow considered their analysis to be beyond the domain of economists, by historians, sociologists, psychologists and other social scientists.[66]

In Rostow's 'system' an important factor influencing capital accumulation is the long-term yield on investment which, not defined precisely, seems to be an expected profit rate adjusted for risk.[67] The relative yields in different industry sectors are seen by Rostow to determine the sectoral composition of investment and, thereby, structural change that accompanies growth.[68] The yield itself is seen to be influenced by the 'potentialities' of innovation and returns to scale;[69] while the extent to which the rate of investment responds to a higher 'yield' will depend on the entrepreneurial attitude toward risk connected in part, to (4) the propensity to seek material advance. Indeed, in Rostow's system the propensities (1) to (5),

shaped by politico-institutional and socio-economic forces, all play a role in determining the rate of growth of the productive power of the capital stock.

In Rostow's theoretical apparatus the process of take-off growth involves a
dynamic interaction between the propensities and the yields in which propensities
(1)–(3), by generating innovation, can causally raise the yields and, in which an
increase in the rate of investment in response to higher yields can, in turn, induce
technical progress. At the same time Rostow believed that a potential constraint to
the expansion of any sector was diminishing returns for a given technology, which
could be overcome by yields being kept up through innovation continuously inducing investment in a process he referred to 'as changing production functions'. This
take-off process involves structural change in which the rapid expansion of the leading sectors, associated with, and, indeed, contributing toward, inducing an increase
in the propensities and thereby yields of new emerging sectors that widens the
investment-driven expansion and puts the economy on the path to self-perpetuating
growth. It is evident though that whereas the propensities are conceived to be slow-
changing according to social and institutional change, the yields are more variable in
response to changes in the propensities and other factors. In this connection, Rostow
refers to the need 'to take account, in history, of the interaction of economic growth
on the propensities themselves'.[70] Indeed, Rostow's theoretical apparatus represents
an attempt to make sense of the complexity of a path-dependent growth process in
which there is interdependence between the major explanatory factors identified,
most particularly, between technical innovation and investment (i.e. capital accumulation). It was indeed from this theoretical apparatus that Rostow formulated his
historical explanation of the take-off process.

1.4 Rosenstein-Rodan's 'big push' model

As Rosenstein-Rodan described it himself, the 'big push' model is essentially
a proposed development strategy for 'launching a country into self-sustaining
growth' by a rapid process of industrialization.[71] He first articulated this strategy
in 1943 for the post-war development of the agrarian-based region of Eastern
and South-Eastern Europe. The central element of the strategy was the establishment of an international institution, to be called the 'Eastern European Industrial
Trust' (EEIT), through which a large capital investment program could be coordinated with the various States in the region. Underlying the big push model of
Rosenstein-Rodan is the idea that a large comprehensive investment program is
required to propel a rapid industrialization process which puts an undeveloped
country (or region) on the path of self-sustaining growth.[72] Without a big, planned
and coordinated investment push by state intervention Rosenstein-Rodan argued
that the process of development would be slow:

> Proceeding 'bit by bit' will not add up in its effects to the sum total of single
> bits. A minimum quantum of investment is necessary, though not sufficient,
> condition of success. This, in a nutshell, is the contention of the theory of the
> big push.[73]

In Rosenstein-Rodan's big push model 'the whole of industry to be created is to be treated and planned like one huge firm or trust', involving the sequencing of coordinated investment according to industry requirements.[74] The priority and central task of this strategy is to provide 'social overhead capital', comprising 'basic industries' providing power, education, transport and other communications infrastructure necessary to induce investment more widely in other industries. Besides this central task, Rosenstein-Rodan argued that complementarity created demand whose supply required ongoing investment to maintain the momentum of development.

The main theoretical rationale for the big push model is what Rosenstein-Rodan calls 'indivisibility' in the development process. There are a number of kinds of indivisibility that he has in mind, which have their origin in Marshall's 'external economies' notion. The first is 'indivisibility in the production function', which requires large scale production to generate increasing returns necessary to produce output at an economically viable cost. On this basis the normal industry structure is seen to be oligopolistic 'with the obvious danger of monopolistic markets'.[75] By reference to Allyn Young's argument of the role of external economies,[76] Rosenstein-Rodan proposed that increasing returns obtained from the growth in the size of firms was also a consequence of the growth of the industry and of the growth of the economic system as a whole. The growth in markets associated with the growth in the economic system as a whole facilitates specialization and technical progress connected with industry networking that is conceived to generate considerable external economies with development. For Rosenstein-Rodan 'the most important instance of indivisibility and hence of external economies on the supply side' is the afore-mentioned social overhead capital since it generates 'investment opportunities' in 'other industries' which 'become available only after long gestation periods'.[77]

Rosenstein-Rodan identifies four different kinds of indivisibilities that characterize social overhead capital. Firstly, it is indivisible in time, by which he means it is historically irreversible and, as a necessary basis for wider industry investment, must be given priority. In the big push strategy social overhead capital may be usefully considered to be the foundation of development. The second kind of indivisibility is that the capital equipment 'has high minimum durability' in the sense it must technically be installed on a large discrete scale so that 'excess capacity will be unavoidable over the initial period in under-developed countries'.[78] An example which perhaps illustrates Rosenstein-Rodan's point is that of a hydro-electrical power plant which, after its installation, will take a long period of time before the production of electrical power approaches near full utilization of its capacity. Significantly, it means a large amount of capital funds must be committed to finance social overhead capital. The third kind of indivisibility of social overhead capital is the long gestation period involved in constructing the infrastructure which thereby requires anticipation of the future need of utility services by industry through planning. The fourth kind of indivisibility which poses an obstacle to development is the need for 'an irreducible minimum social overhead capital industry mix' to get self-sustaining growth off the ground.[79] This refs to the complementarity of the different utility services provided by infra-structure such as power, transport and other communications that is required for industry in general to develop. For this reason Rosenstein-Rodan estimates that an under-developed country will have to invest 'between 30–40 per cent of its total investments' to make substantial progress in its economic development.[80]

In the big push model social overhead capital is crucial for Rosenstein-Rodan because it generates considerable 'external economies' which are seen to be vital to the growth process. It is evident that the strategy relies on the government (or state) playing the key role in financing and providing social overhead capital because it is not a profitable enterprise for the private sector. In the absence of government action social overhead capital would only be established very slowly, bit by bit, and so would any progress toward self-sustaining growth. Moreover, as indicated above, in Rosenstein-Rodan's strategy the provision of social overhead capital involves economic planning by the state: 'Since overall vision is required as well as a cor-rect appraisal of future development, *programming* is undoubtedly required in this lumpy field' as 'normal market mechanisms will not provide an optimum supply'.[81]

Another major indivisibility identified is what Rosenstein-Rodan calls the 'indivisibility of demand', which is based on the notion that the demand for the product of any given industry depends on the aggregate of demand, itself depend-ent on the level of investment by industries in general.[82] According to this notion there is a 'complementarity of demand' such that the profitability of any invest-ment project depends on the number of other investment projects which contrib-ute toward overall demand. In this connection, Rosenstein-Rodan believed that a major obstacle to development for underdeveloped countries was the relatively small size of their domestic market.[83] On this basis, Rosenstein-Rodan argued that greater complementarity of demand lowers 'the marginal risk of each invest-ment' and 'would lead to either higher or cheaper credit facilities and these con-stitute internal economies' to firms.[84] This provides an additional rationale for the big push strategy for an undeveloped country in which a 'minimum quantum of investment' is committed by way of a programme of co-ordinated planning. The minimum size of the push is however reduced by international trade because it enables the world market to partially facilitate the complementarity of demand of a developing country. Nevertheless, Rosenstein-Rodan concludes that inter-national trade cannot eliminate the indivisibility of demand: 'it does not dispense with the need for a big push'.[85]

In addition to the above Rosenstein-Rodan identifies an indivisibility in the supply of savings to finance the large minimum quantum of investment required for self-sustaining development. The problem is that because of their low income underdeveloped countries have difficulty generating the necessary volume of saving. For this reason Rosenstein-Rodan proposed that up to 50 per cent of the funding (i.e. saving) for his big push strategy for post-World War II Eastern and South-Eastern Europe could be supplied by advanced countries through an inter-national trust.[86] The continuation of the development process will nevertheless rely on an increase in the domestic rate of saving: 'a high income elasticity of saving thus constitute the third indivisibility'.[87]

Underlying Rosenstein-Rodan's big push strategy is the notion that markets and the price signals cannot on their own be relied upon in under-developed countries to generate the appropriate sequencing of investment and, especially, to provide the social overhead capital, necessary for development. The 'basic industries' strategically important to development he clearly believed they are naturally dominated by oligopolies and, with the prevalence of economies of scale, are conducive to monopolization. But for Rosenstein-Rodan the problem of indivisibility means that in absence of public investment by the state, social overhead capital would only be provided slowly 'bit by bit'. He believed that a state planning institution was required to carry out the big push investment programme, not only in order to install social overhead capital but to coordinate and sequence industry investment to overcome the problem of demand complementarity. In what appears to be an oblique reference to the national political leadership needed to institute the big push, he commented, 'there may be finally a phenomenon of indivisibility in the vigour and drive for a successful development policy'[88].

1.5 An appraisal through the lens of a demand-led theory of growth

In their contribution to development economics Rostow's 'take-off' and Rosenstein-Rodan's 'big push' have a strong affinity. In different ways both are concerned with the *grand* question of how undeveloped economies can make the decisive step that puts them on the path to self-sustaining growth and development. Rostow's model represents an ambitious attempt to identify from economic history the key factors creating the social, politico-institutional and technical conditions for the decisive take-off in industrial development. From its historical perspective the crucial stage in Rostow's model is in fact the 'pre-conditions to take-off', at which an economy has in place all those key factors which enable the take-off. Hence, Kuznets considered Rostow's sequence of take-off stages were 'analogous' to 'an aeronautical process' in 'putting an aeroplane into flight':

> First there is the checking and fuelling, providing the pre-conditions; then there is the relatively brief take off, during which the driving force is accelerated to produce upward movement; and finally there is the levelling off into self-sustained flight.[89]

Though the aeroplane might of course stall or crash in take-off, the take-off cannot even occur without the pre-conditions being met. Given that Rostow believed the state played a key role in the take-off process, most evident when he elaborates on the development history of Germany and 'Meiji' Japan in the nineteenth century, a central purpose of his model to discover the secrets of growth was to draw lessons for development policy. In this connection the 'big push' is a development policy proposed by Rosenstein-Rodan to essentially achieve Rostow's 'take-off'. Thus, in describing the challenge of economic development Rosenstein-Rodan also used an aeronautical metaphor: '[l]aunching a country into self-sustaining growth is a little like getting an airplane off the ground. There is a critical ground speed which must be passed before the craft can become airborne'.[90] Without sufficient ground speed and thrust the airplane will not get off the ground. While Rosenstein-Rodan was familiar with the kind of institutional factors at the centre of Rostow's historical analysis, the big push is essentially based on theory not history.

A major shortcoming with Rostow's stages model is the supply-side approach to growth, as based on an aggregate production function, which underlies it. Since the capital debates of the 1960s it is well established that the neoclassical aggregate production function (or indeed, the production function for an industry or firm) is only valid in a one-commodity system and not in the general case of heterogeneous commodities used in the production of others. The results of the capital debates undermine the dominant neoclassical supply-side approach to growth (in all its variants, including endogenous growth models) since it cannot be supposed that factor prices systematically regulate to assure that aggregate demand is adjusted in the long run to aggregate output necessary for any supply-determined equilibrium steady-state growth rate.[91] A more promising theory of growth and one not plagued by these theoretical problems is provided by the demand-led approach that has origins in Harrod's growth model.[92] In this approach the growth rate of output is determined by the growth rate of demand in which the growth rate of capital and employed labour are endogenously determined according to the technique of production.

This demand-led approach provides greater clarity in appraising Rostow's 'stages' model of historical development. From the standpoint of the demand-led approach to growth the essential problem of the take-off is one of an undeveloped country being able to generate demand growth when income per capita is relatively low. At the risk of being semantic, the difficulty for poor countries to grow and develop is that they are too poor to generate domestic demand. If however an undeveloped country can find a market for its products in a relatively richer country then they can generate (foreign) demand growth. This perhaps explains why the first nation to take-off, Britain, took longer than most of those that followed because it had to rely more on technical progress to generate higher income per capita and, thereby, higher demand growth in its economic empire. The relatively faster take-off of Germany and the United States in the second half of the nineteenth century, characterized by a rapid absorption of industrial technology, can be much attributed to greater access to lucrative export markets thanks to the established prosperity of the British Empire economy and its liberal policy to international trade. In the case of Germany innovative industrial banking also played a significant role in enabling strong growth in investment and, thereby, domestic demand; whereas the United States benefited from foreign capital, mainly from British lenders. Similarly, the strong post-World War II growth, characterized by a convergence of income per capita of the advanced nations, can be attributed not only to ongoing expansionist fiscal policies but to a liberalization of international trade that in particular enabled Western European countries and Japan to generate strong demand by access to the rich United States market.

From the standpoint of our demand-led approach Rostow's idea of self-sustaining growth when a country reaches the 'stage of maturity' can be well interpreted as achieving a critical level of income per capita, having established institutions in policy-making, finance, education and in innovation-creation that are capable of sustaining ongoing growth in domestic demand.

The demand-led approach to growth can also shed some light on the plausibility of Rosentein-Rodan's 'big push' model for a take-off in growth. There is no doubt that a large-scale investment programme, involving social overhead capital, can in theory generate a considerable lift in demand growth and, thereby, in the growth in output of a developing economy. The real doubt about the success of such a growth strategy led by large-scale planned investment in heavy industry is whether it can be sustained by consumption growth. In absence of a lucrative export market generating foreign demand, the big push requires a rapid increase in income per capita to generate the domestic consumption necessary for the viability of the investment programme and the creation of social overhead capital.[93] Moreover, there is always the danger that unresponsive to market signals of industry needs, programming, often subject to political interference, results in the wrong kind of social overhead capital being constructed.

The problem with Rosenstein-Rodan's 'big push', which the author basically acknowledges, is that it requires a great deal of upfront capital which cannot be internally generated by undeveloped countries with low incomes and it is naïve to expect that it could be provided by international agencies and/or by foreign investors other than as direct foreign capital spending in commercial (usually export orientated) enterprises. This underlies that the essential difficulty for undeveloped countries inducing take-off growth is in generating *sustained* growth in demand when domestic income is low.

Notwithstanding the shortcomings of Rostow's 'stages' model and Rosenstein-Rodan's 'big push' model, they have made highly useful contributions to development economics as much for their grand ambition to discover the secrets to growth and prosperity. It is to his credit that Rostow endeavoured to interpret the history of economic development explicitly by reference to theoretical principles and that he endeavours to employ history to do so. Perhaps for this reason Rostow offers many useful insights even though his theoretical outlook lacks coherency. Similarly, though Rosenstein-Rodan's 'big push' has not proven a successful development strategy, the conceptual thinking underlying it provides useful insights into the challenges for an undeveloped country to take-off into sustained growth. There is no doubt that a lack of social overhead capital can be an obstacle to economic growth and development, not only for undeveloped countries but for advanced ones too. Facilitating the structural network of industries can also generate the external economies of scale that make them internationally competitive. In this regard Rosenstein-Rodan's big push relies on and is decisively constrained by demand growth. It is generating strong sustained demand growth that is the fundamental secret to a country achieving take-off into sustained growth and development which decisively lifts the living standards of its inhabitants.

Notes

1 Rostow and Rosenstein-Rodan would have been well aware of each other's views, especially given that they were both at MIT in the 1950s where development was a major intellectual focus under the auspices of the Centre for International Studies (CENIS), which was concerned with promoting US foreign aid and international policies to thwart the spread of communism to developing countries.
2 W.W. Rostow, *The Process of Economic Growth* (New York: Norton & Company, 1952) on p. 102.
3 W.W. Rostow, 'The Take-off into Sustained Growth', *Economic Journal*, 66: 261 (1956), pp. 25–48, on p. 27.
4 W.W. Rostow, 'The Stages of Economic Growth', *The Economic History Review, NS* 12: 1, (1959), pp. 1–16.
5 W.W. Rostow, *The Stages of Economic Growth: A non-Communist Manifesto* (Cambridge: Cambridge University Press, 1961).
6 For a highly critical response, see P.A. Baran and E.J. Hobsbawm, 'Review of *Stages of Economic Growth* by W.W. Rostow', *Kyklos*, 14: 2, (1961), pp. 234–42.
7 W.W. Rostow, *The Stages of Economic Growth*, p.1.
8 Ibid., p. x.
9 Ibid., pp. x, 38, 59.
10 Ibid., p. 4.
11 Ibid.
12 Ibid., p. 5.
13 Ibid.
14 Ibid.
15 Ibid., p. 6.
16 W.W. Rostow, 'The Stages of Economic Growth', p. 4.
17 W.W. Rostow, *The Stages of Economic Growth*, pp. 17–18.
18 Ibid., p 26.
19 Ibid., pp. 27–31.
20 Ibid., p. 7.
21 Ibid., p 26.
22 Ibid., p 6.
23 Ibid.
24 W.W. Rostow, 'The Stages of Economic Growth', p. 5.
25 W.W. Rostow, *The Stages of Economic Growth*, p. 25.
26 Ibid.
27 Ibid.
28 Ibid., pp. 23–24.
29 Ibid., p. 20.
30 Ibid.
31 Ibid., p. 33.
32 W.W. Rostow, 'The Take-off into Sustained Growth', p. 25.
33 W.W. Rostow, *The Stages of Economic Growth*, p. 7.
34 Ibid., p. 39.
35 Ibid., p. 41.
36 W.W. Rostow (ed.), *The Economics of Take-off into Sustained Growth: Proceedings of a Conference held by the International Economic Association* (London: St Martin's Press, 1963), on pp. xiv–xv.
37 W.W. Rostow, *The Stages of Economic Growth*, pp. 41–46.
38 W.W. Rostow (ed.), *The Economics of Take-off*, pp. xv–xvi. This reference to various case studies assessing the plausibility of Rostow's model of take-off in a volume of conference proceedings, titled *The Economics of Take-off into Sustained Growth*, published in 1963.

39 Ibid.
40 W.W. Rostow, 'The Take-off into Sustained Growth', p. 43; W.W. Rostow, *The Stages of Economic Growth*, p. 52.
41 W.W. Rostow, *The Stages of Economic Growth*, p. 55.
42 Ibid. pp. 54–55.
43 Ibid. p. 46. Referring to its significant role in nationalistic Russia, Germany and Japan, Rostow also argues 'that an enlargement and modernisation of Armed Forces could play the role of a leading sector in take-off' (W. W. Rostow, 'The Take-off into Sustained Growth', p. 46).
44 W.W. Rostow, 'The Take-off into Sustained Growth', pp. 43–44; W.W. Rostow, *The Stages of Economic Growth*, pp. 52–53.
45 W.W. Rostow, *The Stages of Economic Growth*, pp. 46–52.
46 Ibid. pp. 46–50.
47 Ibid., p. 38. The take-off period of other countries nominated by Rostow include Belgium (1833–1860), Sweden (1868–1890), Canada (1896–1914), Argentina (1935–), Turkey (1837–), India (1952–) and China (1952–).
48 Ibid., p. 9.
49 Ibid., p. 59.
50 Ibid., pp. 9, 59.
51 Ibid.
52 Ibid., p. 59.
53 Ibid., p. 10.
54 Ibid., p. 11.
55 Ibid., pp. 73–74.
56 See 'Chart of the stage of economic growth in selected countries' on opening page of W.W. Rostow, *The Stages of Economic Growth*, p. 1.
57 In the opening sentence of this book Rostow declares 'This is an historian's book about economic theory' (W.W. Rostow, *The Process of Economic Growth*, p. 2).
58 Ibid., p.3
59 Ibid., p. 86, fn 9.
60 Ibid., p. 3.
61 Ibid., pp. 4–6.
62 Ibid. pp. 12, 55.
63 Ibid., pp. 13–14. Hicks commented that these propensities 'are clearly intended to regard as in some manner analogous to the propensities which (according to Keynes [in the *General theory*]) determine employment' (J. R. Hicks, 'Review of *The Process of Economic Growth* by W.W. Rostow', *Journal of Political Economy*, 61: 2, (1953), pp. 173–74, on p. 173.
64 W.W. Rostow, *The Process of Economic Growth*, p. 36.
65 Ibid., p. 38.
66 P.A. Baran, 'Review of *The Process of Economic Growth* by W.W. Rostow', *American Economic Review*, 42: 5, (1952), pp. 921–23, on pp. 921–22.
67 W.W. Rostow, *The Process of Economic Growth*, pp. 65–67.
68 Ibid. pp. 80–82, 114–15.
69 Rostow uses the term 'diminishing returns' to investment by which he appears to mean output per unit of capital invested tends to diminish for a given technology, largely because of the decreasing marginal productivity of exploiting natural resources necessary to economic growth (ibid., pp 81–83).
70 Ibid., p. 103.
71 P. N. Rosenstein-Rodan, 'Notes on the Theory of the "Big Push"', in H.S. Ellis and H.C. Wallich (eds), *Economic Development for Latin America: Proceedings of a Conference held by the International Economic Association* (London: MacMillan, 1961), pp 57–73, on p. 57.
72 P.N. Rosenstein-Rodan, 'Problems of Industrialisation of Eastern and South-Eastern Europe', *The Economic Journal*, 53: 210/211, (1943), pp. 202–11; P.N. Rosenstein-Rodan, 'Notes on the Theory of the "Big Push"'.

73 P.N. Rosenstein-Rodan, 'Notes on the Theory of the "Big Push"', p. 57.

74 P.N. Rosenstein-Rodan, 'Problems of Industrialisation', p. 204.

75 P.N. Rosenstein-Rodan, 'Notes on the Theory of the "Big Push"', p. 60.

76 A.A. Young, 'Increasing Returns and Economic Progress', *The Economic Journal*, 38: 152, (1928), pp. 527–42.

77 P.N. Rosenstein-Rodan, 'Notes on the Theory of the "Big Push"', p. 60.

78 Ibid., p. 61.

79 Ibid.

80 Ibid.

81 Ibid., p. 61, my emphasis.

82 Ibid.

83 For an illustration of this notion, see Rodan-Rosenstein's shoe factory example in 'Problems of Industrialisation', pp. 205–06; 'Notes on the Theory of the "Big Push"', p. 62.

84 P.N. Rosenstein-Rodan, 'Notes on the Theory of the "Big Push"', pp. 61–62.

85 Ibid., p. 65.

86 P.N. Rosenstein-Rodan, 'Problems of Industrialisation', pp. 209–11.

87 P.N. Rosenstein-Rodan, 'Notes on the Theory of the "Big Push"', p. 65.

88 Ibid., p. 65.

89 S. Kuznets, 'Notes on the Take-off', in W.W. Rostow (ed.), *The Economics of Take-off into Sustained Growth: Proceedings of a Conference held by the International Economic Association* (London: St Martin's Press, 1963), pp. 22–43, on p. 36.

90 P.N. Rosenstein-Rodan, 'Notes on the Theory of the "Big Push"', p. 57.

91 The general prevalence of 're-switching' and 'capital deepening' means that no inverse functional relationship between factor prices and 'the quantity' (in value terms) of factors of production can be established in a multi-commodity economic system necessary for the adjustment of demand to output consistent with the simultaneous determination of distribution. See P. Garegnani, 'Heterogeneous capital, the production function and the theory of distribution', *Review of Economic Studies*, 37: 3, (1970), pp. 407–36; P. Garegnani, 'Quantity of Capital' in J.L. Eatwell, M. Milgate and P. Newman (eds), *Capital Theory: The New Palgrave* (London: MacMillan, 1990a), pp. 1–78; H.D. Kurz and N. Salvadori, *Theory of Production: A Long Period Analysis* (Cambridge: Cambridge University Press, 1995), pp. 427–64; F. Petri, *General Equilibrium, Capital and Macroeconomics: A Key to Recent Controversies in Equilibrium Theory* (Cheltenham: Edward Elgar, 2004) esp. pp. 206–52.

92 See for example F. Serrano, 'Long Period Effective Demand and the Sraffian Supermultiplier', *Contributions to Political Economy*, 14, (1995), pp. 67–90; M. Smith, 'Demand-Led growth Theory: An Historical Approach', *Review of Political Economy*, 24: 4, (2012), pp. 543–73. The main requirement to avoid the capital problems is that for a given technique prices and distribution be determined separately from the quantity of factors of production and of outputs, leaving them open to be determined by demand. This indeed is a characteristic of the 'surplus' approach to prices and distribution of the classical economists and Marx, as reconstructed by P. Sraffa, *Production of Commodities by Means of Commodities: Prelude to a Critique of Economic Theory* (Cambridge: Cambridge University Press, 1960). On the theoretical structure of the 'surplus approach', see P. Garegnani, 'Value and Distribution in the Classical Economists and Marx', *Oxford Economic Papers*, 36: 2, (1984), pp. 291–325; P. Garegnani, 'Sraffa: classical versus marginal analysis', in K. Bharadwaj and B. Schefold (eds), *Essays on Piero Sraffa: Critical Perspectives on the Revival of Classical Theory* (London: Unwin Hyman, 1990b), pp. 112–40.

93 R. Nurkse, 'Further Comments on Professor Rosenstein-Rodan's Paper', in H.S. Ellis and H.C. Wallich (eds), *Economic Development for Latin America: Proceedings of a Conference held by the International Economic Association* (London: MacMillan, 1961), pp. 74–78.

2 Albert Hirschman

Unbalanced growth theory

Davide Gualerzi

2.1 Introduction

This chapter focuses on the nature of the development process and in particular on its main feature, that of being an unbalanced growth phenomenon. The notion of unbalanced growth is associated especially with the work of Albert Hirschman in *The Strategy of Economic Development* of 1958.[1] Based on the six years Hirschman spent in Colombia, the book lays out a really seminal view of development as a chain of disequilibria opening a research agenda that has been largely set aside today. The problem of development in the world economy of the twenty-first century is certainly different from that observed by Hirschman in the 1950s. Nevertheless induced investment, complementarities and linkages effects are key aspects of today's development patterns. That is why the question of unbalanced growth reaches into the fundamental problems lying ahead for emerging economies.

In the preface to the latest edition of the 1967 book on development projects Hirschman explains that the views on development in *The Strategy* were later complemented by the examination of the political processes[2] and by the critical evaluation of the methods and operational tools for development.[3] He therefore refers to these works as composing a 'trilogy' having the 'overriding common intent to celebrate, to "sing" the epic adventure of development – its challenge, drama, and grandeur'.[4] In the same preface Hirschman explains that the examination of development projects brought to completion his work on development, but at the same time it 'became the bridge the broader social sciences themes of my subsequent writings'.[5]

Hirschman has indeed gone in many different directions in his successive work, going beyond development economics, discussing for instance the 'Responses to the Decline in Firms, Organizations, and States',[6] or the private\public 'cycle'.[7]

In line with the general purpose of bringing back into today's debate the main insights of early development economics, in section 2.2 we first point out Hirschman's peculiar position within development economics. In section 2.3 we outline Hirschman's general view of the development process that stands as the fundamental premise for unbalanced growth. From sections 2.4 to section 2.6 we examine his argument on unbalanced growth and the collision with 'the balanced growth' approach. Section 2.7 examines other views on unbalanced growth, most notably those of Paul Streeten. Sections 2.8 and 2.9 elaborate on the relationship of unbalanced growth with modern theories of growth and structural transformation. The close similarity of these last approaches suggest a possible direction along which to develop Hirschman's views on the development process. In particular, Hirschman's focus on investment decisions indicates that a fruitful line of investigation could be the problem of market formation within developing economies. In that light the analysis of complementarities offers an improvement of the demand side problem of growth, considering more explicitly consumption complementarities.

2.2 Hirschman and development economics

A prominent figure among the early theorists who were émigrés from Continental Europe, Albert Hirschman's work is noticeable for the peculiarity of his intellectual development.[8] Lying in between economic and political theory, a constant in all his work, arguably explains the originality of his views. The 'life history' written by Jeremy Adelman helps to better understand the very special nature of the intellectual journey of Albert Hirschman and the process shaping his ideas.[9] Adelman mentions how in his visit to Francois Perroux: 'He wanted to draw attention to the ways in which perceptions of obstacles were sometimes thornier than the obstacles themselves'.[10] Adelman also recalls Hirschman words about the 'experience of what it is to think dangerous thoughts' referring to his understanding of Machiavelli.[11]. He also describes the number of steps and different influences leading to the study of 'disappointment' as a key force for public action and therefore as a focal point for social sciences.[12]

The Strategy of Economic Development is one of the earlier works by Hirschman in the stage in which development economics was rising and one of the most important seminal contributions in the field. The distinctive point is the notion of unbalanced growth.

As for the other influential contributions – some of which are examined in this volume – they are the result of the intellectual environment and the particular circumstances of the period from the end of WWII to the 1960s. That is what Paul Krugman calls it 'high development theory'[13] arguing that its virtual disappearance from the economic discourse largely depends on the shift in method that occurred in economic theory. Model building became the standard of the profession, and in the process the development theory of Hirschman and Myrdal became to economists 'not so much wrong as incomprehensible'.[14] We can note however that Krugman reconstruction of development economics is very much out of line with what Hirschman argues. Krugman regards as 'the essential high development model' the Rosenstein-Rodan's Big Push argument.[15] But that is precisely the essence of the balanced growth doctrine Hirschman criticizes.

Stiglitz has argued that the lack of formal models cannot tell the story of the decline of development economics. It was the changing intellectual and political context the key element explaining:

I would submit that a far more plausible explanation for the seeming demise of high development theory is that the same currents that led to the dominance of free market ideology in the United Kingdom and the United States were reflected – at least in the United States – in the dominance of those ideas in certain intellectual circles. In short, it was as much the market demand for ideas as the supply of models that was crucial.[16]

Interestingly Hirschman also has an explanation for the rise and fall of development economics. He argues that the sub-discipline, as he calls it, came into being as a result 'of an a priori unlikely conjunction of distinct ideological currents'. Although extraordinarily productive at one point, that created problems subsequently:

[b]ecause of its heterogeneous ideological makeup, the new science was shot through with tensions that would prove disruptive at the first opportunity. Secondly, because of the circumstances under which it arose, development economics became overloaded with unreasonable hopes and ambitions that soon had to be clipped back.[17]

2.3 Hirschman on development

Stiglitz argues that at the core of development theory are still the questions of externalities, technological progress, and returns to scale. Since the point is not the lack of models, what are then the fundamental issues that they miss?

We would argue that it is precisely a theoretical conception of what development is about. That is what we find in Hirschman and it got lost in the recent intellectual history. The non-formalized, discursive approach at theorizing favored by Hirschman was not the stubborn adherence to an 'archaic' method, as suggested by Krugman, but the effort to define the concepts and the framework that are indeed fundamental to the analysis of development. Intellectual progress following the original lines set out by Hirschman should start from what is peculiar and unique to his approach.

In *The Strategy of Economic Development* it is apparent that every aspect of development, as well as the role of government, the pubic sector and institutions at large, depends on the very understanding of the development process. In a nutshell: development depends on inducements mechanisms rather than on identifying obstacles, prerequisites, and missing factors. The point is not how complete and sophisticated that list is, the point is how you break out of the underdevelopment equilibrium. Hirschman observes that the focus shifted from natural resources to capital, to entrepreneurial and managerial abilities and the early notion of human capital. When these failed to provide an explanation the attention turned to the attitudes and value systems. These are important but they are not the fundamental point either. These factors, as much as savings and productive investment, are 'as much a result as a cause of development'.[18]

The methodological premise of the analysis is in the very first sentence of the preface. Hirschman quotes Whitehead: 'The elucidation of immediate experience is the sole justification of any thought; and the starting point for thought is the analytic observation of components of this experience'.[19] His book, Hirschman explains, is based on his own immediate experience in one of the so-called under-developed countries, namely Colombia.

The 'preliminary explorations' as the title of the first chapter reads focuses on the 'primum mobile', the key to the beginning of the development process: 'development depends not so much on finding optimal combinations for given resources and factors of production as on calling forth and enlisting for devel-opment purposes resources and abilities that are hidden, scattered or badly uti-lized'.[20] Thus a 'binding agent' is needed to get the development process started.[21] The preliminary exploration concludes stressing that the investigation concerns the search of effective inducement mechanisms capable of improving and speed-ing up decision-making. Not the deficiency of any particular factor, but 'in the combining process itself' is the obstacle to be overcome.[22]

According to Hirschman it must be understood that underdeveloped coun-tries are latecomers; their development is bound to be 'a less spontaneous and more deliberate process than was the case in the countries where the process first occurred'.[23] Gerschenkron focused on the development process 'as a deliberate attempt at catching up on the part of various groups of economic operators'.[24] The development process is conditioned by the 'relative degree of backwardness' with respect to the early comers, i.e. countries in Continental Europe where industriali-zation had first taken off.

Hirschman however does not share Gerschenkron's point of view on what can set in motion economic operators to bring forward the reforms and the changes in the institutions and values system necessary for development. He questions in particular the idea that operators 'really know all the time what needs to be done to shed backwardness . . . and are therefore able to weigh the costs against the expected benefits of development'.[25] He notes: 'What is a hindrance to progress in one setting and at one stage may be helpful under different circumstances'. He gives the example of the institution of the extended family. The point is that underdeveloped countries have little knowledge of the path ahead and what is needed to achieve the benefits of economic progress. It is only along the way 'rather than a priori that they will determine which of their institutions and char-acter traits are backward and must be reformed or given up'.[26]

It follows that also the binding agent emerges within a 'growth perspective' that 'can only gradually be acquired in the course of growth'.[27] That includes the desire for economic growth but also 'a perception of . . . the road leading toward it'. The break-ing of the 'interlocking vicious circles', to use the expression by Singer,[28] takes place at the level where all the difficulties of human action 'begin and belong, in the mind'.[29]

2.4 Balanced growth

2.4.1 Supply and demand requirements

Economic development is primarily related to the overcoming of 'stagnation' via savings and productive investment. To break out of the underdevelopment equilibrium theorists such as Rosenstein-Rodan, Nurkse, Lewis and Scitovsky focused on balanced growth. But, according to Hirschman, balanced growth is not a useful abstraction, it is misleading and actually impossible.[30]

Paul Streeten offers the following definition of balanced growth: 'is a simultaneous investment in several industries in conformity with the pattern of consumers' demand and of different industries' demand for each others' products'.[31] This is the basic idea Hirschman criticizes. The theory argues that different parts of a developing economy have to grow in step to avoid supply difficulties or meet demand requirements. Rosenstein-Rodan and Nurkse stress the balance in the demand; Scitovsky and Lewis put emphasis on the balance in the supply side. To avoid these problems a large number of new industries must start at the same time, so that they are each others' clients. That is the 'big push'. According to Hirschman, in so doing the theory 'superimposes a new self-contained modern industrial system to an equally self-contained traditional sector'.[32] Rather than facing the problem it assumes something totally unrealistic. How could an underdeveloped economy master the managerial and entrepreneurial skills needed for such a process? Even if planning and the state are brought into the picture the tasks 'simply exceed the capabilities of a society, no matter to whom they are entrusted'.[33] That is why Hirschman argues 'the theory fails as a theory of *development*'.[34]

The other argument for balanced growth concerns external economies. Only a coordinated plan of investment could ensure the appropriation of the external economies generated by the single entrepreneur. The state should step in with centralized investment planning. However, only external economies should be internalized while external diseconomies and social costs should remain external to the central authority. Hirschman asks: can it be done? Although realistic in some case the general idea behind is not. 'Here again, the image . . . must have been that of a backward economic sector which would be pretty much left alone, and a brave new sector to be built from the ground up and in isolation'.[35] At the root of the problem is the fact that *in general, economic development means transformation rather than creation ex-novo*. There is a second point concerning transformation. Traditional ways of living and producing are inevitably disrupted. The rise external diseconomies and social costs then should not be underestimated. That might affect the net results of development.

2.4.2 Scitovsky and balanced growth

The peculiarity of Hirschman views is further highlighted by his criticism of Scitovsky. Although more known for other contributions, Scitovsky did write extensively on economic development. Hirschman makes reference to his work several times in his *Strategy of Economic Development*.

In line with most of the coeval theory, Scitovsky maintains that induced investment creates additional requirements for the production of other commodities and lowers the marginal costs of other commodities because of technical complementarities.[36] However, Hirschman argues, whereas in developed economies these effects 'are expected to take place automatically and almost instantaneously' in underdeveloped countries they are instead 'absolutely basic in determining the expansive path of the economy'.[37] They deserve therefore much more attention and analysis.

Hirschman observes that 'In one of its aspects, the theory stresses the need for the different parts of a developing economy to remain in step to avoid supply difficulties'.[38] That applies to Scitovsky who indeed focuses on balance on the supply side.[39]

Underneath is a fundamental premise 'balanced growth theory results from comparing the initial point of underdevelopment equilibrium with another point at which development will practically have been accomplished'.[40]

Hirschman then has a long quote in which Scitovsky argues that considering two industries and the effects of investment on each other:

> [a new] equilibrium is reached only when successive doses of investment and expansion in the two industries have led to the simultaneous elimination of investment in both . . . We can conclude that when an investment give rise to pecuniary external economies, its private profitability understates its social desirability.[41]

But, Hirschman observes, Scitovsky 'shows a certain impatience' with the process that lies between two equilibrium points. However that is precisely the process of development, and that does not admit shortcuts. Suggesting, as Scitovsky does, 'to reach in a single jump a new point of equilibrium where elimination of investment has been accomplished'[42], is precisely the kind of shortcut one should avoid. That, highlights Hirschman, concludes the fundamental problem of equilibrium analysis; it does not reach into the question of development. 'That nightmare of equilibrium economics, the endlessly spinning cobweb, is the *kind* of mechanism we must assiduously look for as an invaluable help to the development process'.[43] Finally, with respect to the appropriation of external economies, Hirschman recalls that according to Scitovsky entrepreneurs are mistaken in their calculations concerning investment since they are eventually going to be recipients of pecuniary external economies. But then of course that presupposes the existence of a central authority, and that goes into the chapter of planning and state intervention, which needs to be examined and not simply assumed.

To be fair Scitovsky himself says, 'the shortcoming of balanced growth were not forgotten' referring to his critical assessment of 1959.[44] The question is not 'the desirability of matching the structure of output to the structure of domestic demand' but rather the best way to achieve it.[45] Hirschman he says thought that developing economies could aim at balanced growth only in the long run, through a sequential process that he called unbalanced growth.

2.5 Development as a chain of disequilibria

As we will see, Hirschman admits that the notion of balanced growth might be a useful in certain circumstances. But the balanced growth doctrine is certainly not the way to approach the development problem. In *The Strategy* it is precisely the criticism that leads to the alternative. The problem is how development comes about. Focusing on investment decisions Hirschman elaborates the notion of development as a chain of disequilibria.

The pure model of balanced growth rests on the simultaneous start of many activities. A less rigorous but more realistic notion implies that 'the various sectors of an economy will have to grow jointly in some (not necessarily identical) proportion . . . In this form, the balanced growth theory is essentially an exercise in retrospective comparative statics'.[46] Of course, Hirschman argues, growth has proceeded in this way, with growth 'communicated from the leading sectors of the economy to the followers, from one industry to another, from one firm to another'. But rather than the end result we should look at the 'seesaw advance'. The main advantage over balanced growth is that 'it leaves considerable scope to *induced* investment decisions and therefore economize our principal scarce resource, namely, genuine decision-making'.[47]

For Hirschman the fundamental question is that of *induced investment.* He regards the investment response to disequilibrium as a more attainable goal than the ex-novo investment required by balanced growth. That is true regardless of the combination of market and nonmarket forces (public authorities) that might be at work.[48] This is simply a more realistic and operational way to look at development, which appears then as a chain of disequilibria. Whether or not they induce growth depends on circumstances that are of various nature. But this is the mechanism we should focus on. It requires a notion of induced investment appropriate to the study of development; thus the focus should be put on production complementarities. The complementarity effect, argues Hirschman 'provides us with a new concept of *induced* investment'. The conventional notion rests on the response of investment to past increases of output. That is valid only in developed economies, with a fully built up industrial and agricultural structure.

Hirschman draws a fundamental distinction between the role of investment in developed and developing economies. Whereas 'The big dynamic changes in developed economies are expected to originate in 'autonomous' investment', it is not realistic to expect that in underdeveloped economies. Instead 'investment that is induced by complementarity effects may help to bring about a real transformation'.[49] Complementarities are closely linked to the idea that in underdeveloped economies 'investment is undertaken because for one reason or another the ensuing output is expected to find a market'.[50] But then every investment is in a sense induced and that blurs the distinction between induced and autonomous.[51] To solve this problem Hirschman suggests to rank investment projects with respect to external economies. Investment creates external economies but also appropriates external economies. Induced investment can be more clearly identified with projects that are 'net beneficiaries of external economies'. That is however a hard-to-measure criterion. Therefore 'we shall continue to speak of investment inducing other investments and shall simply be aware that there are widely varying degrees of 'inducements'.[52]

2.6 Additional features of unbalanced growth

The unbalanced growth approach above concerns the sectoral-industrial analysis. But it is of more general relevance. It concerns for instance the unbalanced development between agricultural and industry. But economic development is for its very nature unbalanced also spatially; it proceeds by creating growth poles. That results in the problem of the lagging-behind regions. The polarization effects are examined by Hirschman in the last chapter of *The Strategy* – Interregional and International Transmission of Economic Growth – where he returns to the question of the role of public policy and in particular of public investment.

> The most obvious manner in which economic policy affects the rates of growth of different parts of the country is through the regional allocation of public investment. Three principal patterns of allocation can be distinguished: dispersal, concentration in growing areas, and attempts to promote the development of backwards areas.[53]

The deliberate policy attempting to promote the development of lagging-behind regions leads to consider the 'optimal institutional arrangements'.[54]

Institutions and institutional change are central in the recent literature on development theory. Modern political economy is trying to go beyond an almost exclusive focus on markets to discuss also the role of institutions.[55] Ha-Joon Chang has also insisted on this aspect. On the other hand, the debate on the role of the state in development has been re-ignited by the analysis of late industrialization.[56]

Early development economics focused on the cumulative causation arising from an initial stimulus. That is why it insists on the role played government and public investment. But this again would mean singling out one aspect and put it at the basis of the development process. This contrasts with Hirschman view of the development process. As pointed out earlier only the development process itself can define the necessary changes in institutions. They cannot be identified a priori for the institutions most conducive of economic growth are not known in advance and there is no already set road to development.

As for the role of government Hirschman suggests to distinguish governmental activities into two broad categories, that of 'inducing' and 'induced' activities and that of 'unbalancing' and 'balancing' functions, therefore assigning to the government a role that again should reflect the priorities dictated by the development process itself. 'These two tasks may perhaps serve to give ministers and governments a clearer conception of their role within the development process'.[57] What follows is a criticism of the attempt to draw comprehensive development plans. 'The attempt at comprehensive programming usually exacts a high price in terms of articulateness and persuasiveness, qualities that are essential for the plan's ability to come to grips with reality'.[58]

Hirschman further reflection on the argument is contained in *Development Projects Observed*. Here is skepticism about comprehensive planning and planning techniques is grounded on the observation of development projects. The principle of the 'hiding hand' was, he says, 'close to a provocation' compared with the operational character of the technical methods for allocating funds to various projects.[59] Indeed, in this context, nothing could be less 'operationally useful'.[60] But then again one must define the main purpose of the analysis.

While the first chapter of the *Development Projects* is a prologue 'to endow and surround the development story with a sense of wonder and mystery that would reveal it to have much in common with the highest quests undertaken by humankind', the other chapters do offer 'hints, suggestions, and propositions' of more practical relevance.[61] The more practical suggestions concerning the elaboration on uncertainties, 'latitudes', projects design and evaluation, follow from his previous work and therefore much from *The Strategy*.

Balanced growth is mentioned a few times. Although useful for some planning decisions – in particular when the risk of an inadequate demand for a project output is high – balanced growth is an obstacle when considering the basic principles of R&D strategy.[62] In particular 'aiming at a reduction of demand uncertainty through the balanced-growth technique . . . may well increase the supply uncertainties because of the resulting impossibility of applying the R&D strategy'.[63]

2.7 Views on unbalanced growth

Paul Streeten is possibly the second most important advocate of unbalanced growth. His argument on unbalanced bears many similarities to Hirschman views, but it is also different in at least two counts. In first place, it is less imbedded in a view of development, and more in the broader context of its meaning within economic theory. Secondly, it is more prudent on the contrast between balanced and unbalanced growth, offering a careful review of the advantages and disadvantages of the two concepts.

In his 1959 article Streeten observes that Allyn Young advanced a notion of balanced growth later modified by Rosenstein-Rodan. He argues that Allyn Young replaced Smith's division of labour with inducement to invest and that 'the conception of the market . . . carries with it the notion that there must be some sort of balance, that different productive activities must be proportional to one another'.[64] The doctrine he says is widely accepted but 'it is obvious that development means disturbing an equilibrium, upsetting a balance'.[65] His point is that 'in certain conditions unbalance may stimulate rather than impair progress'.[66]

The case for unbalanced growth is then based on the way complementarities affect consumption and production. Streeten distinguishes between static and dynamic complementarities. 'The most important consumption complementarities arise . . . in the process of rising consumption. Similarly, technical complementarities may arise or may become apparent only with the growth of knowledge and inventions'.[67] Regarding consumption it is important that the 'cost of imbalance', due to indivisibilities or 'anabolism of wants', is associated with a higher level of real income and therefore to the opportunities for higher growth. The services of indivisible commodities can be bought, but 'consumption pro-rata, though not impossible, is more expensive. An individual who equates marginal rates of substitution to price ratios will be worse off than one who tolerates some imbalance'.[68] Furthermore, consumption complementarities 'create pressure and a sense of deprivation, which stimulates and guide investment, and guarantee its profitability. Investment opportunities are created by new consumption opportunities which in turn result from unbalance'.[69] Indivisibilities play a central role also in production complementarities. Building capacity ahead of existing demand is justifiable because of economies of scale. But there is an even stronger argument: demand is stimulated by the unbalanced investment, 'by encouraging a cluster of activities' as in the case of railways.[70] The ultimate dynamic complementarities in production concerns invention and innovation 'just as in consumption new voids open up as we move along the path of satisfying existing wants, so investment that is intended to fill existing gaps may lead to innovations that open new gaps'.[71] In other words, the pattern of investment and innovation is stimulated by bottlenecks, but it is at the same time creating new ones calling for more innovation. 'Necessity is the mother of invention, but invention was also mother of necessity'.[72]

Summing up: unbalanced development might be desirable when indivisibilities and costs of expansion are important, 'higher incomes are created than would be in balanced growth'[73], incentives to invention are strengthened. Explicit reference to Hirschman's *Strategy* is made when Streeten observes that unbalances take place where action is needed, therefore economizing in a resource 'often in short supply', the power to take decisions.

In a rather prudent manner Streeten argues that, in the presence of certain conditions, unbalanced growth is a more successful strategy for development. Although is a sense desirable, balance may have to be given up as an overall strategy.

In a reply to Streeten, Nurkse notes that that his interpretation 'of the phrase 'balanced growth' is more limited and less rigid that he makes out to be'.[74] It applies to direct investment, not to overhead investment. Even in that case 'balanced growth is necessary only if export demand is not 'sufficiently' expanding'.[75] Adding the international dimension Nurkse highlights also that 'the complementarities in the make-up of additional consumption can then be implemented through international trade'.[76] In general, and this might be Nurske's most far reaching observation, it is a good idea to distinguish between balanced growth as a method and an objective.

Streeten and Hirschman views have been called into question more forcefully by Nath. He argues that balanced growth is a dynamic concept concerned with change over time. Hirschman 'ridicules' balanced growth treating it as a static equilibrium but in fact it 'is no more concerned with static equilibrium than the equilibrium rate of growth . . . of a dynamic model'.[77] Hirschman criticizes balanced growth for requiring extended state action, but then argues that in some case government may have to take the first step. Coming to Streeten, Nath sustains that the argument about technical progress stimulated by unbalances is inconclusive 'balanced growth does not abolish shortages or scarcities, it only minimizes the social and economic upheaval that they may cause'.[78] As far as the considerations that should guide investment priorities, both Streeten and Hirschman come up with recommendations that are compatible with balanced growth.

In fact Nath defense of balanced growth adds to the understanding of two distinct perspectives on development and development planning. For in the end he argues that balanced growth is practically useful and ultimately it 'demands a programming approach to economic development'.[79] That might not be the entire story, but is an important part of it.

In his reply Streeten dismisses much of Nath criticism.[80] Interestingly Streeten argues that the main weakness of balanced growth is that final markets can be created without a recourse to them, for instance by an expansion of exports. As for intermediate markets he recalls that Nurkse himself came out in favor of unbalanced growth. On development planning he argues that unbalanced growth 'as argued by Hirschman is consistent with, but does not require initial and continued planning'.[81] It requires however a different kind of planning than that associated with balanced growth. But he concedes defects of unbalanced growth theory, such as the underestimation of the resistance to the changes called forth by unbalances, the excessive stress on investment decisions and the underplay of supply limitations. According to Streeten these defects were not absent in his earlier presentation. Indeed at the beginning of his reply he says that the controversy is no longer fruitful, and tells us 'My work in collaboration with Professor Gunnar Myrdal on problems of development in South Asia has clarified and changed my views'.[82]

Streeten is referring to Myrdal's book *Asian Drama*. In the Preface Myrdal acknowledges Streeten contribution on 'developing and elaborating the criticism . . . of the type of model-thinking that characterized the "modern approach"'.[83] In the appendix two of the second volume of Myrdal's book, we can read 'the main controversy respecting balanced versus unbalanced growth has little relevance for the problem central to this appendix: How South Asia countries should plan development. Both doctrines are essentially beside the point'.[84]

2.8 Unbalanced growth and structural change

Overall the 'controversy' clarifies quite well the issues involved in balanced versus unbalanced growth theory. It highlights what seems to be Hirschman's fundamental point: the development process is a disequilibrium process, further qualified by Streeten as a process that in given circumstances may be more favorable to growth.

The issues underlying the controversy have hardly resurfaced in the recent study of development. Nor there has been an effort to develop the insights provided by unbalanced growth theory. It is gone largely unnoticed that unbalanced growth bears a close resemblance to the dynamics that is the focus of the modern theory of structural change and long-term transformation. To be true the theoretical approach is critical of mainstream growth theory that has come to dominate even the field of development, now quite distinct from more broadly defined development studies.

Growth theory is mostly aggregate and theoretical; as such it almost neglects structural change. The changes of the economic structure are instead a defining element of development studies, which are however mostly empirical studies. The theory of structural change is truly concerned with the relationship between change in the economic structure and aggregate growth; at the same time it is 'theoretical'. It arises from the criticism of steady growth models and argues that non-proportional growth is the necessary condition for growth.

Luigi Pasinetti clarifies quite well the relationship between the theory of structural change and the study of development. Not only does he note that the early definition of structural change by Perroux became widesperad and used particularly by 'structuralists' in Latin America, but also that 'The literature on "development economics" has all inevitably been concerned in some way or another with problems of structural change'.[85] He mentions the notions of 'big push' by Rosenstein-Rodan, of 'unbalanced growth' by Streeten and of 'dual economies' by Lewis and Nurkse. According to Pasinetti, since those ideas are hard to formalize development economics has at present a poor reputational standing among theoretical economists.

As for the empirical analyses of Kuznets and Chenery they never attempted any theoretical study of structural change:

> these scholars, on any synthetic presentation of their works, have always very sharply distinguished two separate fields of analysis and research, which they call 'complementary' but which rather uneasily, they keep separate, namely: the field of research concerning changes in the economic structure – which they connect with long-term development, and which they do not integrate into any theory – and the field of research concerning prices and markets, which they do explicitly connect with a specific theory – the Walrasian general equilibrium theory – but which they openly acknowledge as being unhelpful to the investigation of structural change.[86]

Pasinetti structural dynamics approach is grounded on the idea that a changing structure of the economy is a response to unbalances originating from the different pace of technical change among sectors, i.e. different rates of productivity growth. Non-proportional growth concerns the supply side *and* the demand side. Therefore Pasinetti's structural dynamics opens an entire new chapter concerning the changes in consumption composition.

The role of imbalances is even more explicit in the theory of *transformational growth*. Transformational growth theory is presented by Edward J. Nell in several contributions. Nell argues that in a Keynesian perspective the analysis of accumulation must ultimately focus on demand growth.[87] In other words, we need a theory of the growth of demand.

Demand growth is generated endogenously from within the process of transformation. It proceeds from the 'structural development' of the market, i.e. through changes of demand composition and the rise of new markets. Market expansion driven by population and/or income growth can be accommodated in a steady growth framework. The expansion of existing markets (more or less mature) can be explained by the diffusion path of new products, shaped by the product life cycle and by the income-driven dynamics associated with the Engel curve. The more difficult problem is that of new markets. Nell argues that there are two major sources of new markets: the evolution of the social structure and the development scenarios driven by the major facts of historical transformation (this is the case of the enclosures and the creation of an urban-industrial setting in the early stage of capitalism) or, in more abstract terms, by structural imbalances.

'For growth to start up, the economy must become imbalanced . . . [when] a structural imbalance is regularly reproduced it becomes a trend'.[88] This creates an incentive and an opportunity for innovation of a specific type. Initially this will happen in a few industries and in a few places and these will become centers of innovation and investment. Notice that 'this is not a one-time, exogenously caused imbalance; it is an imbalance which results from an ongoing process, an imbalance which will be reproduced if corrected'.[89]

Transformational growth describes the growth pattern that characterized the development of advanced industrial economies as a result of the operations of the market.[90] At the center of the transformation is the development of the market, not purely its expansion. On the other hand Pasinetti structural dynamics inevitably poses the question of the rise of new markets.[91]

2.9 Development, consumption complementarities and market formation

Admittedly neither Pasinetti's structural dynamics nor the transformational growth approach are concerned with developing economies *per se*. There is nevertheless a striking similarity between development as a chain of disequilibria and the mechanism by which structural imbalances drive the process of transformation. The focus on demand composition, the evolution of consumption, and the formation of markets suggests a new perspective on induced investment and development linkages. New markets arising from the process of transformation address the question of the interdependence between investment decisions and the growth of interlocking markets. We find evidence for this new perspective in Hirschman's argument about complementarities and recalling that in developing economies induced investment is clearly associated with the transformation of the economic structure.

In line with the idea that a community should be capable of taking investment decisions when faced by bottleneck and supply constraints Hirschman focused on production complementarities. These are largely dictated by technical requirements. But the notion of induced investment can be more fully articulated considering also consumption complementarities.

Hirschman recalls that there is 'a rigid type of complementarity in use (best treated as derived demand)' and a 'looser, "developmental" type of complementarity (entrained want)'.[92] An example of the first one is cement and steel rods in construction, an example of the second is new office building strengthening demand for various goods and services. He then goes on with an interesting description of what the complementarities might be:

> from modern office furniture and equipment (still fairly rigid), to parking and restaurant facilities, stylish secretaries, and eventually perhaps to more office buildings as the demonstration effect goes to work on the tenants of the older buildings. Here again, failure to arrange for all these complementarity items from the start could be denounced as 'poor planning' . . . an attempt to telescope the whole process would be futile because of the virtually infinite number of complementarity repercussions, and because of the uncertainties about a good many of them.[93]

In a footnote he provides some more details:

> Development itself constantly extends the range of complementarities that are rigidly compelled and necessarily simultaneous: the optional equipment of one period becomes the standard equipment of the next, as a result of social and cultural pressures and needs rather than because of purely technological factors[94].

It seems only fair to say that there is a certain amount of evidence on the importance of consumption complementarities and a hint in the effects they might have in the rise of new markets. The new possible research agenda on market formation can help to articulate the problem of the interlocking of markets in the consolidation of development. The uncertainties seem to be clearly associated with the open-end process by which consumption evolves and new markets arise. This line of investigation finds support in some passages cited above from Streeten's 1959 article. They could be further analyzed in an effort to make more precise the role of market formation in the development process.

The plausibility of moving in this direction finds further support recalling the link between demand and supply adjustment that is so central to development economics. The fact that they need to grow in step one another is the main reason for the big push. Hirschman argues that if we focus on the balancing of demand and supply at two equilibrium points we miss the fundamental aspect of the unbalance, which is that of providing the incentive to decision making. Consumption complementarities add to the motivations and the consequences of induced investment, while market formation proceeds from consumption complementarities and it is part of the process of transformation driven by induced investment.

Complementarities are no longer a purely technology matter but more accurately reflect the relationship between technology, investment and change of consumption patterns, i.e. the transformation associated with the development process. This clarifies Hirschman's claim that transformation and development mean different things in developed and developing economies. In one case they are primarily associated to autonomous investment (creating new products, new processes, even entire new industries); in the other, they are the result of induced investment, with production complementarities setting limits according to technical feasibility and consumption complementarities guiding the rise of new markets. That completes Hirschman's view of unbalanced growth. It offers a more accurate view on development linkages and the role of investment.

2.10 Concluding remarks and research questions

In this chapter we focused on the highly original theorizing of the development process contained in Hirschman's *Strategy of Economic Development* and we argued that a new research agenda can arise from it. That should be regarded as complementary to the study of institutions and the role of the state in today's drastically different circumstances than those in which development economics first arose. Hirschman's conceptualization of the development problem and his analysis of the development process as a chain of disequilibria takes us beyond balanced growth, which Krugman regards as the basic model of high development theory. Market formation, although hardly discussed as such, is implicitly contained in that basic model.[95] It is now more clearly grounded in the notion of development as chain of disequilibria.

More work is clearly necessary to focus on the question of today's development trends. However the relationship between investment and the expansion of the domestic market appears fundamental for the current phase of transformation facing the emerging economies. Fundamental aspects of the problem are consumption complementarities, the evolution of consumption patterns and the rise of new markets. That suggests an enlarged view of development linkages and a new research agenda.

Hirschman notes that the term 'South', as opposed to the industrialized North, is taken to indicate the lagging behind regions. But then he observes that 'The term 'South' as used here does not include undeveloped – i.e., largely unsettled – areas'.[96] One can only speculate on what unsettled really means. This appears however a curious distinction in today's world. Especially through 'globalization' there seem to be very few corners of the world that are not affected by 'development'. That calls for an approach that rather than backwardness looks at the interaction between development and underdevelopment. This of course is the question of dependency, which remains largely outside Hirschman perspective. That also might be subject to a rethinking.[97]

Revisiting the unbalanced nature of the development process and the notion of dependency seem promising venues to respond to the changes occurred in the very question of development in the profoundly different circumstances of the world economy today.

Notes

1 A.O. Hirschman, *The Strategy of Economic Development* (New Haven: Yale University Press, 1958).
2 A.O. Hirschman, *Journeys Toward Progress. Studies of Economic Policy-Making in Latin America* (New York: The Twentieth Century Fund, 1963).
3 A.O. Hirschman, *Development Projects Observed* (Washington DC: The Brookings Institution, [1967] 1995).
4 Ibid., p. viii.
5 Ibid., p. xii.
6 A.O. Hirschman, *Exit, Voice, and Loyalty: Responses to Decline in Firms, Organizations, and States* (Cambridge MA: Harvard University Press, 1970).
7 A.O. Hirschman, *Shifting Involvements* (Princeton: Princeton University Press, 1982).
8 This is one of the areas of economics where the contributions by German-speaking émigrés are most significant see H. Hagemann, 'Dismissal, Expulsion, and Emigration of German-speaking Economists after 1933', *Journal of the History of Economic Thought*, 27: 4, (2005), pp. 405–20; H. Hagemann, 'German-speaking Economists in British Exile 1933–1945', *Banca Nazionale del Lavoro Quarterly Review*, LX: 242, (2007), pp. 323–63.
9 J. Adelman, *Worldly Philosopher. The Odyssey of Albert Hirschman* (Princeton: Princeton University Press, 2013).

10 Ibid., p. 435.
11 Ibid., p. 491.
12 Ibid., ch. 18.
13 I am here making reference to the article in Paul Krugman web site, dated 2005, see P. Krugman, 'The Fall and Rise of Development Economics' (2005), at http://web.mit. edu/krugman/www/dishpan.html, [accessed 20 January 2015]. The original article was published in 1993, see P. Krugman, 'Toward a Counter-Revolution in Development Theory', *Proceedings of the World Bank Annual Conference on Development Economics* (Washington DC: World Bank, 1993) pp. 15–38.
14 P. Krugman, 'The Fall and Rise', p. 1.
15 Ibid., p. 2.
16 J. Stiglitz, Comment on 'Toward a Counter-Revolution in Development Theory' by P. Krugman, *Proceedings of the World Bank Annual Conference on Development Economics* (Washington DC: World Bank, 1993), pp. 39–50, on p. 42.
17 'The Rise and Decline of Development Economics', *Essays in Trespassing, Economics to Politics and Beyond* (Cambridge: Cambridge University Press, 1981), pp. 1–24, on p. 2.
18 A.O. Hirschman, *The Strategy*, p. 3.
19 A.N. Whitehead, *Process and Reality* (New York: Macmillan, 1930).
20 A.O. Hirschman, *The Strategy*, p. 5.
21 Ibid., p. 6.
22 Ibid., p. 25.
23 Ibid., p. 8.
24 Ibid.
25 Ibid., p. 9.
26 Ibid., p. 10.
27 Ibid., p. 11.
28 H.W. Singer, 'Economic Progress in Underdeveloped Countries', *Social Research*, 16, 1949, pp. 1–11.
29 A.O. Hirschman, *The Strategy*, p. 11.
30 'It is only fair to warn the reader that I heartily disagree with the "balanced growth" doctrine', A.O. Hirschman, *The Strategy*, p. 50.
31 P. Streeten, 'Unbalanced Growth', *Oxford Economic Papers. New Series*, 11: 2, (1959), pp.167–90, on p. 176.
32 Hirschman, *The Strategy*, p. 52.
33 Ibid., p. 54.
34 Ibid.
35 Ibid., p. 56.
36 T. Scitovsky, *Welfare and Competition. The Economics of a Fully Employed Economy* (Chicago: R.D. Irving, 1951).
37 Hirschman, *The Strategy*, p. 42.
38 Ibid., p. 51.
39 T. Scitovsky, 'Two Concepts of External Economies', *Journal of Political Economy*, 62: 2 (1954), pp. 143–51.
40 Hirschman, *The Strategy*, p. 65.
41 T. Scitovsky, 'Two Concepts of External Economies', pp. 148–9.
42 Hirschman, *The Strategy*, p. 66.
43 Ibid., emphasis added.
44 T. Scitovsky, 'Balanced Growth' in J. Eatwell, M. Milgate and P. Newman (eds) *The New Palgrave – Economic Development* (New York–London: W.W. Norton, 1987), pp. 55–8, on p. 57 and T. Scitovsky, 'Growth – Balanced or Unbalanced?', in T. Scitovsky, *Papers on Welfare and Growth* (London: Allen and Unwin Ltd., [1959] 1964), pp. 97–110.
45 T. Scitovsky, 'Balanced Growth', p. 57.

46 Hirschman, *The Strategy*, p. 62.

47 Ibid., p. 63.

48 'There is no implication that any disequilibrium whatsoever will be resolved by some combination. But if a community cannot generate the "induced" decisions and actions needed to deal with the supply disequilibria that arise in the course of uneven growth, then I can see little reason for believing that it will be able to take the set of "autonomous" decisions required by balanced growth', ibid., p. 64.

49 In his example, more demand for beer may not only lead to an increase of brewing capacity but to the establishment of a brewery, ibid., p.70.

50 Ibid.

51 For an interesting discussion of the two concepts see J.U. Melville, 'Autonomous and Induced investment', *The American Economic Review*, 42: 4, (1952), pp. 587–9.

52 Hirschman, *The Strategy*, p. 71.

53 Ibid., p. 190.

54 Ibid., p. 199.

55 See for instance D. Acemouglu, S. Johnson and J.A. Robinson, 'Institutions as a Fundamental Cause of Long-Run Growth' in P. Aghion and S.N. Durlauf (eds), *Handbook of Economic Growth*, Vol. 1 (Amsterdam: North Holland, 2005), pp. 385–472.

56 H-J. Chang, *Institutional Change and Economic Development* (London: Anthem Press, 2007); A. Amsden, *Asia's Next Giant: South-Korea and Late Industrialization* (Oxford: Oxford University Press, 1989), A. Amsden, *The Rise of the "Rest": Challenges to the West from Late-Industrializing Economies* (Oxford: Oxford University Press, 2001).

57 Hirschman, *The Strategy*, pp. 204–5.

58 Ibid., p. 205.

59 Hirschman, *Development Projects Observed*, p. viii.

60 Ibid., p. ix.

61 Ibid.

62 Ibid., p. 78.

63 Ibid., p. 84.

64 P. Streeten, 'Unbalanced Growth', p. 167.

65 Ibid., p. 170

66 Ibid., p. 171.

67 Ibid., p. 173.

68 Ibid., p. 174.

69 Ibid., p. 175.

70 Ibid., p. 180.

71 Ibid.

72 Ibid., p. 181.

73 Ibid.

74 R. Nurkse, 'Notes on 'Unbalanced Growth'', *Oxford Economic Papers*, 11: 3, (1959), pp. 295–7, on p. 295. Nurkse died on May 6, 1959. James Tobin put together the few fragments of what was probably a longer reply to Streeten.

75 Ibid.

76 Ibid., p. 296.

77 S.K. Nath, 'The Theory of Balanced Growth', *Oxford Economic Papers*, 14: 2 (1962), pp. 138–53, on p. 148.

78 Ibid., p. 151.

79 Ibid., p. 152.

80 P. Streeten, 'Unbalanced Growth: A Reply', *Oxford Economic Papers*, 15: 1, (1963), pp. 66–73.

81 Ibid., p. 67.

82 Ibid., p. 66, footnote.

83 G. Myrdal, *Asian Drama. An Inquiry into the Poverty of Nations* (Allen Lane: The Penguin Press, 1968), on p. xvii.

84 Ibid., p. 1932.
85 L.L. Pasinetti, *Structural Economic Dynamics* (Cambridge: Cambridge University Press, 1993), on p. 9.
86 Ibid., p. 10.
87 E.J. Nell, *The General Theory of Transformational Growth* (Cambridge: Cambridge University Press, 1998).
88 Ibid., p. 19.
89 Ibid.
90 The focus is not on the market's allocation function but rather on its mode of operation as an institution of change.
91 See D. Gualerzi, *The Coming of Age of Information Technologies and the Path of Transformational Growth* (London: Routledge, 2010); D. Gualerzi, 'Towards a Theory of the Consumption–Growth Relationship', *Review of Political Economy*, 24: 1, (2012), pp. 15–32.
92 Hirschman, *The Strategy*, p. 68.
93 Ibid., p. 69.
94 Ibid., footnote 7.
95 See D. Gualerzi and A. Cibils, 'High Development Theory, CEPAL, and Beyond' in J.L. Cardoso, M.C. Marcuzzo and M.E. Romero Sotelo (eds), *Economic Development and Global Crisis. The Latin American Economy in Historical Perspective* (Abingdon: Routledge, 2014), pp. 139–58.
96 Hirschman, *The Strategy*, p. 187.
97 It could be argued that precisely the focus on consumption patterns and market formation could provide the link between the unbalanced nature of the development process and dependency theory. Market formation proceeds indeed from the 'importation' of a model of mass consumption and the ensuing transformation of the production and consumption sphere.

3   The brilliant fifties

International trade as a cause of underdevelopment

Cosimo Perrotta[1]

3.1 Before the start

The years 1949–50 are a turning point in the theory of international trade. The Heckscher-Ohlin law was completed by Paul Samuelson;[2] while a new course started, linked to development economics. The Heckscher-Ohlin law is the modern version of the Ricardian comparative costs law. It maintains that, in a free trade context, different endowments in the productive factors tend to equalize the price of the factors, either by moving factors abroad or through commodities' exchange.

This modern version apparently overcomes the static nature of the Ricardian law, which implied the absolute non mobility of factors through countries. But in fact it is even more restrictive and unrealistic – now the development of a country does not depend on its production, but on its natural resources. According to the new version, it would be irrational for a country with land in excess to industrialize (Samuelson's example refers to the USA themselves!).

In the previous decades the supporters of the Ricardian law had given valuable contributions. In 1950 Rostow surveyed those of them devoted to a complex question: how to measure the terms of trade. He concluded that the variables were too many for establishing a general rule in such a measure.[3]

However these are also the years in which – thanks to the 'discovery' of the gap between developed and backward economies – decisive criticisms are put forward against the Ricardian law. Besides the Marxist and radical theories of imperialism, ostracized by the academy, we find Hirschman's 1945 book on national power and foreign trade, which effectively connects political and economic analysis with a mercantilist-like approach.[4] Hirschman sees international trade as a strategy for power, which aims at imposing a nation's interest on others. He speaks of domination, disequilibrium, cumulative effect and dependence in foreign trade, and of exploitation between nations. In this perspective he also examines the problem of the terms of trade.

As early as in 1949, Balogh notes that Samuelson's model cannot apply when the two countries have strong differences in their development level – Samuelson himself acknowledged it – or have different customs.[5] Besides, the quantity of capital cannot be fixed; it depends on the possibilities of investment. When there are such big differences, Balogh added, free trade, for the sake of an immediate advantage, can put in danger the weaker country's development.[6]

The most effective attack to the old theory was moved by Prebisch and Singer, in 1949–50. By analyzing the terms of international trade, they explained that the gap between developed and underdeveloped countries was increasingly widening.

3.2 Singer and Prebisch: the widening gap

After Rosenstein-Rodan's pioneering article of 1943 on backwardness and industrialization, Raúl Prebisch and Hans Singer show that backwardness is not a simple pre-industrial stage. It tends to become permanent because of perverse trade relationships.[7]

Prebisch uses the concepts of centre (developed countries) and periphery (poor countries). Like Balogh, he states that the comparative costs law holds only when the trading countries have a similar level of development.[8] In the last years, he says, technical progress has been faster in industry (thus in the rich countries) than in agriculture (which still dominates poor economies). Despite this, the advantages have gone mainly to the rich countries. He reports the data, of a UN document, about the declining terms of trade of the poor countries since 1876.

Prebisch believes that the contrary should happen:

> Had the rise in income in the industrial centres and in the periphery been proportionate to the increase in their respective productivity . . . given the higher productivity of industry, the price relation would have moved in favour of the primary products.[9]

He explains such an 'inconsistence' this way: during the upward phase of the business cycle, western wages grow, following the other prices. But during the downward phase they do not diminish, because of the unions' pressure. However such inelastic tendency of western wages does not affect negatively western profits. In fact, the consequent increase in costs can be charged on the importers of western goods, that is on the poor countries, and especially on their wages. In fact, in the poor countries, competition is not so strong and unions are not well organized. Even if, he adds, the periphery wages were rigid, the tendency would not change. In this case western countries would not export any longer; then they would import less primary products from the periphery. This compels the poor countries to accept the diminution in their terms of trade, in order to keep exporting.[10] As a remedy, Prebisch pleads for industrializing Latin American agriculture and increasing its productivity.[11]

Hans Singer too refers to another UN publication which showed the same decline in prices of the third world export since the 1870s.[12] Then, he says, the specialization principle of the Ricardian law works to the detriment of the poor countries. Besides, investments in the poor countries come from western economies, then all the advantages go to the West. This kind of specialization hinders poor economies from industrializing, that is from developing. Even if the benefits of specialization, based on the comparative advantages, were equally distributed, what really matters is the exclusion from industrialization.[13] This creates a vicious circle which generates exploitation.[14]

The decline in the prices of third world goods cannot be due to their increase in productivity, says Singer. Productivity increased more in manufactures. Like Prebisch, he maintains that this should have raised third world incomes. In fact the opposite happened. Technical progress in manufacture raised income for western producers, whereas technical progress in primary productions has lowered the prices of primary goods, to the advantage of western consumers.[15]

Singer, as Furtado will do later, adds that this tendency is reinforced by primary goods' scarce income elasticity.[16] But this argument does not hold – there is not inelasticity in natural resources, nor in the non-essential foodstuff exported by the poor countries, such as coffee, cocoa, tea, bananas, etc.

Finally Perroux, in a number of essays published between 1948 and 1959, describes economic dynamics in contrast with the neo-classical equilibrium approach. An economy develops by concentrating in some focal points the main productive factors. Some enterprises are more productive and drive development. This causes polarization. Growth poles in turn generate a dominant economic area, or nation, to which dependent economies aggregate in a subordinate position.[17]

These authors deny the harmonic classical vision. According to them, international trade is made of conflicting interests. Moreover the distribution of gains depends on the kind of goods exchanged. Primary products, without manufactures, are insufficient to create development.[18] The same principles had been held by the mercantilists. But development economists ignored their thought.

Singer and Prebisch also point out that specialization, when applied to strongly unbalanced partners, increases differences – as it is proved by monoculture, which was stressed by Brankovic.[19]

Balogh, Singer, Prebisch, Perroux, and even Hirschman, discovered polarization; which, contrary to equilibrium, pushes productive factors towards the more developed areas, where they are better remunerated or are more easily employed. The opposite tendency is the diffusion of development. In Singer terms, polarization creates divergence, diffusion creates convergence.

The cultural novelty of these analyses should not be undervalued. The justification of the international division of labour between western industry and non-western primary production was deeply rooted in economic thought. As Boianovsky shows, it even had a representative in List, the great development theorist.[20]

3.3 The unsolved problems in the Prebisch-Singer theory

The revolution in the trade theory left some analytical problems unsolved.

3.3.1 Primary and manufactured goods: too simple a distinction

The equation 'primary exports = declining terms of trade' is oversimplified. In the 1970s some poor countries started exporting manufactured goods, but their exports still suffered unfavourable ratios.[21] On the other hand mechanized agriculture allowed some industrial countries – USA first – to be the most competitive exporters of primary products, with favourable terms of trade.[22]

The explanation is that manufactured export from the poor countries was produced with low level technology, while the agricultural export from the developed economies was produced with high technology. Then it was technology level, not the primary nature of products, responsible for the loss of the third world.

This is confirmed by another fact. In the third world's primary export there were two very different types of goods. One is natural resources (such as various metals, wood, rubber, cotton, wool, chemical and biological ingredients, etc.). The other is 'leisure food', so to say, like cacao seeds, coffee beans, tea leaves, exotic fruits, tobacco, etc. However the two types of goods have a common feature: they are both raw materials for western industry. Then it is the value added in western manufactures which makes the difference that affects the terms of trade.

3.3.2 Import substitution also requires export substitution

Prebisch and Singer did not go deep into the remedies, but their analysis pushed many poor countries in the 1960s to implement an import substitution policy. The aim was to produce at home (with high technology) the industrial products previously imported; it was not to employ productively one's own natural resources. These countries were interested in substituting imports, but not exports. This was one of the major causes which made their project fail.

This kind of import substitution led to import from western countries even more costly goods (the means of production); moreover without the financial system, the infrastructures and the skilled human capital that were indispensable to implement industrial production. Besides, the GATT and western countries imposed the poor countries not only to export primary products at very low prices,[23] but also to accept any western manufactured goods.[24] Thus the so called developing countries were deprived of the only means to develop, i.e. raw materials, increase in demand, growth of human capital.

In fact the underdeveloped countries ended up by financing with the export of raw materials the import of western industrial means of production. The consequence was the worsening in their terms of trade. Until they drowned into debts.[25]

It is worth comparing this experience of import substitution with that of mercantilism. The latter strategy was to extend manufactures thanks to the internal employment of natural resources (both labour and raw materials), either domestic or imported. In the 16th century Starkey maintained that development depended on keeping one's own raw materials and working them at home. Ortiz wrote much the same. This concept was repeated again and again, until Cantillon in 1730 expressed it in a brilliant example, showing that the country which exports its resources impoverishes, whereas the one which imports and uses them in production 'gains twice'.[26]

Mercantilists saw in all goods two components: matter and labour. The country should make any effort to export goods with much labour (i.e. with value added) and to import goods with much raw matter which, in turn, activates production.

The last great mercantilist, James Steuart writes that it is better to export finished products rather than semi-processed goods, and semi-processed goods rather than raw materials. And adds: when a country is forced to export its own raw materials in exchange for manufactured goods, it is better for it to stop trading abroad and to try and develop domestic manufactures.[27]

Had the poor countries in the 1960s–70s followed this old example, by using labour-intensive technologies, may be they would have developed, slowly but definitely sooner.

3.3.3 Productivity differentials

The main flaw in Prebisch-Singer's thesis regards the effects of productivity increase. First of all, Prebisch confuses productivity increase with business cycle, by using the argument that 'cycle is the proper way of growing in capitalist economy and the increase in productivity is one of the main factors of growth'.[28] This linkage has no meaning. Business cycle and increase in productivity are different processes, independent from one another.

What is odd is the idea that the increase in western productivity should improve the terms of trade of the poor country. Even in a market with perfect competition, the innovator does have an advantage; because he can sell cheaper or have a higher per unit return than his competitors. Such an advantage is temporary by definition, because competition forces the other producers to adopt the same innovation as soon as possible. This is Ricardo's way of approaching the problem. According to him, foreign commerce, like innovation, usually produces only temporary advantages for profits. Marx, on the contrary, while starting with the same approach, tends to think of a permanent advantage of the more productive and more developed economy.[29] Recently Pradella has signalled similar other passages of Marx in order to show that this author describes a process of dualism in capitalist development.[30]

But when international exchange is between very unequal producers, we are far from perfect competition, and the advantage of the innovator can be permanent. In this case there are neither atomistic competitors nor perfect mobility of productive factors. Western and multinational enterprises have an oligopolistic and monopsonic position. To this, also the dominating position of western social system must be added.

Technical progress prospers in developed economies, and forms a sort of growing sedimentation at many levels: production process, social organization, infrastructures, human capital formation, skill, law, etc.[31] In the 1950s all this was expressed by using the Marshallian concept of external economies. As Arthur Lewis puts it:

> the productivity of investment in B [the developing country] depends not only on B's natural resources and its human institutions, but also on the efficiency of all other industries whose services the new investment would require to use . . . The productivity of one investment depends upon other investments having been made before.[32]

Much earlier Smith had noted: 'A great stock, though with small profits, generally increases faster than a small stock, with greater profits. Money, says the proverb, makes money'.[33]

3.3.4 Wage differentials and productivity

The problem of productivity's effects can be examined, not only from the viewpoint of the market structure, but also from that of the differences in wages. It is true – as Prebisch and Singer state – that an increase in productivity usually lowers wages, but only as percentage of the overall investment, not in comparison with the wages of the less advanced production. Prebisch and Singer's argument paradoxically implies that wages in elementary production should increase faster, thanks to the technical progress of the advanced production. Of course, the contrary holds. Thanks to the cumulative advantages given by technical progress, the gap between developed and underdeveloped countries widens.

As early as in 1728 Daniel Defoe explained the advantage of a high level production. England, he writes, cannot compete with China and India in international trade on the basis of production costs, because Asian workers are in wretched conditions and have very low wages. England, instead, having the highest wages in the world, can compete on the basis of the high quality of her products, which derives from high wages.[34]

Wages apart, Jacob Viner, in order to deny the declining terms of trade of the poor countries, used an argument similar to Defoe's:

> It may perhaps take more pounds of coffee, or of cotton to buy a lamp today than it did in 1900, but today's coffee and cotton are, I presume, not appreciably better in quality than those of 1900; whereas today's electric lamp is incomparably superior to the kerosene lamp of 1900.[35]

This argument is correct, but it does not disprove the poor countries' declining terms of trade. On the contrary, Viner unawares confirms Prebisch' and Singer's main thesis: western industry has a growing productivity, whereas the poor countries are stuck to the production of raw materials and cannot use the latter to industrialize; then their productivity cannot increase. Despite the Prebisch-Singer's shortcomings, the widening gap they described was real. It still works today for the poorest countries.

3.4 W. Arthur Lewis: the two-sectors economy

3.4.1 A two-sectors model of development

In 1954 Arthur Lewis overturns the role of low wages in backward economies (his analysis explicitly adopts the classical economics' categories). Wages, instead of being the weak point in growth projects, can be the way towards development. Lewis transforms the twofold concept of centre-periphery in the concept of dual economy: in the poor countries we can have an industrial (capitalist) sector and a subsistence (non-capitalist) sector living together.

The subsistence non-capitalist sector provides food and the other elementary goods which form the wages for the capitalist workers. That sector has an unlimited supply of labour, which is generated by hidden unemployment.[36] The latter is widespread in agriculture, but also in the mean services, retail trade, household labour and servants' labour; it is kept high by the increase in population.

The marginal productivity of these workers is near to zero; then wages are at the subsistence level. This is the real advantage of a dual economy: capital is highly rewarded because it is the scarce productive factor. As long as the unlimited supply of labour holds, wages will be at the minimum level, and all the advantages of capital formation and of technical progress will add to profit. The latter increases proportionally to the expansion of the capitalist sector.

In an underdeveloped economy, Lewis explains, saving is low not because people are poor but because profits are few. As long as capitalist accumulation goes on, there is a displacement of wealth in favour of the élites and their incomes (profits and rents). This allows to save without reducing the part of national product destined to subsistence.[37] In such a model wages can start increasing only when capitalist accumulation will drain the unlimited supply of labour.

In a sense, Lewis provides a view alternative to the concept of the vicious circle of poverty,[38] put forward by Singer. But he goes too far in making cheap labour the main factor of development. First of all, had developing countries waited to dry up all their hidden unemployment, they would still look forward to starting a development process. Second, cheap labour can be the way towards development only for a while, as Lewis himself acknowledges.[39] In the long run other factors are needed, especially the growth of human capital and of technical progress.[40] It is true that production based on low wages can be competitive even for centuries, as it has been in Latin America. But in this case it does not promote, rather it hinders development. In actual fact Latin America did not develop for centuries.

Anyway Lewis' model was a great achievement. As Sunna shows, it raised many criticisms but also inspired important new results.[41]

3.4.2 The dual model in international trade

We should keep in mind Lewis's shortcomings when dealing with the last part of his essay, where his model is applied to foreign exchange. Lewis adopts Ricardo's law of comparative costs. But he admits that it does not apply to a situation with a strong difference between developed and underdeveloped economies: 'In the classical world all countries have labour surplus. In the neo-classical world labour is scarce in all countries. In the real world, however, countries which achieve labour scarcity continue to be surrounded by others which have abundant labour'.[42]

The author seems uncertain between diffusion and polarization; between his original approach, based on profitability deriving from cheap labour and scarce capital, and the opposite one, based on profitability due to the general system's productivity and external economies: 'it may be more profitable to invest capital in countries which already have a lot of capital than to invest it in a new country. If this were always so, no capital would be exported, and the gap between wages in countries with a labour surplus and non-surplus would not diminish but would widen. In practice capital export is small, and the gap does widen, and we cannot at all exclude the possibility that there is a natural tendency for capital to flow towards the capitalized, and to shun the undercapitalized'.[43]

Lewis concludes that many capitalists, despite the excess labour and the subsistence wages in their country, prefer to invest in the developed economies because of their higher productivity. Then it is not certain that capital returns tend to fall: 'The yield may fall or it may not; we cannot foretell'.[44]

In these pages there is an unresolved tension between the Ricardian approach and the evidence of reality. The author tries, unconvincingly, to apply Ricardo's law, based on labour cost, to the relationship developed-underdeveloped countries. According to this law, in marginal terms, the poor country with excess labour should have convenience to export foodstuff and import manufactured goods. But Lewis cannot accept such a 'divergence between the actual and what it ought to be'. Such a discrepancy, he writes, has deceived both economists and governments. The latter have allowed, or were pushed to allow, the destruction of their own industries by cheap foreign imports. Then a protection policy is needed.[45] Just the opposite of Ricardo's plea for free trade.

The last sentence of the essay perfectly synthesizes Lewis' contradiction:

> The Law of Comparative Costs is just as valid in countries with labour surplus as it is in others. But whereas in the latter it is a valid foundation of arguments for free trade, in the former it is an equally valid foundation of arguments for protection.[46]

As a matter of fact the comparative costs law proved to be unsuitable to explain the exchange between developed and underdeveloped economies. It works just – and within highly unrealistic assumptions too – for countries with a similar level of development, and it assumes a static situation with given endowments of resources.[47]

Besides the law implies a perfect internal mobility of the productive factors and their perfect immobility internationally.[48] The assumption is so unrealistic that Lewis supposes the opposite case: a perfect international mobility of capitals and of labour. But this version is untenable too. It implies again that wages cannot grow and development cannot start in poor countries until the whole mass of hidden unemployment in the world disappears.

Actually factors are partially mobile both inside and abroad but overall they are more mobile inside. The increase in wages is possible before the disappearance of labour surplus, because it also depends on many other conditions.

3.5 Cumulative process, dependence, oligopolies, diffusion

3.5.1 Myrdal: the cumulative process

In 1957 Gunnar Myrdal provides a complete overview of the dualistic world economy. He applies to underdevelopment the Swedish concept of cumulative process; and gives a general framework to the previous achievements.

Myrdal maintains that the main assumption of the traditional theory is unfounded, i.e. the tendency of economic systems towards a stable equilibrium, where different processes counterbalance each other generating a static situation. In fact, he says, the opposite dynamic tendency holds: variations push economic factors in the same direction. Such a tendency emphasizes the consequences of a certain occasional change.[49] The change can be upward or downward, it can foster growth or recession. In any case it increases differences, and creates a cumulative spiral.[50]

Myrdal recalls the Bible: 'who has more will receive more, who does not have will lose also what he possesses'.[51] While Marrama reminds a graphic epigram of the Roman poet Martial: 'If you are poor, you will always be poor. Nowadays wealth is given only to the rich'.[52]

Beside development's polarization, there is also the opposite tendency to its diffusion. However the international movements of capitals, labour and goods do not counterbalance the tendency to regional disparities; on the contrary, the latter was strongly reinforced in the colonial age.[53]

According to Myrdal the decline in prices of the poor countries' export is due to western policies, which encourage production of primary products in the third world. He echoes Lewis: in the poor countries, with surplus and unskilled labour, any improvement in technology goes to the advantage of western importers, in the form of lower prices;[54] whereas the poor country which exports gets only inflation.[55] He confirms that hidden unemployment can become an advantage for development.[56]

Developing countries should be allowed to adopt import restrictions, protection of infant industries, support to their export, and a policy of import substitution[57] Since many infant industries are suffocated by the narrowness of the domestic market, they need to export. Trade regulations in the poor countries cannot be based on the Heckscher-Ohlin's idea, but may implement a dynamic version of the comparative costs law.[58]

In general, Myrdal says, a dynamic approach enlarges the scope on development processes. It includes the social, 'non-economic', factors, which give 'quality' to development. Non-economic factors are as important as the economic ones for investments' efficiency. In conclusion, Myrdal criticizes once again the static approach and its unrealistic assumptions like free trade, *laissez-faire* and harmony of interests.[59]

In another famous book, Myrdal notes that western countries, in order to build up the welfare state, concentrated on their own national interests, to the detriment of the poor countries.[60] The latter too should pursue a nationalist policy to support development and their own welfare state. These are the necessary premises for a welfare state at the world level.

3.5.2 Furtado: underdevelopment as dependence

During the years 1952–60, Celso Furtado published a series of essays, then collected in a book which is a powerful picture of the theories, history and analysis of development and underdevelopment. Furtado speaks of dependence. He states that underdevelopment derives from the way in which western capitalism expanded; but it is not a necessary consequence of development.[61]

Since the beginning western capitals went to countries with non-capitalist economies in order to take away natural resources and raw materials. This created a primary industry (mines and plantations) which employed a small percentage of natives, whose wages were determined by the traditional/subsistence economy. In the small countries, where land is scarce, the profits of this industry were exported to western countries. In the big ones, where there is an unlimited supply not only of labour but also of land, profits were partly re-invested internally. The first countries have a lower dualistic structure, the second a higher one, more complex and with a certain potential of growth.[62]

In both cases Furtado speaks of 'bastard capitalism', functional to, and directed by, other countries. In underdeveloped countries any increase in the yields of the export and industrial sectors goes to the advantage of the rich, by increasing luxury consumption. Consequently wages are steadily low, and this fact provides competitive prices in export.

While repeating Prebisch's argument, Furtado also explains the origin of technical progress. In developed economies, competition in the demand for labour tends to increase wages, and consequently costs. To lower costs again, entrepreneurs promote technical progress. The latter, says Furtado, usually consists in substituting primary productive factors (land and labour) with capital.[63]

In underdeveloped countries capitalists do not need technical progress because of the excess in labour supply (as Myint notes, even when labour is getting scarce, poor countries' entrepreneurs prefer to promote migrations from China and India rather than promoting technical progress).[64]

Thus economic dualism also becomes a technological dualism, and underdevelopment becomes dependence on the dominant economies. The technical gap tends to widen. It strengthens incomes' concentration, hinders innovations and makes disequilibrium permanent.[65] The dependence of these economies is confirmed by the import of luxuries, consumed by the rich. In these conditions, and this seems an answer to Lewis, labour surplus instead of being absorbed tends to endure.[66]

3.5.3 Balogh: increasing returns and oligopolies

Also Thomas Balogh published in 1960 a collection of previous articles on international exchanges, with the meaningful title *Unequal Partners*. The book opens with a vast 'Theoretical Introduction', which can be considered as a perfect synthesis of the new ideas.[67]

Balogh's basic principle is that exchange conditions shift so frequently that static equilibrium analysis is useless. It implies stability, symmetry, reversibility of relationships; atomistic units in perfect competition and given endowments.[68] But the actual relationships are determined by national differences in the development stages, national oligopolies and divergent shifts also inside the national economies. The traditional theory of international trade has contributed to inequality and instability rather than to policies for a balanced development.[69]

Exchange generates specialization, and the latter drives to oligopolies. Traded commodities change continually their prices, because of the variations caused by exchange itself. Many of these changes are irreversible; such as the devastating specializations induced in the weaker partners.[70]

In particular Balogh devotes insightful analyses to the three connected factors which make equilibrium impossible: capital accumulation which increases labour and land productivity, returns to scale and technical progress. All these factors produce increasing returns. This makes the traditional hypothesis of given endowments impossible. In fact, increasing returns spread unequally. This shows that exchange does not equalize factors' remunerations, as the classical theory maintains.

Balogh extends the concept of infant industry to areas and countries where development is starting. They too need protection.[71]

3.5.4 Hirschman: polarization and diffusion

Finally, in 1958 Hirschman showed that, in development, polarization and diffusion are always weaved together.[72] The prevalence of one or the other depends on the particular economic process and on the political context – whether it is regional development in a national dualistic economy or it is development in two different countries. A wise economic authority should treat the different processes according to their own nature and according to the context.

3.6 The comparative costs law is incompatible with development

Nurkse and Chenery tried to make the Ricardian law dynamic at the practical level.[73] But they missed the main point expressed by the above critics of the law: in the long run the real advantage in international exchange goes to the production which has a faster technical progress. On turn, a rapid technical progress derives from a big amount of human capital and social capital accumulated.

The 1950s critics stressed two main flaws of the law. Its static nature, and its indifference to the type of goods exchanged (whether they are raw materials or technological products). It is worth noting that precisely these flaws confer the law that rigorous aspect which appeals to so many economists. It is well known that often economists are attracted more by logical coherence than by the correspondence to reality.

From another viewpoint, the law is basically spoiled by its separation between necessaries and comforts. Contrary to Smith, Ricardo maintains that, in a favourable foreign trade, the consequent increase in profits cannot be permanent, because profits 'speedily subside to the general level'. He explains: 'the rate of profits can never be increased but by a fall in wages'; and 'there can be no permanent fall of wages but in consequence of a fall of the necessaries on which wages are expended'.[74]

Note that the same thing holds for technical progress. Foreign exchange and technical innovation make wages fall and profits rise only if they make wage goods cheaper. If, instead, they concern goods 'consumed by the rich', profits will have no alteration.

If comforts or luxuries become cheaper, says Ricardo, we will pay for a greater quantity of goods the same 'portion of the produce of the land and labour' of the nation. But, since these goods do not concern workers' consumption, i.e. wages, profits will not vary; although cheaper comforts increase our enjoyments.[75]

Then the law excludes the two main factors of development: the increase in workers' consumption, which gradually extends from the strict necessary to comforts; and the contribution to the increase in productivity provided by the usual consumers of comforts, i.e. the middle classes. This means to exclude from accumulation skilled people (civil servants, professionals, technicians, teachers, etc.), and the products of their labour (public administration, health care, education, infrastructures, skill).

Consequently the terms of trade and the gap between strong and weak economies cannot be explained. The gap actually widens because of two connected processes which occur in the stronger economy: increase in consumption and increase in productivity.

Even technical progress is seen by the Ricardian law as an exception. Not to mention the Duesenberry effect, recalled by Nurkse and Myint.[76] Then the law ignores all the basic processes of development and of international trade.

The scope of the law is so narrow and useless that Ricardo's eulogy of it appears ideological. He writes: 'under a system of perfectly free commerce each country naturally devotes its capital and labour to such employments as are most beneficial to each. This pursuit of individual advantage is admirably connected with the universal good of the whole'.[77] Ricardo concludes: 'It is this principle which determines that wine shall be made in France and Portugal, that corn shall be grown in America and Poland, and that hardware and other goods shall be manufactured in England'.[78]

If you put, in lieu of Ricardo's examples, silver from Peru, coffee from Brazil or bananas and gold from Africa, you will have the picture of world underdevelopment and of the secular exploitation of non-western countries. This can explain why Myrdal insists that the Ricardian law is the link between western interests and economic theory.[79]

The modern version of the law – that of Heckscher, Ohlin and Samuelson – does not improve things. It implies that the most abundant factor of production is also the cheapest, then the most productive. But, first, abundance not always means cheapness. Human capital is not cheap even when it is abundant. Second, cheapness not always means higher productivity, even in the narrow sense of profitability. In the case of natural resources and of elementary labour, at least in the long run, it means a low or decreasing productivity.

3.7 After the fifties: a note

The main principles of the new international trade theory were put forward during the 1950s. After that decade the literature provides useful, but no longer original, treatments, that rely mainly on Prebisch-Singer's and Lewis' analyses. During the 1960s neo-classical authors contested the meaning attributed by development economists to the historical records of the terms of trade; and criticized the import substitution policy.[80] Meanwhile the new approach became increasingly radical, and merged with the theories of imperialism, especially those of Marxist derivation.[81]

The 1970s were shaken by Emmanuel's book – with a fortunate title, *L'échange inégal* – which seemed to provide the definite international trade theory from a radical-Marxist viewpoint. However, Emmanuel's analysis does not hold. The author starts from a mix of the Prebisch-Singer's approach and Lewis' analytical tools. The core of his thesis is expressed by this statement: if there is an increase in productivity in the export sector of the poor country, and its wages are blocked at a very low level 'for some independent reason', the surplus gain has to go to somebody else. The latter cannot be the poor countries' entrepreneur, because competition equalizes profits internationally. Then the gain goes to the consumer of western countries, which import those goods at lower prices.[82]

Emmanuel describes this as a process of exploitation, in the Marxist sense, at the international level. Yet the Marxist concept of exploitation has nothing to do with the consumer's advantage, as the contemporary Marxists soon pointed out.[83] Nor it has anything to do with the relationships, however unfair, between countries. But what matters more is that Emmanuel discards the increase in productivity, due to technical progress, as the main factor of development. Because of this, not only Joan Robinson, but even Samuelson could rightly criticize him.[84]

In the late 1970s development economics began declining, as Hirschman noted soon.[85] In the 1980s the free trade doctrine started a long-lasting revival. It was based on the comparative advantages law and the connected ideas of fair competition, equilibrium and harmony. Poor countries were (and are) accused to be the cause of their own poverty, for not being committed enough to free trade policies. The latter are seen as the antidote to the assistance disease, which supposedly spoils the chances of development. In the last decades, in western universities, students have been educated in the full ignorance of what had happened to the international trade theory in the period 1950–1980.

In the last years, along with the deepening of economic crisis, the concepts of the fifties have emerged again, particularly the criticism of free-trade as a policy for development. This attitude was revived either by authors coming from the old literature,[86] or by new authors.[87] Of course the situation is so deeply changed that most of the old analyses cannot be automatically applied to the present processes. However the categories of the 1950s – like dualism, cumulative processes, conflicting interests in trade, widening gap, economic dependence, the couple polarization-diffusion, etc. – on the one hand still have a meaning, on the other they need to be re-shaped in order to explain the new situation.

3.8 Today: old concepts, new problems

Today the processes of international trade singled out in the 1950s often have different effects.

3.8.1 Lewis model's application

Arthur Lewis wanted to show the poor countries a way to industrialize. In his 1954 essay, he never wrote that his model was based on selling abroad the industrial goods produced with subsistence wages. However, since Lewis did not hint at an increase in domestic consumption, the majority of his readers rightly understood his development model as based on industrial export.[88] Later on Lewis himself stressed that increase in export was the priority to start development.[89]

Lewis' model was neglected, in actual policies, at least for two decades. Actually it could be suitable just for production of low technical level and elementary products. Then it could only be a labour-intensive production, with low returns and a slow increase in capital and in investments.[90]

But, as we have seen, in the 1960s many poor countries aimed at a fast development chose the unsuccessful way of heavy industrialization. We also saw that, as Myrdal remarked, in the same period the implementation of the welfare state led western countries to discard third world development. This means that western countries employed internally the huge mass of wealth that neo-colonial policies were drugging from the poor countries to them.

Finally in the late 1970s the so called Asian Tigers started to apply steadily Lewis' model. In the Eighties it was applied on a large scale in China. Today we can say that at least China, India, Brazil, partly Mexico and South Africa, are applying it.

However the emerging countries' development is due not merely to the application of Lewis's model. Beside the labour surplus, these countries have a huge domestic market which can absorb part of the new products, first of all the means of production.

Moreover Lewis's model is applicable only for a short period. In fact India and China are already promoting high-tech production, research, high education and specialization, and huge infrastructures. In China wages are already growing, despite the enormous reserve of unlimited supply of labour still present in the countryside.

3.8.2 Development diffusion and western saturation

The authors of the fifties proved that trade based on specialization does not lead to equilibrium and to the diffusion of development. On the contrary, it leads to polarization, dependence, and a widening gap between developed and poor countries. Then they pleaded for industrializing underdeveloped countries. However, when industrialization finally started in the emerging countries, in the 1980s, this was mainly due to western investments, rather than to the domestic capital formation. Beside the traditional exploitation of natural resources, western capitals were now directed to produce in some countries industrial goods, mainly for export.

At the beginning the new investments implemented just a low level of industrial production, like the assemblage of western high-tech components, or very simple final products, or semi-processed goods. This means that western investments were (and are) looking for lower wages. However in the long run the search for low wages also applies to more complex or refined types of production.

At first sight, industrialization of the emerging countries seems the consequence of diffusion, the tendency which is contrary to polarization. The classical approach considered diffusion as the normal output of development. It was best described by Smith, as Lewis reminds. Smith writes: 'When profit diminishes merchants are very apt to complain that trade decays; though the diminution of profit is the natural effect of its prosperity, or of a greater stock being employed in it than before'. The profit's fall, Smith adds, leads a part of investments to migrate to countries with scarce capital. There they can yield high profits, even together with raising wages (what is happening today in China). In the developed economy the capital flow outside decreases supply, raises prices, lowers wages and increases profits.[91]

In the 1980s the massive capital shift started to change radically the international division of labour. Western manufactures moved abroad and western internal production was directed mainly to high-tech or cultural goods, and specialized services.[92] These changes seemed to confirm the tendency to diffusion, to the equalization of productive factors' returns, to equilibrium, and to advantages for all. Moreover they apparently disproved the theories of the 1950s. In any case the experience of the last decades proves that, besides polarization, also diffusion is generally at work in international economic relationships.

However, in the last twenty years, the capital flow has become unbridled. In the developed areas it is now dismantling manufacture, increasing unemployment, and worsening wages and working conditions. All this cannot derive from the normal tendency to counter the decline in profits through diffusion. It rather derives from saturation. The latter has two main causes. First, mature economies, after the welfare state, could not expand their traditional consumption any more. Secondly the great increase in productivity due to new technologies makes traditional jobs more and more redundant.

Western countries tried to overcome saturation by liberalizing the export of both capital and commodities, the so called globalization. These policies speeded up industrialization and competitive growth in the emerging economies; but did not absorb the huge western excess in capitals and goods; nor did they free the majority of poor countries from exploitation of natural resources and of elementary labour.[93]

Thus, despite the tendency to diffusion and to the equalization of productive factors' returns, globalization is driving the world economy increasingly far from equilibrium, reciprocal advantages and harmony of interests.

3.8.3 Hic sunt leones

This expression (the lions' land) appeared in the maps of ancient Romans to indicate that part of Africa unexplored and dangerous. The present crisis too is largely unexplored and unknown. Its processes are upsetting the meaning of many basic concepts of the 1950s' development economics. Such changes will require new and extended analyses. Here we can just mention some of them.

3.8.3.1 Hidden unemployment

It appears again, at the top of development. No more in agriculture or in mean services, rather in industry and in some modern services (cars, building, domestic devices, clothing, foodstuff, entertainment, information, insurance, etc.). Thus the infinite reserve of labour, with zero marginal productivity, analyzed by Lewis, now appears again in mature economies; not because of the lack of capital and investments but because of an excess of capital and investments.

3.8.3.2 Labour-intensive production

In mature economies, this expression means no longer elementary production, with scarce capital and much unskilled labour. New investments have the highest percentage of labour, but the skilled one. This is for a number of reasons; although all of them are a consequence of the same evolution. The material supports of the new products, both as means of production and for final consumption, are very cheap. The cost of today's goods consists mainly in labour (think of computers, robotics, biotechnologies, information technologies, etc.). Production is increasingly dematerialized; labour is more and more skilled (its cost increases). In the end capital-intensive production is today the backward one. Labour-intensive advanced production is at the same time the more productive and the one which destroys much more jobs than the new one it creates.

3.8.3.3 Dualism

The present world economy is no longer dual; it is at least threefold: mature economies, emerging countries, and poor countries. In each of these groups the economic dynamics follows a different rationale. Besides the diffusion process, there is no more one simple process of polarization, but several contrasting tendencies.

3.8.3.4 Dependence

Today there are new types of dependence, or interdependence, in addition to the traditional one. For instance, western countries are now in competition with emerging countries in exploiting the natural resources of the poor areas. But at the same time they are being forced by emerging countries to change their basic sectors of production too rapidly, before the new sectors of production can develop sufficiently.

3.8.3.5 Saturation and profit

Saturation is the future of the bigger part of production based on profit. This means that capitalist production is going to change radically. Competition between countries and the terms of trade will be no longer based on the increase in productivity, in the sense of production of higher profits. The production of increasingly higher profits can lead an economy to become weaker rather than stronger.

Notes

1 I thank Claudia Sunna for her useful suggestions and her effective help in the source hunting.
2 P.A. Samuelson, 'International Trade and the Equalisation of Factor Prices', *The Economic Journal*, 58: 230 (1948), pp. 163–184; P.A. Samuelson 'International Factor-Price Equalisation Once Again', *The Economic Journal*, 59: 234 (1949), pp. 181–197.
3 W.W. Rostow, 'The Terms of Trade in Theory and Practice', *Economic History Review*, 1 (1950), pp. 1–20, on p. 3 and fn at pp. 4–5; T. Balogh, 'Investimenti all'interno e investimenti all'estero', in T. Balogh *Unequal Partners* (Italian trans. *Una società di ineguali*, Torino: Einaudi, [1960] 1967), pp. 220–235, on pp. 227–229 confirms Rostow's argument.
4 A.O. Hirschman, *National Power and the Structure of Foreign Trade* (Italian trans. Bologna: il Mulino, [1945] 1987), pp. 57–159.
5 'But have we not perhaps proved too much? At times in the historic past . . . important differences in wages and other factor prices have persisted', despite the mobility of factors. It can happen, among other cases, when 'different regions of the world are extremely different in factor endowments', P.A. Samuelson 'International Trade', p. 178.
6 T. Balogh, 'Modelli statici e problemi attuali', in T. Balogh *Unequal Partners* (Italian trans. [1949] 1967), pp. 210–219, respectively on pp. 215, 17–18.
7 It is uncertain whether one of the two authors suggested to the other the first idea and who was him.
8 R. Prebisch, 'El desarrollo económico de la América Latina y algunos de sus principales problemas', reprint in *Desarrollo económico*, 26: 103 [1949] (1986), pp. 479–502, on p. 482.
9 Ibidem, p. 482b; quotation from R. Prebish 'The Economic Development of Latin America and its principal problems' (27 April 1950) p. 10, New York.: ECLA, at http://repositorio.cepal.org/bitstream/handle/11362/ 29973/002.df?sequence=1 [accessed 10 November 2014].
10 Prebisch, 'El desarrollo económico', p. 485a.
11 Ibid., pp. 479, 496–497.
12 H.W. Singer, 'The Distribution of Gains between Investing and Borrowing Countries', *American Economic Review*, 40: 2 (1950), pp. 473–485, on p. 477, fn. 4.
13 Ibid., pp. 476–478.
14 Ibid., pp. 345–348.
15 Ibid., pp. 477–481.
16 C. Furtado, *Desenvolvimiento e subdesenvolvimiento*, partly included in *Théorie du développement économique* (Italian trans. Bari: Laterza, [1961] 1972), on pp. 237, 243; H.W. Singer, 'The terms of trade fifty years later. Convergence and divergence' *Zagreb International Review of Economics and Business*, 1:1 (1998), at http://gesi.sozphil.uni-leipzig.de/fileadmin/media/Global_Studies/Download_Content_EMGS/Preparatory_readings/Singer_-_The_Terms_of_Trade_Fifty_Years_Later_-_Convergence_and_Divergence. pdf, on p. 2 recalls the Engel curve [accessed 15 October 2014].
17 F. Perroux, *L'économie du 20.me siècle*, (Italian trans. Milano: Comunità, [1948–1959] 1966), on Vol. I, pp. 33–100; Vol. II, pp. 145–272; Vol. VI, pp. 584–590.
18 For a different view, see R. Nurkse, 'Some International Aspects of the Problem of Economic Development', in A.N. Agarwala, S.P. Singh, (eds) *The Economics of Underdevelopment* (Oxford: Oxford University Press, [1952] 1958), pp. 256–271, on p. 261.

19 Monoculture is the organizing of an entire economy on a single export, i.e. tropical primary good or mineral. It was imposed to many colonies; then it made those countries extremely dependent on western economies, see S. Brankovic, *Il problema dei paesi sottosviluppati* (Milano: Feltrinelli 1959), ch. 2, pp. 12–21.

20 M. Boianovsky 'Friedrich List and the Economic Fate of Tropical Countries', *History of Political Economy*, 45: 4 (2013), pp. 647–691.

21 Singer is aware of that, see H.W. Singer 'The Terms of Trade Fifty Years Later', pp. 1–2.

22 Moreover Europe and US give a heavy financial support to their agriculture. Then they practice a disguised form of dumping.

23 For two interesting readings on this, see J. Perkins, *Confessions of an Economic Hit Man* (Italian trans. Roma: Minimum fax, 2004) and M. Alacevich, *Le origini della Banca Mondiale* (Milano: Bruno Mondadori, 2007).

24 See the detailed analysis by J. Stanovnik, *I paesi in via di sviluppo nell'economia mondiale* (Italian trans., Milano: Feltrinelli, 1965). He proved the strict western protectionism against the finished or semi-processed industrial products of the poor countries. The free trade proclamations only served to make non-western countries buy western industrial products, and sell their primary products to the West. The GATT is the General Agreement on Tariffs and Trade; substituted in 1994 by the WTO (World Trade Organization).

25 See S. Pollard, *The International Economy since 1945* (Italian trans., Roma-Bari: Laterza [1997] 1999), on pp. 97–111.

26 T. Starkey, *A Dialogue between Pole and Lupset*, (London: Royal Historical Society – University College, [1529–32] 1989) on p. 115; L. Ortiz, *Memorial a Felipe II*, in *Anales de Economia*, 63, [1558] (1957), pp. 117–200; R. Cantillon, *Essai sur la nature du commerce en général* (London: Macmillan, [1730] 1931), on pp. 225–243; see also pp.15–16; 64–95.

27 J. Steuart, *Principles of Political Oeconomy* (Chicago: Chicago University Press, [1767] 1966), on vol. II, pp. 291–292, 296. For more documentation, see C. Perrotta, *Consumption as an Investment* (New York–London: Routledge 2004), on ch. 10.

28 R. Prebisch 'El desarrollo económico', p. 484b.

29 D. Ricardo, *The Principles of Political Economy and Taxation* (New York: Dutton, [1821] 1973), on p. 78; K. Marx, *Il Capitale*, Vol. 3 (Italian trans., Roma: Editori Riuniti [1864–1865]1972), on ch. 14.5, pp. 289–290. However Marx's view was not static like that of Ricardo.

30 L. Pradella, *Globalisation and the Critique of Political Economy. New insights from Marx's writings* (Abingdon–New York: Routledge, 2015), see especially pp. 148–153.

31 Marx had an intuition of this; see K. Marx, *Il Capitale,* Vol. 1, (Italian trans., Roma: Editori Riuniti, [1867] 1964), on ch. 20, p. 614.

32 W. A. Lewis, 'Economic Development with Unlimited Supply of Labour' in A.N. Agarwala, S.P.Singh, (eds.) *The Economics of Underdevelopment* (Oxford: Oxford University Press, [1954] 1958), pp. 400–449, on p. 438.

33 A. Smith, *The Wealth of Nations*, A. Skinner ed., (Harmondsworth: Penguin [1776] 1974), on p. 195.

34 D. Defoe, *Plan of the English Commerce* (New York: Kelley [1728] 1967), on pp. 36–68.

35 J. Viner, 'The Economics of Development' in A.N. Agarwala, S.P.Singh (eds) *The Economics of Underdevelopment* (Oxford: Oxford University Press, [1953] 1958), pp. 9–31, on p. 27.

36 Hidden or disguised unemployment means an excess of workers employed, without which the final product would be the same. This concept, with a different meaning, was introduced by Joan Robinson in the 1930s (see chapter 4 below), P.N. Rosenstein-Rodan, 'Problems of Industrialization of Eastern and South-Eastern Europe', in A.N. Agarwala, S.P. Singh, (eds) *The Economics of Underdevelopment* (Oxford: Oxford University Press, [1943] 1958), pp. 245–255, on p. 245; and R. Prebisch 'El desarrollo económico', pp. 495–496 applied it to backward agriculture.

37 W.A. Lewis, 'Economic Development', pp. 416–418; 448.
38 According to this concept, in a backward economy factors act as a hindrance to one another: low incomes depress consumption; low consumption discourages investments; then production does not grow; then incomes keep being low. The same logic applies to productivity, skill, attitude to risk, etc., see R. Nurkse, *Problems of Capital Formation in Underdeveloped Countries* (Italian trans. Torino: Einaudi, [1953] 1965), on pp. 7–9.
39 W.A. Lewis, 'Economic Development', pp. 434–435.
40 Ibid., p. 438.
41 See Chapter 4 below.
42 W.A. Lewis, 'Economic Development', p. 435.
43 Ibid., pp.438–439.
44 Ibid., p. 439.
45 Ibid., p. 444.
46 Ibid., p. 449. However the protection of infant industries was approved also in other approaches of the times, see R. Nurkse, *Problems of Capital Formation,* ch. V.1, pp. 124–130.
47 In this sense see also the criticisms of R. Nurkse, *Patterns of Trade and Development*, (Italian trans., Milano: Etas Kompass, [1959] 1970), on p. 39; and H. Myint, 'An interpretation of economic backwardness' in A.N. Agarwala, S.P.Singh, (eds.) *The Economics of Underdevelopment* (Oxford: Oxford University Press, [1954] 1958), pp. 93–132.
48 See D. Ricardo, *The Principles*, ch. 7.
49 G. Myrdal, *Economic theory and Underdeveloped Regions* (Italian trans. Milano: Feltrinelli, [1957] 1966), on ch. 2, pp. 22–31.
50 Ibid., ch. 3, pp. 31–34.
51 Ibid., p. 23.
52 '*Semper pauper eris si pauper es, Aemiliane./ Dantur opes nullis nunc nisi divitibus'* in V. Marrama, *Saggio sullo sviluppo economico dei paesi arretrati* (Torino: Boringhieri [1958] 1963), on p. 94.
53 G. Myrdal, *Economic theory*, ch. 5; see also H. Myint, 'The Classical Theory of International Trade and the Underdeveloped Countries' in B. Jossa (ed.), *Economia del sottosviluppo* (Bologna: il Mulino [1958] 1973), pp. 353–377, on p. 365.
54 G. Myrdal, *Economic Theory*, ch. 5, p. 58.
55 Ibid., ch. 7, p. 95.
56 Ibid., p. 97.
57 Ibid., pp. 95–99.
58 Ibid., pp. 96–97; 144.
59 Ibid., ch. 11, pp. 143–152.
60 G. Myrdal, *Beyond the Welfare State* (New Haven-London: Yale U. P., [1960] 1965), on ch. 10.
61 C. Furtado, *Desenvolvimiento,* pp. 209, 216.
62 Ibid., pp. 209–217.
63 Ibid., p. 237.
64 H. Myint, 'The Classical Theory', p. 357.
65 C. Furtado, *Desenvolvimiento*, pp. 218–221.
66 Ibid., pp. 227, 242.
67 T. Balogh, 'Investimenti all'interno', pp. 5–69.
68 Ibid., pp. 5–6, 15–19.
69 Ibid., p. XVI.
70 Ibid., pp. 17–32.
71 Ibid., p. 39.
72 A.O. Hirschman, *The Strategy of Economic Development* (New Haven: Yale University Press, 1958), on ch. 7.
73 R. Nurkse, *Patterns of* Trade, see also R. Nurkse, *Problems of Capital Formation*, ch. IV, pp. 115–123. H. Chenery, 'Comparative Advantages and Development Policy' in B. Jossa (ed.), *Economia del sottosviluppo* (Bologna: il Mulino [1961] 1973),

pp. 295–333. For an accurate and sympathetic history of the evolution of the comparative costs law, see A. Maneschi, *Comparative Advantage in International Trade. A Historical Perspective* (Cheltenham UK–Northampton USA: Elgar, 1998).

74 D. Ricardo, *The Principles*, pp. 78–80.

75 Ibid.

76 R. Nurkse, 'Some international aspects', ch. 3, pp. 70–74; H. Myint 'An interpretation', p. 118. According to the Duesenberry (or imitation) effect, people's economic satisfaction depends less on the absolute level of their income than on the comparison they do with the upper class' income.

77 D. Ricardo, *The Principles*, p. 81.

78 Ibid.

79 See also Furtado (1961, IV.3, p. 234).

80 See C. Oman and G. Wignaraja, *The Postwar Evolution of Development Thinking* (Italian trans. Milano: LED, [1991] 2005), on pp. 128–130.

81 Ibid, chs. 5–6.

82 A. Emmanuel, *L'Échange inégal* (Paris: Maspero [1969] 1979), on p. 135.

83 See C. Bettelheim, 'Remarques théoriques' in A. Emmanuel (ed.), *L'Échange iné-gal* (Paris: Maspero [1969] 1979), pp. 297–341; C. Palloix, 'The Internationalization of Capital and the Circuit of Social Capital' in H. Radice (ed.), *International Firms and Modern Capitalism* (Harmondsworth: Penguin, 1975), pp. 63–88; S. Amin, 'The End of a Debate', re-published as Part IV of *Imperialism and Unequal Development*, (English trans., Hassocks: Harvester, 1977).

84 J. Robinson, *Aspects of Development and Underdevelopment* (Cambridge: Cambridge University Press, 1979); P.A. Samuelson, 'Illogic of Neo-Marxian Doctrine of Unequal Exchange', in D.A. Belsley, E.J. Kane and P.A. Samuelson (eds.), *Inflation, Trade and Taxes* (Columbus: Ohio State University Press 1976), pp 96–107, on pp. 100–105).

85 A.O. Hirschman, 'The Rise and Decline of Development Economics', *Essays in Trespassing, Economics to Politics and Beyond* (Cambridge: Cambridge University Press, 1981), pp. 1–24.

86 See H.W. Singer 'The terms of trade fifty years later'; S. Amin, *Capitalism in the Age of Globalization* (London: Zed Books, 1997) and the essays collected in F. López Castellano (ed.) *Desarrollo: Crónica de un desafío permanente* (Granada: Editorial Universidad de Granada, 2007).

87 We confine ourselves to mention M. Damian, J.C. Graz (eds), *Commerce international et développement soutenable* (Paris: Economica, 2001); S. Lall, 'World Trade and Development', in R.Beynon (ed.), *The Routledge Companion to Global Economics* (London–New York: Routledge, 2001) pp. 21–46; H.J. Chang, *Bad Samaritans. The Myth of Free Trade and the Secret History of Capitalism* (New York–Berlin–London: Bloomsbury, 2008), ch. 3.

88 See R. Nurkse, *Patterns of Trade*, p. 42.

89 See W.A. Lewis, *Development Planning* (Italian trans., Milano: Feltrinelli, [1966] 1968), pp. 34–40.

90 For a different view, see A.O. Hirschman, *The Strategy*, pp. 120–25; pp. 150–52. For a detailed analysis of the requirements of the export sector in a poor country, see C. Furtado, *Desenvolvimiento*, pp. 240–243).

91 A. Smith, *The Wealth of Nations*, ch. 9, pp. 194–196. Smith referred to colonies, but his description also applies, *mutatis mutandis*, to emerging countries.

92 As early as in 1958 Hirschman had foreshadowed this situation: A.O. Hirschman, *The Strategy*, ch. 8, p. 152 f.n.

93 See C. Perrotta 'Economic Development. Past and Present', in J.L. Cardoso, M.C. Marcuzzo and M.E. Romero (eds), *Economic Development and Global Crisis* (New York–Abingdon: Routledge, 2014), p. 15.

4 Dual Development Models in historical perspective

Claudia Sunna

4.1 Introduction

The seminal article of William Arthur Lewis on 'Economic Development with Unlimited Supplies of Labour' of 1954 opened an important season of research on economic development issues based on Dual Development Models (DDM). After the publication of Lewis' article, the concepts of 'dualism' and 'dualistic economy' was permanently linked to this author. Anyway, as we will see in this chapter, firstly during the 1950s other *pioneers* of development economics could appreciate the notion of dualism and the application of this concept to explain development processes, and secondly the same concept of dualism was evident in the observation of crucial features of the backward countries.

It is possible to define the importance of the approach of DDM looking at the theoretical and policy developments that stemmed, and still are, from this analytical tool.

During the so-called season of 'high development theory',[1] between the 1950s and the 1960s, a common features of many rationales of development economists was to give account of dualism inside developing countries. Dualism is a very wide concept as it can be applied to different economic situations and historical phases inside countries and in the international relations between countries. The definition of dualism, starting from the 1950s, relies on the internal characteristics of Less Developed Countries (LCDs) and was mainly referred to the simultaneous operation of two dissimilar economic sectors, endowed with different levels of technology, and characterized by different markets for outcomes, different cultures of production, different institutional status, and so on.

The first occurrence of this concept, during the 1950s, was the sociological theory of Julius Boeke that studied the coexistence inside colonial Indonesia of two sectors of social and economic activities: the traditional domestic sector, and the modern capitalist sector, driven by the Dutch. The sociological model of Boeke was centred on the discrepancy between market-oriented western economic institutions and informal traditional Indonesian institutions. According to Boeke, the attempt to modernize the Indonesian society through interventions dropped from different backgrounds would not produce appreciable results.[2] Higgins criticized Boeke's approach and pointed out that the main features of dualism was the different technological endowment between sectors.[3]

At the core of the dualistic analysis it is possible to individuate the historical process that led to the formation of economic activities by the colonizing countries alongside the traditional economy of the conquered countries. However these activities were functional to the export of raw materials or to the organization of the colonies' economy according to the interests of the motherland. Economic activities that have these characteristics are best described as a static productive sector of 'enclave', meaning that they do not produce any effect on the traditional economy. Conversely, as we shall see in the following pages, the dualistic models are based on intersectoral relationships within the LDCs and are essentially dynamic.

Development economists, starting mostly after the publication of Lewis' article, concentrated on the definition of dualism and on the dynamic of economic growth processes that could be derived starting from this situation. In other terms, they simply observed the coexistence of the two economic sectors and tried to give account of this phenomenon through economic and historic lens.

This approach was, in some sense, in opposition to the group of development economists concentrated on the analysis of industry and on the relations between industries. From this last approach derived the 'balanced growth theory' of Rosenstein-Rodan, Ragnar Nurske and the stage approach of Walt Rostow.[4]

The starting premise of Dual Development Models was that within the economies analyzed there were two sectors – the modern-capitalist and the traditional-backward. The explanation of the processes of development stemmed from the dynamics of transformation and expansion of the capitalist sector, which ultimately leads to the demise of dualism.

In this chapter, section 4.2 is devoted to the analysis of Lewis' dual development model. In section 4.3 it will be analyzed the debates generated by Lewis' model while in section 4.4 the dualistic analysis of Celso Furtado and Albert Hirschman are studied. The theoretical and policy consequences of DDM will be analyzed in Section 4.5. The last section will outline some concluding remarks.

4.2 The Lewis' model

The author which is always linked with Dual Development Models is William Arthur Lewis and, in particular, his 1954 article 'Economic Development with Unlimited Supplies of Labour'.

Lewis clearly states at the beginning of his article that in order to study development there is the need to turn toward classical economists and, in particular, toward the assumption of 'unlimited supply of labour . . . available at the subsistence wages'.[5] The point is that Lewis explicitly denies the usefulness of the Keynesian apparatus in order to explain the process of economic growth and, also for this reason, he refers to the classical macroeconomic framework. Let's follow Lewis argumentations:

> When Keynes's *General Theory* appeared, it was thought at first that this was the book which would illuminate the problems of countries with surplus labour, since it is assumed an unlimited supply of labour at the current price,

and also, in its final pages made a few remarks on secular economic expansion. Further reflections, however, revealed that Keynes's book assumed not only that labour is unlimited in supply, but also, and more fundamentally, that land and capital are unlimited in supply – more fundamentally both in the short-run sense that once the monetary tap is turned the real limit to expansion is not physical resources but the limited supply of labour, and also in the long-run sense that secular expansion is not embarrassed not by a shortage but by a superfluity of saving. Given the Keynesian remedies the neo-classical system comes into its own again. Hence, from the point of view of countries with surplus labour, Keynesianism is only a footnote to neo-classicism – albeit a long, important and fascinating footnote. The student of such economies has therefore to work right back to the classical economists before he finds an analytical framework into which he can relevantly fit his problems.[6]

As explained in a later contribution, Lewis abandoned any neoclassical and Keynesian assumptions because of the need to explain the variability of resources. In particular he needed to drop the assumption that the supply of labour was fixed.[7]
In the words of Lewis:

> an unlimited supply of labour maybe said to exist in those countries where population is so large relatively to capital and natural resources, that there are large sectors of the economy where the marginal productivity of labour is negligible, zero, or even negative.[8]

The classical theoretical apparatus, especially in the version of Smith and Ricardo, allowed Lewis to explain the historical and analytical context in which the industrial revolution matured, that is to say through what processes the capitalist firm had spread as a predominant system of production. For Lewis the dualistic model and the classical approach allowed to explain how the process of capitalist development revolved 'on the higher than average propensity to save from profit income'. Accordingly, savings would be re-invested in the capitalistic sector and the result would be 'the rise of the share of profits in the national income in the initial spurt of economic development'.[9]

One of the fundamental ingredients of the Lewis model, in the 1954 version, is surplus labour. This is, in other terms, the concept of 'disguised unemployment' originally brought forward by Joan Robinson referring to mass unemployment during the 1930s within a strictly Keynesian framework.

According to Robinson, when there is a lack of effective demand, workers are not simply pushed out of the labour market (i.e. they are not simply idle) but they shift toward the informal labour market where productivity is lower.[10] The overall effect is, apart from no appreciable consequence on the level of unemployment, the presence of a two-sector labour market, the regular and the informal, with productivity differentials between the sectors. Furthermore, as a consequence, if a rise in effective demand takes place workers may came back to the regular sector (if their productivity is still at the level of the regular sector).

Streeten warns that there are some 'obvious' reasons that prevent the use of this concept referred to underdeveloped countries. In particular, the informal sector of developed countries might be compared to the subsistence rural sector of underdeveloped countries but 'it is not true that an increase of effective demand [in underdeveloped countries] would, by itself, absorb the excess of population in industry. Clearly a series of additional measures would be necessary'.[11] The point is that there are structural differences between developed and underdeveloped countries (in the level of capital invested, of labourers' skills, of infrastructures or social overhead capital, and so on) that don't allow the functioning of the process described by Joan Robinson.[12]

However the concept of disguised unemployment in itself was readily and extensively utilized during the first season of development economics often transformed into the concept of underemployment.[13] This last concept was referred to the lack of means of production's supply (especially capital and technical knowledge) and not as a result of a fall of effective demand. Underemployment was then considered as a distinctive feature of underdeveloped countries' agricultural sector. The crucial point was that a migration of workers from the agricultural sector would not have produced a fall in the total production of that sector. This was because, as specified by Lewis before, the marginal productivity of the agricultural sector was considered to be very low and sometimes even negative.

Paul Rosenstein-Rodan defined disguised unemployment as a distinctive feature of underdeveloped countries. He considered as a starting hypothesis of his famous 'big-push' model of 1943 the existence of an 'agrarian demographic excess'.[14] This feature for Rosenstein-Rodan, 'although a weakness, may represent a source of development and strength'.[15] This was due to the fact that the migration of workers from the agricultural unproductive sector toward the newly settled capitalist sector might generate the fundamental stimulus to economic growth.

Given the assumption of 'unlimited supply of labour', Lewis builds a two-sector model with capitalists and the capitalist sector on one side and the majority of the population and the subsistence or traditional sector on the other side. The subsistence sector consists of traditional agriculture and low productivity services like casual jobs, petty retail trading and domestic works.

The main economic characteristics of the two sectors are the following. For the traditional sector: the employment only of rudimental forms of capital, very low or even negative level of labour marginal productivity (workers are unproductive in the Smithian sense) and wages are at the level of biological subsistence. Due to the low level of productivity, there is disguised unemployment not only in the agricultural sector but also in the services sector.

The capitalistic sector employs only a minority of the active workers – at a level that doesn't causes the rise in the wage of the traditional sector. Workers are productive as they use reproducible capital. Wages are determined according to the marginal productivity of labour and they are slightly above the subsistence level. That is because the products of the capitalistic sector may be sold at a price that is above the cost of labour.

The growth of the capitalistic sector allows the growth of profits, the expansion of credit and savings up to the point in which still exists an *unlimited* supply of labour. According to Lewis 'the supply of labour is therefore unlimited so long as the supply of labour at this price [of subsistence] exceeds the demand'.[16] So the supply of labour is virtually unlimited because it is reinforced by three different sources: the subsistence sector, women entrance in the labour market, and finally population growth. As a conclusion Lewis maintains that:

> It is clear enough that there can be in an overpopulated economy an enormous expansion of new industries or new unemployment opportunities without any shortage of unskilled labour becoming apparent in the labour market. From the point of view of the effect of economic development on wages, the supply of labour is practically unlimited.[17]

In 1958, after four years from the publication of the dual model, Lewis started to specify some controversial aspects of his approach. Firstly, the model was to be interpreted for its contribution to the analysis of development processes and did not have a normative character.[18] In second place, Lewis specified that from the model derived two stages of development. The first stage is in operation, 'so long as unlimited labour is available at a fixed real wage' and 'the share of profit in the national income will increase', then a *turning point* is reached when 'anything which raises wages relatively to profits will check the speed at which the rate of profit on capital is increasing'.[19] Finally, when the reservoir of unlimited labour is exhausted by the development of the capitalistic sector, the second stage is reached and 'classical economics ceases to apply' as we re-enter in the neoclassical framework characterized by the scarcity of all factors of production and by their inelasticity of supply.[20]

Overall, the impact of this 'modified classical model' was really impressive. As recalled by Lewis 'some such model was needed at the time of writing, since the dynamic models then in use assumed constant savings and profits ratios'.[21] Charles Kindleberger, for instance, promptly applied the Lewis model to explain the process of economic growth of Europe after WWII.[22] In other peripheral countries, like Italy during the 1950, the dual model raised a great deal of debate around the proper form of intervention in order to reduce the share of surplus labour in Southern regions.[23]

On the other hand a more recent flow of analysis, which uses on the background the Lewis' model, is related to the empirical testing for developing countries, like China or Brazil, of the achievement of the turning point in the level of real wage.[24]

4.3 The debates on the Lewis' model

After 1954 Lewis, due to the debate on the zero or negative marginal productivity issue raised by his article, was forced to respond to his critics and was led to elucidate the concept of unlimited supply of labour[25]. At the beginning, the debate was raised mainly by Theodor Schultz and was referred to the issue of zero or negative marginal productivity of the subsistence sector that, from the very beginning of this debate, was interpreted to be located in agriculture.

Lewis and Schultz were both in the committee established by the United Nations in order to study employment problems of underdeveloped countries in 1951[26]. As explained by Tignor, the analytical implications of the disguised unemployment discussed and finally stated in the UN report 'were far-reaching. They implied that the marginal productivity or the additional product of many additional workers was zero, perhaps even negative – a stance that should have been anathema to free market neoclassical economists, especially those who specialized in agriculture'.[27] Schultz initially refused to sign the final version of the report but, in the end, unenthusiastically accepted to sign.

Schultz, in his book on *Transforming Traditional Agriculture*, tried to demonstrate that the surplus labour assumption and the zero marginal productivity argument in the Lewis model were not valid.[28] He used an 'epidemic test' to explain that after the 1918–19 influenza in India, the increase in deaths caused by the epidemic had contributed to decreased production in the following years. Lewis defines the data provided by Schultz as 'doubtful statistics' and, in any case, argues that the statistical test should have shown that the decrease of the population had taken place '*only* from the small family farms and other underemployed pockets'.[29]

Since the first reply to his critics of 1958 Lewis was forced to elucidate that in his model:

> the dynamic force is capitalistic accumulation, resulting in the expansion of capitalist employment. . . . One could have a model in which the dynamic force was located in the self-employed sector . . . For example, growth could be due to the expansion of peasant agriculture.[30]

Anyway, as we will see, most analysis on the Lewis model interprets the definition of dualism between an industrial sector and an agricultural sector.[31]

Other critics of the Lewis model from a neoclassical perspective were Peter Bauer and Jacob Viner.[32] Bauer argued that 'the assumption of stagnation in the agricultural sector give Lewis' apparently dynamic model a static bias which is at times misleading'.[33] This is because 'Lewis' discussion of capital formation ignores the establishment, extension, and improvement of agricultural properties, as well as certain other less important categories of agricultural investment'.[34] On the same vein Viner argued that it was impossible to consider that a farm cannot improve the productivity of the land through a more careful management.[35]

In response to these criticisms, J. Fei and G. Ranis constructed a model in which maintained the Lewis hypothesis of surplus labor in the traditional sector, i.e. in agriculture, but to the latter they assigned the role of engine of the development process since, the entering of technical innovations in agriculture would have raised the production function in agriculture and would have enabled an increase in productivity. Agriculture constituted in this way a sector parallel to the capitalist where the increase in the share of savings necessary to the accumulation process would be generated.[36]

Another criticism against Lewis' model underlines that while in the model it is assumed a smooth migration process from overpopulated and underemployed rural area toward the full employed urban capitalistic sector, on the contrary, the flux of migration produced a typical structure of unemployment that it is precisely located in the urban areas while in the rural areas there is no population pressure.[37]

Furthermore, it has been noted that for Lewis there was no problem in the formation of a capitalistic class of entrepreneurs able to reinvest their profits into the modern sector.

Lewis replies to the criticisms pointing out that, in his model, he assumed a 'capitalist' and a 'subsistence' sector, and not a rural and an urban, or an industrial sector and an agricultural sector. What in essence, in the definition of Lewis, distinguishes the two sectors is basically the use of capital. However, in the article on his model written in 1979, Lewis uses another terminology calling the two sectors the modern and the traditional and drops the 'surplus labour' hypothesis.[38]

According to Lewis it is possible to remove the assumption of zero marginal productivity of labour in the subsistence sector without affecting the basic features and functioning of the dual development model. It is sufficient to assume that the level of wages is exogenous and determined conventionally to the subsistence level, according to the classics, and that is at a level lower than in the capitalist sector.[39] The exogenous level of wage, as Ranis points out, 'cannot be determined by the usual tools of economic analysis' because it incorporates information on social attitudes of that particular moment in the stage of development.[40] In addition, within the model, the only way to prevent the premature interruption of the development process is to allow the real wages of the capitalist sector to remain anchored to the subsistence wage for a period of time necessary to raise the share of profits in the national income. This outcome is consistent with the Kuznets' analysis on the trend of the distribution of income during the development process.[41] In the *Theory of Economic Growth*, Lewis sustains that one of the characteristics of the colonial government was precisely to keep down the real wage level of the subsistence sector for not allowing the growth of wages in the capitalist sector.[42]

As for the issue of unemployment in the development processes of the sixties, Lewis in 1965 explained that, in a dualistic model, unemployment grows 'because the traditional sector is expelling labour too rapidly' and 'the modern sector is taking too few because it is highly capital intensive'.[43] In this case, therefore, the process of transfer of labour from the traditional sector to the capitalist sector is too fast and it can occur the eventuality that the higher wages of the capitalist sector will attract too many employees compared with the actual capacity of employment. As we will see in the last section, this application of the dual model is very effective to explain both internal migration and the emergence of large cities in LDCs, and the formation of an informal sector inside the economy which, in many ways, replaces the traditional sector.

In respect to the criticisms on disguised unemployment we think that the last written explanation of Lewis is apt to close this dispute:

What was the basis of near infinite elasticity [of labour]? Critics fastened on disguised unemployment among small farmers in half-dozen overpopulated countries, but this was only one item in a long catalogue covering four pages of the first article. Other items were: technological unemployment [. . .]; underemployment in urban areas, in what now has come to be called the informal sector; the movement of women from the household into the labour market; and the increase of population.[44]

So in this passage Lewis seems to admit that, even if disguised unemployment in the rural sector was a debatable feature of his famous construction, there were many other points that still supported his unlimited supply of labour model.

It is worth noting that the criticisms over this model could be used also as a measure of how much it influenced subsequent debates on economic development.[45]

4.4 Furtado and Hirschman on dualism

Within development economist Celso Furtado and Albert Hirschman, widely commentated the Lewis' model. In the case of Furtado, he wrote in 1952 an ample comment on the Lectures that Ragnar Nurkse gave in Brazil in 1951. The lectures, in a revised version, were published in 1953 with the title *Problems of Capital Formation in Underdeveloped Countries*.[46]

In discussing the problems of capital formation and development brought forward by Nurkse, Furtado in some passages of the text used all the ingredient of the Lewis' model, adding some interesting aspects. Furtado says 'the increase in the physical productivity of labour is, in the main, the fruit of capital accumulation. However the relation between those two phenomena – increased productivity and capital accumulation – must be studied very closely if we are to understand the difficulties to be overcome in the initial stages of the process of development'. He adds:

> the main obstacles in the path of development . . . are encountered at the lowest level of productivity. Once the process of growth has been launched, the movement's own dynamic ensure that part of the increase in income is set aside for capital investment. A backward community has a very great tendency to remain stagnant without been able, on its own, to set the process of development in motion. The initial impulse to overcome those difficulties has always come from sources outside the community.[47]

In this passage the source of novelty, compared with Lewis' model, regards the reflection on the *primo mobile* (i.e. the initial impulse) of development processes. Lewis does not elaborate on the subject of the causes of the dynamic in the processes of economic development inside a dualistic model, while, according to Furtado, the process of development is a deliberate choice for underdeveloped countries.

Another interesting aspect of Furtado's approach lies in the role of the demand inside the dual development model. He underlies that the increase in productivity produces the growth of the level of income in the 'sector affected' (that means both agricultural and manufacturing capitalist sectors). At the beginning of the process of development the increase in income is absorbed by profits, which allows a sort of Marxian primitive accumulation. But 'once the process of growth is consolidated and the demand for labour increases, real wages will tend to rise'.[48] This in turn will affect the distribution of newly created income between consumption and investments. In conclusion, 'the additional consumer demand will affect prices in certain sectors and will ensure that new investments will be channelled towards them . . . The way demand develops is a basic factor governing the direction of the new investment'.[49]

According to Boianovsky, even if in Furtado there is a clear analysis of the Lewis' model ingredients and processes (i.e. the connection between an elastic labour supply from the subsistence sector and high profits in the capitalistic sector), 'it was only after the publication of Lewis's classic 1954 paper that the full analytical implications of the unlimited labour supply assumption for the theory of development became clear'[50]. This is probably true, anyway, as we have seen before, Furtado added some interesting point to the analysis of Lewis.

Before concluding this section it is interesting to look also at the analysis on DDM of Albert Hirschman.[51] In this article of 1957, 'Investment Policies and "Dualism" in Underdeveloped Countries', Hirschman define the two sectors as North and South. He says 'The North–South split is nothing but a special aspect of the often noted "dual" character of underdeveloped countries where the hypermodern exists side by side with the traditional, not only in techniques of production and distribution, but also in attitudes and in ways of living and of doing business'.[52] The main feature of this dualism is, according to Hirschman, given by the existence of two different wage levels for the industrial sector and for the preindustrial or non-industrial sector. This dualism is explained in terms of different legislation over wages in the two sectors and by the higher cost of living that labourers in the industrial sector must afford (due to urbanization). Hirschman also described the dualism in terms of 'the partial character of industrial penetration into underdeveloped countries . . . , i.e. the feeling that the economic structure is a rather incongruous mixture of the new and the old'.[53]

The main aim of Hirschman analysis is to look closer to the type of investment needed in this situation of dualism. 'The most efficient use of capital in underdeveloped countries is not in capital-intensive industries *qua* capital-intensive; it is in industries that open new product horizons for the economy and these industries are likely to be more capital-intensive then others'. The point then, subsequently developed in his *Strategy of Economic Development* of 1958, is that the process of capitalistic accumulation must be qualified and deeply studied in order to understand which is, for a particular underdeveloped country, the type of investment needed[54].

In conclusion, according to Hirschman, 'dualism brings with it no doubt many social and psychological stresses, but it has some compensating advantages and represents in a way an attempt by the economy of an underdeveloped country to make the best of its resources during a transitional phase'.[55]

4.5 The applications of Dual Development Models

As we have seen in the previous section, starting from the 1950s, Dual Development Models opened a vast range of reflections. It is possible to look at the many applications of this conceptual framework of dualism up to our days, at least in four different theoretical directions.

The first regards the development of studies on human capital; the second is the group of dual development neoclassical models, the third regards the emergence of the approach that studies the rural-urban and international migration phenomena and, finally, the analysis on the so-called informal economy.

4.5.1 Human capital

The development of the subject of human capital is strictly related to the Lewis' dual model. As we have seen before, one of the most important and lasting criticisms to the dual model had been brought forward by Schultz and, as we have seen, had 'forced' Lewis to change one of the fundamental characteristics of his model. Ironically, when Lewis was awarded of the Nobel Prize in 1979, he shared it with Theodore Schultz precisely for his contribution on the role of investment in human capital, particularly in agriculture.[56]

Hirschman commented this half-prize as a clear sign of the attack of neoclassical economics (or Monoeconomics, in his words) to the separateness of Development Economics as a discipline:

> whereas in the natural or medical sciences Nobel prizes are often shared by two persons who have collaborated in . . . a given scientific advance, in economics the prize is often split between one person who has developed a certain thesis and another who ha mightily to prove it wrong.[57]

Leaving aside the irony of this situation, human capital subject, quickly developed as a very fruitful field of investigation within the so-called problem of 'residual factor' in the construction of the aggregate production function.[58]

4.5.2 Dual neoclassical models

During the sixties and the seventies an extension of the debate around the Lewis' model was conducted inside the neoclassical theory with the contributions, to name the most debated, of D. Jorgenson, A.K. Dixit, and the model of A.C. Kelly, G. Williamson and R.J. Cheetham.[59] All these models basically departed from the Lewis assumptions framework in order to extend to the dualistic approach the neoclassical growth theory.

Dixit, which was at MIT during the raising tide of the neoclassical growth theory,[60] searched the appropriated level of capital intensity given that, the wage rate in the capitalist sector overcome the marginal product of the traditional sector. But, according to Lewis, 'this issue is largely political, and our models throws no light on it'.[61]

In Jorgenson model, on the other hand, there is a form of surplus labour that does not conduce to a zero or negative marginal productivity of labour. This is because when the institutional wage in agriculture is above the marginal productivity of labour, the latter could be still positive. Furthermore, the two sectors produce different goods and they trade with each other in the closed economy. So the growth of the capitalist sector can be slowed down if the adverse terms of trade are in operation.

In this case, to Lewis, the model loses its explanatory power as far as 'it is a good model for studying the economic history of countries before about 1870 . . . [when] transportation costs were so high that countries had virtually to be self-sufficient in basic necessities'.[62] In other terms, before the application of innovations that dramatically reduced transportation costs around the world, it made sense to assume a closed economy. After 1870, if the capitalist sector need foodstuff and raw materials from the agricultural sector, and the prices are against its terms of trade, then he simply goes on the international market to buy it.

In conclusion, for Lewis, the neoclassical sophistication left untouched the basic crucial features of his model, namely 'the abundance of labour at the current wage' and 'the notion that in the due course wages will rise faster then profits until some upper levelling-off is reached'.[63]

4.5.3 Migrations

In the Lewis' model the dynamic process of growth is characterized by with wage differentials between sectors. Then a migration of labour from the traditional sector to the capitalist sector occurs. In the case of the emergence of unemployment, this migration process, as we have seen previously, appears to be somewhat problematic because it takes place in a context of urban overpopulation. In this regard, Lewis, in 1972, points out that 'there is much less resistance today then there was in 1954 to the idea of an unlimited supply of labour being available to the capitalist sector, since swelling urban unemployment has emerged as the biggest problem of the seventies, *as a result of the modernization process itself*'.[64]

Since the end of the sixties, thanks to the early contributions of M. Todaro and J. Harris, a very articulated area of study related to economic analysis has developed on the subject of migration between sectors and on the processes of urbanization.[65]

In these models the migration processes are explained starting from the wage differentials between sectors that result from unbalanced growth of output between the capitalist and traditional sectors (or between urban and rural sectors). As a consequence the flows interrupt only when the wage gap between sectors is absorbed. The main difference between migration models and Lewis approach can be traced to microeconomic foundations of the former family of models while Lewis observed the process of labour migration from a macroeconomic perspective.

4.5.4 Informal economy

The last point of this brief survey on the 'effects' of the Lewis' model on development economics should recall the issue of the survival of the informal economy inside the broad picture of the capitalistic sector.

This is an unexpected outcome of the model of Lewis as far as, as we have seen in the precedent points, dualism was interpreted as a temporary feature during the process of economic development. At the same time, the task to define and to face the survival of the informal sector of the labour market, has become one of the most fruitful field of research inside development economics, sociology and political science.[66] The fact that this is a relatively not well established sector of research is given by the fact that there is an ample variability in the terms used for the definition of this phenomenon. According to Schneider and Enste is it possible to find more or less the same concept recorded as: 'underground economy, illicit work, informal sector, irregular sector, leisure economy, alternative economy, black economy, hidden economy, unofficial economy, parallel economy, shadow economy, unobserved economy, unrecorded economy'.[67]

4.6 Concluding remarks

According to Krugman the decline of Development Economics as an independent sub-discipline of economic research is due to the fact that 'development theorists were unable to formulate their ideas with the precision required by an increasingly model-oriented economic mainstream and were thus left behind'.[68] The fecundity of applications and ramifications of DDM and the uninterrupted flow of analysis that we studied in this work is in sharp contrast with this judgement. On the contrary, according to Ranis, the Lewis' model 'really contributed in a major way to the transition to growth theory, to the notion of development phases and sub-phases, en route to modern economic growth'.[69]

Starting from the Lewis' model all the debates generated revolve around the basic assumption related to the path and to the process of change of intersectoral factors inside the dual economy. As we have seen, the dynamic aspects of these models are the still-living territory in which development economics still produce interesting and useful analytical tools.

To sum up, since 1954, the Lewis' model explains the development processes from the theoretical context of England's first industrial revolution. Over the years, however, Lewis has always tried to upgrade the approach to this classical interpretations, which was essential for his research project, without giving up the two essential elements that characterize all the reasoning: 'the abundance of labour at the current wage' and 'the notion that in the due course wages will rise faster then profits until some upper levelling-off is reached'. As we have seen in section 4.5, the latter is probably the weakest point of the Lewis model, given the fact that dualism, in the labour market and in the economic sectors of advanced and less developed countries, seems to be a permanent feature instead of being a transitional process.

Progressively the Lewis model has become an essential tool for studying the processes of development after WWII. Lewis believes that the LDCs showed characteristics similar to the pre-capitalist phase of advanced countries, however, as opposed to Rostow, he did not build a deterministic model in which all countries will sooner or later go through the same stages in the development process. In *The Theory of Economic Growth* Lewis is very clear on this point. He refused the neoclassical and the Marxian stage approach in which development seems to be inevitable and teleological.[70]

The aim of Lewis is to show which processes are crucial to foster the spread and expansion of the capitalist enterprise from a context where the only abundant factor is unskilled labour.

The debate on the Lewis' model have never questioned the basic category of the Dual Economy. Ultimately the concept of dualism, in the sense of the simultaneous coexistence within a system of structurally different economic sectors, also in the version given by Furtado and Hirschman, is one of the major 'discovery' of this season of development economics.

Notes

1 P. Krugman, 'Toward a Counter-Revolution in Development Theory', *Proceedings of the World Bank Annual Conference on Development Economics* (Washington DC: World Bank, 1993) pp. 15–38.

2 J.H. Boeke, *Economics and Economic Policy of Dual Societies as Exemplified by Indonesia* (New York: Institute of Pacific Relations, 1953).

3 B. Higgins 'The "Dualistic Theory" of Underdeveloped Areas', *Economic Development and Cultural Change*, 4:2, (1956), pp. 99–115. For an overview on this debate, see G. Ranis 'Analytics of Development: Dualism', in H.B. Chenery and T.N. Srinivasan (eds), *Handbook of Development Economics*, Vol. 1 (Amsterdam: North Holland, 1988), pp. 73–92; C. Oman and G. Wignaraja, *The Postwar Evolution of Development Thinking*, Italian trans. *Le teorie dello sviluppo economico dal dopoguerra a oggi* (Milano: LED, [1991] 2005), on pp. 93–95.

4 P.N. Rosenstein-Rodan, 'Problems of Industrialization of Eastern and South-Eastern Europe' in A.N. Agarwala and S.P. Singh, (eds) *The Economics of Underdevelopment* (Oxford: Oxford University Press, [1943] 1958), pp. 245–255; R. Nurkse, *Problems of Capital Formation in Underdeveloped Countries* (Oxford: Oxford University Press, 1953); W.W. Rostow, 'The Take-off into Sustained Growth', *Economic Journal*, 66: 261 (1956), p. 25–48. On the debate between 'balanced/unbalanced' development approach see chapter 2 above, on the theory of Rostow see chapter 1.

5 W.A. Lewis, 'Economic Development with Unlimited Supply of Labour' in A.N. Agarwala and S.P. Singh, (eds) *The Economics of Underdevelopment* (Oxford: Oxford University Press, [1954] 1958), pp. 400–449, on p. 400.

6 Ibid., pp. 400–401.

7 W.A. Lewis, 'Development Economics in the 1950s', in G.M. Meier and D. Seers (eds), *Pioneers in Development* (New York–Oxford: Oxford University Press, 1984a), pp. 121–137, on p. 132; see also G. Ranis, 'Labour Surplus Economies', in J. Eatwell,

M. Milgate and P. Newman (eds), *The New Palgrave – Economic Development* (New York–London: Macmillan, 1987), pp. 191–198.

8   W.A. Lewis, 'Economic Development', p. 402.

9   W.A. Lewis, 'Reflections on Unlimited Labour' in L.E. Di Marco (ed.), *International Economics and Development. Essays in Honour of Raul Prebisch* (New York: Academic Press, 1972), pp. 75–96, on p. 75.

10 J. Robinson, 'Disguised Unemployment', *The Economic Journal*, 46: 182, (1936), pp. 225–237, on pp. 225–226.

11 P. Streeten, 'Disguised Unemployment and Underemployment' in G.R. Feiwel (ed.) *Joan Robinson and Modern Economic Theory* (New York: New York University Press, 1985), pp. 723–726, on p. 723.

12 A different explanation was given by Eckaus as far as he considered the fact that 'factor-market imperfections which limit factor mobility create employment problems in underemployed areas with low per capita incomes and limited capital resources which are not different in kind but are much different in degree from those existing in the more advanced countries', R.S. Eckaus, 'The Factor Proportion Problem in Underdeveloped Areas', *The American Economic Review*, 45: 4, (1955), pp. 539–565, on p. 565. On the different definitions of disguised unemployment see W.C. Robinson, 'Types of Disguised Rural Unemployment and Some Policy Implications', *Oxford Economic Papers*, 21: 3, (1969), pp. 373–386; A. Bhaduri, 'Disguised Unemployment', in J. Eatwell, M. Milgate and P. Newman (eds), *The New Palgrave – Economic Development* (New York–London: Macmillan, 1987), pp. 109–113.

13 See A.J. Navarrete and I. Navarrete, 'Underemployment in Underdeveloped Economies' in A.N. Agarwala and S.P. Singh, (eds) *The Economics of Underdevelopment* (Oxford: Oxford University Press, [1953] 1958), pp. 341–347.

14 P.N. Rosenstein-Rodan, 'Problems of Industrialization', p. 245. He developed also a methodology in order to measure underemployment, see 'Disguised Unemployment and Underemployment in Agriculture' in *Monthly Bulletin of Agricultural Economics and Statistics*, 6: 7–8, (1956), pp. 1–70. For a discussion on that methodology see P. Streeten, 'Disguised Unemployment'.

15 P.N. Rosenstein-Rodan, 'Natura Facit Saltum: Analysis of the Disequilibrium Growth Process', in G.M. Meier and D. Dudley (eds), *Pioneers in Development* (New York–Oxford: Oxford University Press, 1984), pp. 207–221, on p. 208.

16 W.A. Lewis, 'Economic Development', p. 403.

17 Ibid., p. 406.

18 W.A. Lewis 'Unlimited Labour: Further Notes', *The Manchester School*, 26: 1, (1958), pp. 1–32, on p. 31.

19 Ibid., pp. 18–19.

20 Ibid., p. 26.

21 W.A. Lewis, 'Reflections on Unlimited Labour', pp. 75–76.

22 C.P. Kindleberger, *Europe's Postwar Growth: The Role of the Labor Supply* (Cambridge, MA: Harvard University Press, 1967); Id. *Economic Laws and Economic History* (Cambridge: Cambridge University Press, 1989), pp. 21–42.

23 See L. Spaventa, 'Dualism in Economic Growth', *Banca Nazionale del Lavoro Quarterly Review*, 12:51, (1959), pp. 386–434; H.B. Chenery, 'Development Policies for Southern Italy', *The Quarterly Journal of Economics*, 76: 4, (1962), pp. 512–547.

24 See for instance: N. Islam and K. Yokoda, 'An initial look at China's industrialization in light of the Lewis growth model, *East Asia Economic Perspectives*, 17: 2, (2006), pp. 103–132; M. Banik, 'Dualism, Structural Change a the Development Experience of Brazil', Working paper, *Economic Development, INTS*, (2011).

25 See W.A. Lewis 'Unlimited Labour: Further Notes', Id. 'Reflections on Unlimited Labour'; Id., 'The Dual Economy Revisited', *The Manchester School*, 47: 3, (1979), pp. 211–229; Id., 'Development Economics in the 1950s', pp. 132–134.

26 The report of the committee had the title *Measures for the economic Development of Under-developed Countries*. For a reconstruction of the debate inside the committee see G.M. Meier and R. Baldwin, *Economic Development. Theory, History, Policy* (New York: John Wiley and Sons, 1957), on pp. 281–283; and R.L. Tignor, *W. Arthur Lewis and the Birth of Development Economics*, Princeton, NJ: Princeton University Press, 2006), on pp. 84–86.

27 R.L. Tignor, *W. Arthur Lewis*, pp. 85–86.

28 T.W. Schultz, *Transforming Traditional Agriculture* (New Heven: Yale University Press, 1964), on ch. 4.

29 W.A. Lewis, 'Reflections on Unlimited Labour', p. 82. On this debate see also A. Bhaduri, 'Disguised Unemployment', pp. 112–113; G. Ranis, 'Arthur Lewis' Contribution to Development Thinking and Policy', *The Manchester School, 72: 6*, (2004), pp. 712–723, on p. 717.

30 W.A. Lewis 'Unlimited Labour: Further Notes', p. 9.

31 See M. Figueroa, 'W. Arthur Lewis versus the Lewis Model. Agricultural or Industrial Development?', *Manchester School*, 72: 6, (2004), pp. 736–750, on p. 743–744. Starting from the fifties the analysis on the intersectoral balance in the process of economic growth has received wide attention. See, for example, N. Kaldor, *Causes of the Slow Rate of Economic Growth in the United Kingdom* (Cambridge: Cambridge University Press, 1966); Id. 'The Problem of Intersectoral Balance', in N. Kaldor, *Causes of Growth and Stagnation in the World Economy* (Cambridge: Cambridge University Press, 1996), pp. 39–54; H.B. Chenery and M. Syrquin, *Patterns of Development 1950–1970* (London: Oxford University Press, 1975); L. Taylor and P. Arida, 'Long-run Income Distribution and Growth', in H.B. Chenery and T.N. Srinivasan (eds), *Handbook of Development Economics*, Vol. I (Amsterdam: North Holland, 1988), pp. 161–194; A.P. Thirlwall, *The Nature of Economic Growth* (Cheltenham: Edward Elgar, 2002).

32 R.L. Tignor, *W. Arthur Lewis*, pp. 98–101.

33 P. Bauer, 'Lewis' Theory of Economic Growth', *The American Economic Review*, 46: 4, (1956), pp. 632–641, on p. 634.

34 Ibid., p. 635.

35 In R.L. Tignor, *W. Arthur Lewis*, p. 86;

36 G. Ranis and J.C.H. Fei 'A Theory of Economic Development', *The American Economic Review*, 51: 4, (1961), pp. 533–565; J.C.H. Fei and G. Ranis, *Development of the Labour Surplus Economy: Theory and Practice* (Homewood, IL: Irwing, 1964).

37 P. Leeson, 'The Lewis Model and Development Theory', *The Manchester School*, 47: 3, (1979), pp. 196–209. The analysis of the debates around Lewis' model is in A. Dixit, 'Models of Dual Economies', in J. Mirrlees and N.H. Stern (eds), *Models of Economic Growth* (London: MacMillan, 1973), pp. 325–352; R. Findlay, 'On W. Arthur Lewis' Contribution to Economics', *The Scandinavian Journal of Economics*, 82: 1, (1980), pp. 62–79.

38 W.A. Lewis, 'The Dual Economy Revisited', p. 211; see also Id. 'Reflections on Unlimited Labour', p. 77, where Lewis admit that regarding the zero marginal productivity of labour aspect of his model 'it was probably a mistake to mention marginal productivity at all. since this has merely led to an irrelevant and intemperate controversy'.

39 W.A. Lewis, 'Reflections on Unlimited Labour', pp. 77–79.

40 G. Ranis, 'Labour Surplus Economies', p. 194; see also K. Kirkpatrick and A. Barrientos, 'The Lewis Model after 50 years', *Manchester School*, 72: 6, (2004), pp. 679–690, on pp. 683–687.

41 S.S. Kuznets, 'Economic Growth and Income Inequality', *The American Economic Review*, 45, (1955), pp. 1–28.

42 W.A. Lewis, *The Theory of Economic Growth*, Italian trans., *Teoria dello sviluppo economico* (Milano: Feltrinelli, [1955] 1963), on p. 408.

43 W.A. Lewis, 'A Review of Economic Development', *The American Economic Review*, 55: 1–2, (1965), pp. 1–16, on p. 12.

44 W.A. Lewis, 'Development Economics in the 1950s', p. 133.

45 See R.L. Tignor, *W. Arthur Lewis*, ch. 3.

46 I would like to thank Mauro Boianovsky for suggesting me that Furtado had dealt with the issue of dualism in the process of economic development.

47 C. Furtado, 'Capital Formation and Economic Development' in A.N. Agarwala and S.P. Singh, (eds) *The Economics of Underdevelopment* (Oxford: Oxford University Press, [1952] 1958), pp. 309–337, on pp. 318–319.

48 Ibid., p. 321.

49 Ibid.

50 M. Boianovsky, 'A View from the Tropics: Celso Furtado and the Theory of Economic Development in the 1950s', *History of Political Economy*, 42, (2010), pp. 221–266, on p. 252. As recalled by Boianovsky, Furtado in a letter of 1955 to his colleague at CEPAL Juan Noyola wrote 'I call your attention to Lewis's work . . . I regard it as the best single piece ever written about the theory of development. He follows exactly the same approach adopted by us in our preliminary studies for planning techniques. I am convinced that if we had not been discouraged to 'theorize' at that stage, we would have been able to present two years ago the basic elements of a theory of development along the lines of this important contribution by Lewis", ibid.

51 A.O. Hirschman, 'Investment Policies and "Dualism" in Underdeveloped Countries', *The American Economic Review*, 47:5, (1957), pp. 550–70.

52 Ibid., p. 557.

53 Ibid,. p. 560.

54 As Hirschman put it 'the industrial processes that have least to fear from the competition of the South [non industrial sector] are those which are entirely outside the technological and capital capabilities of the local handicraft and small workshop industries . . . , for instance, of chemicals, petroleum refining, basic iron and steel, cement', ibid., p. 559.

55 Ibid., p. 562.

56 See T.W. Schultz, 'Investment in Man: An Economist's View' in *The Social Service Review*, 32: 2, (1959), pp. 109–117; Id., 'Capital Formation by Education', *Journal of Political Economy*, 68: 6, (1960), pp. 571–583; Id., 'Investment in Human Capital', *The American Economic Review*, 51: 1, (1961), pp. 1–17.

57 A.O. Hirschman, 'The Rise and Decline of Development Economics', *Essays in Trespassing, Economics to Politics and Beyond* (Cambridge: Cambridge University Press, 1981), pp. 1–24, on p. 8.

58 See H.W. Arndt, *Economic Development. The History of an Idea* (London: The University of Chicago Press, 1987), on ch. 3.

59 D. Jorgenson, 'Surplus Agricultural Labour and the Development of a Dual Economy' *Oxford Economic Papers*, 19:3, (1967), pp. 288–312; A.K. Dixit, 'Optimal Development in the Labour-Surplus Economy', *Review of Economic Studies*, 35, (1968), pp. 23–34; A.C. Kelly, G. Williamson and R.J. Cheetham, *Dualistic Economic Development: Theories and History* (Chicago: University of Chicago Press, 1972); for a survey on these models see C. Oman and G. Wignaraja, *The Postwar Evolution*, pp. 102–4; R. Kanbur and J. McIntosh, 'Dual Economies', in J. Eatwell, M. Milgate and P. Newman (eds), *The New Palgrave – Economic Development* (New York–London: Macmillan, 1987), pp. 114–121.

60 M. Boianovsky and K.D. Hoover, 'In the Kingdom of Solovia: the Rise of Growth Economics at MIT, 1956–1970', *History of Political Economy*, Annual supplement, 46, (2014), pp. 198–228.

61 W.A. Lewis, 'Reflections on Unlimited Labour', p. 91.

62 Ibid.

63 Ibid.

64 Ibid., p. 85, emphasis in the original.
65 M.P. Todaro, 'A Model of Labor Migration and Urban Unemployment in Less Developed Countries', *The American Economic Review*, 59: 1, (1969), pp. 138–148; J.R. Harris and M.P. Todaro, 'Migration, Unemployment and Development: A Two-Sector Analysis', *The American Economic Review*, 40: 1, (1970), pp. 126–142; see also J.G. Williamson, 'Migration and Urbanization' in H.B. Chenery and T.N. Srinivasan (eds), *Handbook of Development Economics*, Vol. 1 (Amsterdam: North Holland, 1988), pp. 425–465.
66 As an example, see A. Portes, M. Castells and L.A. Benton (eds), *The Informal Economy. Studies in Advanced and Less Developed Countries* (Baltimore and London: The Johns Hopkins University Press, 1989); F. Schneider and D.H. Enste, *The Shadow Economy. An International Survey* (Cambridge: Cambridge University Press, 2004); R. La Porta and A. Shleifer, 'The Unofficial Economy and Economic Development', *Brookings Papers on Economic Activity*, (2008), pp. 275–352; F. Schneider (ed.), *Handbook on the Shadow Economy* (Cheltenham: Edward Elgar, 2011).
67 F. Schneider and D.H. Enste, *The Shadow Economy*, p. 6.
68 P. Krugman, 'Toward a Counter-Revolution', p. 28.
69 'Arthur Lewis' Contribution to Development', p. 715.
70 W.A. Lewis, *The Theory of Economic Growth*, pp. 164–166.

5 The structuralist research program in development economics

Mauro Boianovsky

5.1 Approaches to development economics

The December 1974 meetings of the American Economic Association, held in San Francisco, featured a session on 'A reassessment of development economics'. The session featured a paper by Hollis Chenery – World Bank's vice-president for development policy from 1972 to 1982 – on 'The structuralist approach to development policy'.[1] Chenery argued that development economics should be grouped under three main approaches, according to their respective methodologies: neoclassical, neo-Marxist and structuralist. Gradually, Chenery's classification became restricted in the literature to a binary division between neoclassical and structuralist models of development economics, especially after Oxford economist Ian Little turned it into the organizing principle of his book on economic development.[2] Cristóbal Kay, for instance, has suggested that the 'essential antithesis' of development economics is between neoclassical and structuralist theories.[3]

According to Chenery, structuralist development economists aim at detecting 'specific rigidities, lags, and other characteristics of the structure of developing economies that affect economic adjustments and the choice of development policy'.[4] In Little's words, 'the structuralist sees the world as inflexible', whereas the neoclassical vision of the world is one of flexibility, in which people respond to incentives by adapting 'readily to changing opportunities and prices'.[5] In Chenery's account, the structuralist approach had been put forward by Paul Rosentein-Rodan, Ragnar Nurkse, W. Arthur Lewis, Albert Hirschman, Gunnar Myrdal, Hans Singer, Raul Prebisch, Celso Furtado and other authors who turned development economics into a new field of economic theory in the 1940s and 1950s – the 'years of high development theory', as famously described by Paul Krugman. From that point of view, the methodology of early development economics was essentially structuralist, in the sense of focusing on the failure of the market price mechanisms to bring about economic growth and improve the standard of living. By the time Chenery in 1975 presented his proposal of a unified theoretical framework for structuralist analysis, structuralism was still strongly influential in the formulation of economic development policy and theory. This started to change in the late 1980s, when the neoclassical approach became increasingly dominant as part of the neoliberal wave in economics and other fields.[6]

The origins of structuralism in that broad sense may be traced back to the emergence of the doctrine of market failures and economic planning in England during the 1930s and 1940s.[7] However, the term 'structuralism' started to be used in economics only in the late 1950s and early 1960s, in connection with the interpretation, by some Latin American economists (particularly Juan Noyola, Celso Furtado and Osvaldo Sunkel)[8], of the relation between inflation, external disequilibrium and development in the region. Since those economists were at the time members of the United Nations Economic Commission for Latin America (CEPAL in Spanish and Portuguese), economic structuralism in the strict sense became mainly associated with that organization.[9] Nowadays, it is common to distinguish between Anglo-Saxon and Latin American economic structuralism. Anglo-Saxon structuralism has been based on a combination of Lewis's concept of a dual economy, Rosenstein-Rodan's notion of complementarity in demand caused by increasing returns and externalities, Nurkse's vicious circle of poverty, and Hirschman's backward and forward linkages. Together, they have originated the view of economic underdevelopment as a low-level equilibrium trap caused by an extensive coordination failure. Furtado's study of the historical process of development by 'external induction' with technology as an 'independent variable' determined abroad led him to define an underdeveloped structure as one in which 'the full utilization of available capital is not a sufficient condition for complete absorption of the working force at a level of productivity corresponding to the technology prevailing in the dynamic sector of the economy'.[10] This structural definition has been accepted as an alternative to general descriptions in terms of statistical indicators such as income per capita etc.[11] It means that underdeveloped countries are not just backward, but hybrid systems with the prevalence of a technology that does not correspond to the pattern of the available factors of production.

5.2 Structuralist methodology and dependency theory

Latin American structuralism of the 1950s and 1960s had many points in common with the Anglo-Saxon version, not just because Nurkse, Rosenstein-Rodan, Chenery and others visited Latin America often at the time. However, as pointed out by Jameson, and Blackenburg, Palma and Tregenna, the defining characteristic of the Latin American structuralist school has been its methodology.[12] From that perspective, Latin American economic structuralism may be interpreted as a specific form of the structuralist methodology originally introduced by F. De Saussure in linguistics, C. Lévi-Strauss in anthropology and J. Piaget in psychology, among other predominantly French social scientists. According to Blackenburg Palma and Tregenna, the structuralist methodology 'advocates a focus on the system in its totality and on the interrelations between its elements, rather than on individual elements in isolation'.[13] This is well expressed by Prebisch's division of the international economic system into 'center' and 'periphery' with distinct economic structures, and the analysis of their respective economic dynamics as determined by their interaction.[14]

However, the use of the noun 'structuralism' to describe (a substantial part of) Latin American economics gained currency only later. It was in the methodological appendix added to the French edition of his book on development economics that Furtado referred, for the first time, to 'le structuralisme économique' as a Latin American school of thought.[15] He argued that economic structuralism was 'not directly related to the French structuralist school', that is, to scientific classic structuralism as developed by Lévi-Strauss and others. Whereas the latter was defined by its anti-historicism, Latin American economic structuralists often included historical studies as part of their research agenda. Instead of the synchronic analysis of French classic structuralism, Furtado and other Latin American structuralists deployed diachronic analysis of socio-economic phenomena, with careful discussion of the historical processes of economic development.[16] Hence, their method has been labelled 'historical-structural'.[17]

The 'historical-structural' ('historico-estructural' in Spanish) method made its first appearance in volumes produced by Chilean economist Osvaldo Sunkel in 1970,[18] and by Brazilian sociologist Fernando H. Cardoso and Chilean historian and sociologist Enzo Faletto in 1969.[19] In both cases, it was introduced as an element of (self)criticism of CEPAL's structuralism of the 1950s and early 1960s, in the context of the formulation of dependency theory and its application to Latin American socio-economic development. The historical-structural method at its inception represented not just a criticism of aspects of CEPAL's early structuralism but also largely a rejection of Lévi-Strauss's structuralism in favour of dialectics.[20]

The context of the new historical-structural approach was the poor economic performance and, especially, the persistence of poverty in most Latin American economies despite the implementation of import-substituting industrialization strategy supported by CEPAL since the 1950s. This led to the formulation of 'dependency theory' as the rebellious offspring of structuralism, with focus on an integrated world-system in which centre and periphery are interconnected.[21] Sunkel described how a 'self-critical position inside the structuralist school' was developed at the time at both methodological and ideological levels. 'It became clear that structuralism did not examine Latin American reality as a totality that explains itself as a product of its historical evolution'. The proposed new method should approach reality from a 'structural, historical and totalizing' point of view, based on the notions of 'process, structure and system'.[22]

The historical-structural method in economics and political and social sciences is usually associated with Cardoso and Faletto's influential essay of 1969, regarded as the foundational contribution to dependency theory.[23] The method is described in section 3 – 'Structure and process: reciprocal determinations' – of the second chapter of that book, even though the term itself was not used but only the expression 'historical-structural characteristics'. The analysis of economic and social development, claimed the authors, should 'go beyond the structural approach, reinstating it in an interpretation elaborated in terms of the "historical process"'.[24] This was not about the 'naïve' perspective of searching for the temporal origins of each social situation in succession, but the view that 'historical becoming can only be explained by categories that attribute meaning to facts and, consequently, are historically referred'. Such categories should express the distinct moments and 'structural characteristics of the historical process'.[25] Cardoso and Faletto described their method as a 'dialectical approach' that was both structural and historical. It aimed at studying not just the relations that sustain a given structure, but also those that oppose it and lead to its transformation: 'thus our methodology is historical-structural'.[26]

Dependency theory became central to Furtado's research agenda in the 1970s.[27] His 1978 essay on culture, creativity and dependency was the high-point of his intellectual effort in the field.[28] Furtado came closer to classic structuralism as he distinguished sharply between *structure* (form) and *process* (causality), the two building blocks of cognitive work. The 'principle of causality' was associated with the use of continuous analytic functions in physical sciences, inadequate to describe the discontinuities of social reality. The practice of social sciences had led them to adopt a 'structural approach' which until recently had not warranted attention from an epistemological perspective. It was clear to Furtado that the advance of social sciences could only come from the 'structural approach'.[29]

The issue was relevant to the theory of development, which dealt with transformation – in the 'morphogenic sense of the adoption of forms which are not just an unfolding of pre-existent ones'. The future, therefore, cannot be derived from the information contained in the structure.[30] Furtado's suggested solution was to reconcile structure and process by introducing the notion of *creativity*, understood as the 'human faculty to intervene in causal determinism, enriching any social process by introducing new elements'.[31] 'Structural discontinuities' are produced when the actions of several innovative acts converge. Economic development results from technical progress, seen as the ability of men to create and innovate based on what Max Weber called 'substantive' and 'formal' rationality.[32] Furtado's concept of creativity has since become one of the philosophical underpinnings of Latin American economic structuralism.[33] Furtado's use of the expression 'historical-structural approach' as subtitle of his book should be seen as an attempt to build a bridge between structure and process by means of the notion of discontinuity.[34] This was largely consistent with Lévi-Strauss's structuralism but distinct from the dialectical meaning of 'historical-structural' in Sunkel and Cardoso and Faletto.

History was important, according to Furtado, because 'our structuralism, as developed in the 1950s, stressed the importance of noneconomic parameters in macroeconomic models. Because the behaviour of economic variables depends heavily on those parameters – which take form and evolve in a historical context – one cannot separate the study of economic phenomena from their historical context. This observation is of particular relevance to socially and technologically heterogeneous economic systems, such as those in underdeveloped countries'.[35] According to Furtado:

> A linear model, which is the simplest instrument of economic analysis, leads to the determination of the numerical values of a vector of variables (endogenous) from the known values of another vector of variables (exogenous). The way the second vector determines the first, that is, the set of precise relations between the variables, forms the *structural matrix* of the model. If the values of the parameters are specified, the relations between variables take on precise characteristics and define a *structure*. This way, to each model corresponds an undetermined number of structures . . . It is in this sense that the term 'structure' is used here.[36]

From that perspective, the criticism advanced by T.N. Srinivasan that 'neither the origin of the rigidities nor their persistence is adequately explained in behavioural terms by structuralists'[37] is unwarranted, as the explanation was based on historical analysis.[38] As pointed out by Marchal, if economic structures are described exclusively in terms of exogenously and often non-economic given data, without any attempt to logically reproduce the invariants of the model through abstract reasoning (of the kind argued by Lévi-Strauss), their explanatory value may be seriously reduced.[39] Xavier Ragot has argued, on precisely those grounds, that Latin American economic self-proclaimed structuralists do not really belong to structuralism, as they allegedly lack a self-contained model.[40] However, the 'transformation of parameters into variables' through historical investigation, mentioned by Marchal in passing, was one of the features of Latin American structuralism.

5.3 Economic development and macroeconomic imbalances

Latin American economic structuralism originated in the 1950s, as an effort to interpret the connections between economic development and macroeconomic imbalances in the region, under the guise of external disequilibrium and inflation. Historical and statistical investigation of the 'deep structures' underlying Latin American economies identified two main features of the development of peripheral economies exporters of commodities.[41] The first is balance of payments constrained growth, that is, the proposition that the rate of economic growth at the periphery depends on the relation between the income-elasticities of imports and exports, originally advanced by Prebisch and later rediscovered by Thirlwall in the 1970s.[42] This was accompanied by the falling terms of trade thesis, formulated independently by Prebisch and Singer. The policy conclusion was that only industrialization could lead to economic development, through planed import-substitution process.

Although Latin American structuralists contributed to the theory and practice of economic planning through the deployment of input–output tables and other planning techniques, their argument was not usually formalized mathematically. Chenery and his associates modelled one of the structuralists' basic insights about balance of payments and economic growth – the two-gap model – in the 1960s. Lance Taylor, Chenery's graduate student at Harvard in the 1960s, would carry out a substantial part of the effort to formalize the structuralist argument,[43] usually adapting and elaborating on post-Keynesian Cambridge models of growth and distribution. In his turn, Taylor influenced a number of students at MIT and the New School.[44] By 1986, Kenneth Jameson regarded Taylor's mathematical 'new structuralism' as the key to revival of the structuralist tradition in economics, after its apparent stagnation in the 1970s. The kind of mathematical argument used by Taylor and his associates was seen as congenital to the structuralist approach.[45]

The Prebisch-Singer thesis of declining terms of trade between primary products and manufactures has attracted the lion's share of the literature on the structuralist approach to trade and growth.[46] Whereas the terms of trade argument and its criticism of comparative advantages belong in the 'real' trade theory domain, the study of balance of payments dynamics is a matter of open monetary macroeconomics.

Although those issues are interconnected, they should be kept analytically separated, as illustrated by June Flanders's distinction between a 'balance of payments problem' and a 'real income problem' in Prebisch.[47] One of the main theses of the structuralist approach was the proposition that there are two distinct bottlenecks restricting the rate of growth in developing countries – domestic saving and the shortage of foreign exchange. Under the assumption that a significant share of investment depended on the availability of imported capital goods, the 'transformation of savings into real investment' through foreign trade was an alternative way to interpret balance of payments constrained growth in the context of the Harrod–Domar growth model.[48] During the 1960s that view would become known as the 'two-gap' approach after models designed by Hollis Chenery, Ronald McKinnon and others, with no reference to Latin American original insights though.[49] According to Lance Taylor Furtado's chapter 5 of the 1964 book *Development and Underdevelopment* 'presages the two-gap model very neatly'.[50] Chenery started working on the two-gap model when visiting CEPAL headquarters in Santiago in the late 1950s.[51]

By 1951, Prebisch started to refer to disparities in income-elasticities of demand for imports – for primary commodities at the centre and for manufactures at the periphery.[52] For well-known reasons, 'the income-elasticity of primary imports in the centres tends to be lower than unity'.[53] The income-elasticity of imports of manufactures at the periphery was supposed to be at least equal to unity because of demand for foreign capital goods.[54] External disequilibrium produced by these 'dynamic differences . . . cannot be maintained; income must either be reduced permanently to a level where imports may be adjusted to the capacity to import, or the level of income is maintained by substituting imports with domestic products'.[55]

Estimates for the period 1940–1953 pointed to 0.66 and 1.58 as the income-elasticities of US imports of primary commodities and Latin American imports of industrial goods, respectively.[56] Prebisch would provide a numerical example, but this time he pointed to the implications of income-elasticities discrepancies for the rate of growth in the periphery instead of balance of payments disequilibrium. Assuming that the rate of growth of income per-capita in the centre is 3 per cent, and that income-elasticities of demand of imports of primary commodities (produced at the periphery) and industrial goods (produced at the centre) are 0.80 and 1.30 respectively, then, 'in a balanced development process, peripheral income cannot increase faster than 1.84 per cent per year', so that imports and exports grow at the same rate of 2.40 per cent'.[57]

The constrained rate of growth of income per capita in the periphery is given by the rate of growth of the centre times the income-elasticity of its exports of primary commodities to the centre, divided by its income-elasticity of imports from the centre. Prebisch provided yet another numerical illustration of his proposition that 'the growth of exports places an upper limit on the rate of development in a peripheral country. This limit is set by the intensity with which the demand for imports expands with the growth of per capita income'.[58] Clearly, according to Prebisch the balance of payments posed a constraint for economic growth in the periphery, not for industrialized countries.

The model implied that a permanent increase in the relative rate of growth of the periphery can only be achieved by raising the income-elasticity of its exports (through the introduction or expansion of industrial exports) and/or decreasing the income-elasticity of its demand for imports through import-substituting industrialization. Import-substitution through tariff protection aimed at changing 'the composition of imports, not their volume'.[59] Hence, Prebisch's ideal tariff system was designed to allocate scarce foreign exchange, not to bring down the total demand for imports.[60] This type of protection – which 'encourages the structural changes required by economic development without provoking a reduction in imports below the volume corresponding to the capacity for external payment' – should be distinguished from the kind of protection which exceeds those limits and 'adversely affects world trade'.[61] The optimal degree of industrialization was determined by the rate of growth of exports, in the sense that the lower the proportion of the increase of labour force absorbed by exports, the greater should be the extent of industrialization.

The foreign exchange constraint was expressed by the amount of exports 'upon which [Latin American] countries depend to transform their savings into imports of capital goods'.[62] The development bottleneck may consist of foreign exchange rather than domestic saving if the rate of growth allowed by exports is lower than the rate allowed by saving. The economy features unemployment, excess aggregate supply and excess domestic saving. Hence, unemployment is caused by an effective demand problem, but of a different kind from developed countries', as clarified by Furtado:

> It is pertinent to consider a problem specific to under-developed countries – namely, that of the possibility of transforming saving into real investment. It is well known that in a developed economy saving does not necessarily imply growth, since in this case it is the level of effective demand that conditions the process of accumulation. Similarly (but for other reasons), saving in an under-developed economy is not always an effective cause of growth. There must also be the possibility of converting this saving into real investment – a possibility dependent upon the capacity to import.[63]

Reducing consumption would have little effect on growth, since marginal domestic resources set free could not be turned into imports of capital goods because of the external restriction. The foreign exchange constraint reflects the inability of the economy to provide the composition of output required by its rate of investment, which frustrates its willingness to save and invest.[64] Furtado pointed out that 'as long as exports do not increase *pari passu* with the demand for imports, the process of growth will create disequilibria which take the form of an excess internal production and of an unfavourable balance of payments'.[65] With given relative prices (exchange rate, terms of trade and real wages), excess demand for traded goods is accompanied by excess supply of domestic goods along the lines of Walras's Law. 'Excess of outward demand means, on the one hand, insufficient internal demand – always assuming that there is no monetary expansion – and, on the other, the drawing down of reserves'.[66] There is macroeconomic balance in the demand and supply of goods as a whole, but 'structural imbalance' caused by the fact that the composition of production and consumption at a given level of income does not match.[67]

CEPAL's approach to external disequilibrium has been formalized by Arida and Bacha in 1987 through a fix-price model of the disequilibrium macroeconomics type.[68] Arida and Bacha argue that a disequilibrium regime of 'structural deficit' of the balance of payments features excess supply of goods and labour. External disequilibrium results not from an excess domestic demand, but from insufficient external demand. However, as noted by Arida and Bacha, depending on the price-elasticities of exports and imports, Walrasian equilibrium may be reached and the structural regime eliminated through exchange rate devaluations. While relative price adjustment can close the gap, it cannot do so without reducing the rate of growth and/or bringing about an inefficient allocation of resources.[69]

Due to its increasing oil exports, Venezuela was regarded as an important exception to the widespread Latin American balance of payments constraint.[70] In May 1957 Prebisch assigned Furtado to investigate the economic peculiarities of Venezuela, where he stayed for three months. It was his last assignment at CEPAL. The outcome was an anonymous report drafted by Furtado in August 1957, titled 'The recent development of the Venezuelan economy (exposition of some problems)'. It was recently published in Portuguese version.[71] The opening sentence states that, despite being 'the underdeveloped economy with the highest income per capita in the world', Venezuela presented all the 'structural characteristics' of underdeveloped economies, such as large productivity differences between economic sectors, low consumption standards of most of the population, low participation of manufacturing industry in labour force absorption, etc.[72] Furtado's report aimed at explaining the apparent paradox of the persistence of an underdeveloped productive system despite a rate of growth of income per capita of 5 per cent between 1945 and 1956. He found the explanation in the effect of oil production and exports on Venezuelan economic structure.

The productivity difference between the oil sector and the rest of the economy was illustrated by the fact that the former employed only 2.5 per cent of the labour force in 1956, but represented 29.1 per cent of total output. The increase of the import coefficient was determined by the overvaluation of the Venezuelan currency, as a direct consequence of the oil boom. The appreciation of the Venezuelan bolivar raised the dollar value of money-wages, which hurt the profitability of other exports and sectors of the economy, and encouraged imports.

> The absorption of the increasing supply of foreign exchange was accompanied by a strong appreciation of the Venezuelan currency, which resulted in money-wages much higher than in those countries where average productivity is much superior, and which compete in the Venezuelan market with domestic production . . . The terms of the problem are simple enough: the average level of money-wages – calculated in foreign exchange – is above the average productivity level. Therefore, any tradable good comes with advantage into the Venezuelan market despite the existence of 'normal' protection.[73]

This is an early formulation of the proposition known as 'Dutch disease' in trade literature.[74] The rise in the relative price of non-traded goods in terms of traded goods means a real appreciation of the currency. De-industrialization was the main structural consequence of the overvaluation of the Venezuelan bolivar. As recalled by Furtado, 'for the first time I had before my eyes the phenomenon of those economies which grow supported by a very high productivity sector producing a non-renewable resource. As much as they grow rich, they do not achieve autonomous growth, and may come down like a castle of cards'.[75]

Latin American structuralists discussed also another macroeconomic issue, closely related to external disequilibrium: inflation. The controversy between 'structuralists' and 'monetarists' dominated economic debates in the region. Indeed, the English adjectives 'monetarist' and 'structuralist' were introduced by Roberto Campos in his influential contribution to the Hirschman volume of 1961 that gave international visibility to the debate.[76] Campos would also coin the nouns 'monetarism' and 'structuralism'.[77] The Latin American structuralist-monetarist debate of the late 1950s and early 1960s, therefore, took place sometime before the monetarist controversy that would pervade macroeconomics in the United States and Europe a few years later. It was only after Karl Brunner in 1968 used the word 'monetarism' – apparently independently of Campos – and Kaldor launched his attack on Milton Friedman, that the term penetrated the Anglo-Saxon literature, although the meaning was to some extent distinct.[78] Before that, the expression was generally used in association with the Latin American debate, as witnessed by Martin Bronfenbrenner and Franklyn Holzman's discussion of the position of the 'so-called 'monetarists', the Latin American opposition to *estructuralismo*', with references to essays in the Hirschman volume of 1961.[79]

Latin American structuralists focused on the relation between economic development and inflation, which they interpreted as the outcome of unbalanced growth accompanied by changes in the composition of demand in economies with inelastic supply functions and relative downward rigidity of (mainly industrial) money prices. 'Propagation mechanisms' in the system – that is, the ability of economic agents, including the government through fiscal deficits, to keep or increase their shares in output – also known as 'social conflict inflation', 'wage-price spiral' or 'income struggle', turn relative price changes into inflation.[80] Instead of the structure of demand and supply, monetarists underlined their respective levels, with emphasis on excess aggregate demand caused by a sustained expansion of the money supply associated with fiscal deficits. There was some disagreement within the structuralist camp about the analytical role of fiscal deficits in inflation analysis. According to Sunkel's broad political meaning of structural factors, 'structural deficiencies in the tax system'[81] should be regarded as one of the sources of basic inflationary pressures, which raised the criticism of the Argentine economist Julio Olivera that 'one thing is structural inflation and another is structural proneness to inflation'.[82] Olivera distinguished sharply the ('non-monetary theory') of structural inflation, provoked by 'real' changes in the relative prices of rapidly growing sectors, from ('monetary') inflation caused by shifts in aggregate demand or supply.[83] Sunkel, on the other hand, stated that his purpose was not to replace the cost-push and demand-pull explanations by a new inflation theory, but to use those and other categories in order to highlight the interdependence between inflation and economic development.[84] In particular, in Sunkel's view it was 'not enough to observe that money supply increases because of demands from the public sector', but 'to examine the reasons why the government systematically incurs deficits', which are part of the 'basic inflationary pressures'.[85]

The debate, therefore, differed from the demand–pull vs. cost–push discussion that was going on in the US and in the UK at the time, since the structuralist approach included both demand and cost elements. Moreover, changes in money supply were perceived by structuralists as essentially endogenous to the inflationary process. Their starting-point was that, as far as the analysis of inflation in underdeveloped countries is concerned, 'money itself is a veil', as put by Juan Noyola in 1956[86] in the discussion that followed the presentation of his paper and reaffirmed in Olivera's call to 'lift up the 'monetary veil' . . . to search beneath the monetary surface, into the underlying region of physical flows, real prices, and sectional disequilibria'.[87] This did not imply disregarding the role of money, for, as put by Sunkel, structuralists 'had not get rid of the monetary veil to replace it by a screen'.[88] It did imply treating credit and money supply as passive factors in the inflationary process, that is, as part of the propagation mechanism.[89]

The timing of economic policy and the stabilization costs associated to it was a crucial issue for structuralist economists. One of the main assertions of Latin American structuralism was that any attempt to bring inflation down, for a given economic structure, was bound to bring about a permanent reduction in the rate of economic growth. The structuralist position was, therefore, based on the implicit assumption of a non-vertical long-run Phillips curve, with the proviso that the relevant tradeoff was between inflation and growth, instead of unemployment. The monetarists, on the other hand, believed on a long-run vertical curve and sometimes even on a negative relation between inflation and economic development. From that perspective, the debate was not about the specification of the aggregate demand side – since both camps agreed that the velocity of circulation of money conventionally defined was generally stable – but on how to interpret the dynamics and composition of aggregate supply, and the double relation between economic development and inflation: inflation as the consequence of unbalanced growth, and the effects of inflation itself on the economic growth process.

5.4 The road ahead: neostructuralism

After the largely successful orthodox attack on structuralist theory and policy in the 1980s,[90] the revival of structuralism in economics came mainly through a new generation of CEPAL economists who in the late 1980s and in the 1990s established 'neostructuralism' as the 'first fully articulated development discourse to challenge directly the hegemony of neoliberal ideas'.[91] Latin American neostructuralism was born at CEPAL as a reaction to the macroeconomic crisis that beset the region throughout the 1980s, accompanied by negative economic growth rates, in contrast with the economic success of the so-called Asian Tigers. The leading economist at CEPAL at the time was Fernando Fajnzylber, who put forward a careful analysis of the role of technological progress in a process of economic growth accompanied by equity in income distribution.[92] This represented a shift in CEPAL's analytical framework, which had stressed in the 1950s and 1960s the role of demand dynamics in economic development. As put by Sunkel, one of the members of the 1950s generation and a leading formulator of neostructuralism 30 years after:

> it is not demand and markets that are critical. The heart of development lies on the supply side: quality, flexibility, the efficient combination and utilization of productive resources, the adoption of technological developments, an innovative spirit, creativity . . . public and private austerity, an emphasis on saving, and the development of skills to compete internationally. In short, independent efforts undertaken *from within* to achieve self-sustained development.[93]

Schumpeter's framework, which had been disregarded by structuralists in the 1950s as invalid for developing countries,[94] would become an essential ingredient of CEPAL's neostructuralism, especially in the guise of evolutionary theory developed since the 1980s in England and the US to analyse technical progress.[95]

Neostructuralist economists argued for greater trade openness in order to achieve 'authentic' competitiveness based on systemic absorption of technical progress, instead of 'spurious' competitiveness founded on low real wages. As pointed out by Love, this represented a renunciation of the traditional structuralist notion of the 1950s – that any kind of industrial activity was warranted if it raised national productivity, with protection allowing rents for firms operating below international productivity patterns.[96] Whereas CEPAL economists have claimed that neostructuralism is a continuation and further elaboration of the original structuralist research program,[97] others, especially Leiva, have argued that there has been a substantial change, entailing abandonment of Prebisch's center–periphery system and a new view of the roles of market and state in economic development.[98] The notion of balance of payments constrained growth is still very much part of neostructuralists research agenda, often combined with Neo-Schumpeterian elements. This is clear in Cimoli and Porcile's definition of economic development as 'the process by which a country transforms its productive and employment structures based on learning and the accumulation of technological capabilities'.[99] They also point out that structuralist theory (old and new) regards asymmetries in the dynamics of learning as a central force explaining why two different structures (centre and periphery) emerge in the world economy. Latin American neostructuralism has come to maturity in a recent collection of essays published by CEPAL, which includes chapters on development macroeconomics and cyclical instability, structural change and technical progress, and inequality and welfare.[100]

The founding document of Latin American neostructuralism was CEPAL's United Nations 1990 report about development with equity, coordinated by Fajnzylber and Rosenthal.[101] It argued for greater trade openness (in contrast with import substitution industrialization and protectionism associated with classical structuralism), high real exchange rate and overall macroeconomic stability.[102] As put by C. Kay, neostructuralists 'take account of the new reality brought about by neoliberal globalization'. They believe that through a 'state-guided restructuring of the region's links with the world market' it is possible to achieve higher rates of growth and benefit larger parts of the population.[103] This entails internal restructuring of the economy in order to attain systemic and sustainable competitiveness accompanied by higher equity.

Latin American neostructuralism has joined forces with North American new structuralism in the 2009 book by José Antonio Ocampo (former secretary-general of CEPAL), Codrina Rada (University of Utah) and Lance Taylor (New School).[104] The book is organized around the notion of structural transformation and the dynamics of production structures and policies that facilitate the diffusion of innovations generated in the centre. The analysis is based on the growth-productivity connection established by the Kaldor-Verdoorn technical progress function, with its emphasis on increasing returns and interaction between demand and supply aspects of the economic growth process. From that perspective, neostructuralism may be seen as part of a broad heterodox approach to economics. However, as indicated by Justin Lin's (former World Bank chief economist) recent book, structuralism is also back as part of changes introduced into orthodox neoclassical development economics after the end of the Washington Consensus.[105]

Notes

1. H.B. Chenery, 'The structuralist approach to development policy', *American Economic Review*, 65, (1975), pp. 310–16.
2. I. Little, *Economic development* (New York: Basic Books, 1982), ch. 2.
3. C. Kay, 'Structuralism', in R.J. Barry Jones (ed.), *Routledge encyclopedia of international political economy* (London: Routledge, 2001), pp. 1502–11.
4. H.B. Chenery, 'The structuralist approach', p. 310.
5. I. Little, *Economic development*, pp. 20, 25.
6. See W. Ascher, 'The evolution of postwar doctrines in development economics' in A.W. Coats (ed.), *The post-1945 internationalization of economics*, Annual supplement to *History of political economy* (Durham: Duke University Press, 1996), pp. 312–36; C. Kay,. 'Latin American structuralist school'.
7. H.W. Arndt, 'The origins of structuralism', *World Development*, 13, (1985), pp. 151–59.
8. See M. Boianovsky and R. Solís 'The origins and development of the Latin American structuralist approach to the balance of payments, 1944–1964', *Review of Political Economy*, 26, (2014), pp. 23–59.
9. See D. Hunt, *Economic theories of development: an analysis of competing paradigms* (New York: Harvester Wheatsheaf, 1989), on ch. 5; C. Mallorquín, *Ideas e historia en torno al pensamiento económico latinoamericano* (Mexico City: Plaza y Valdés, 1999), on ch. 3; J.L. Love, 'The rise and decline of economic structuralism in Latin America', *Latin American Research Review*, 40, (2005), pp. 100–25; O. Rodríguez, *El estructuralismo latinoamericano* (Mexico City: Siglo XXI and CEPAL, 2006).
10. C. Furtado, *Development and underdevelopment* (Berkeley: University of California Press, 1964), translation by R. Aguiar and E. Drysdale of *Desenvolvimento e Subdesenvolvimento* (Rio: Fundo de Cultura [1961]), on p. 141; and C. Furtado

'The external disequilibrium in the underdeveloped economies', *Indian Journal of Economics*, 38, (1958), pp. 403–10, on p. 404.

11 See D. Hunt, *Economic theories of development*, p. 49.

12 K.P. Jameson, 'Latin American structuralism: a methodological perspective' *World Development*, 14, (1986), pp. 223–32.; S. Blackenburg, J.G. Palma and F. Tregenna 'Structuralism' in S. Durlauf and L. Blume (eds), *The New Palgrave dictionary of economics*, 2nd edition (London: Macmillan, 2008) pp 69–74.

13 S. Blackenburg, J.G. Palma and F. Tregenna 'Structuralism', p. 69.

14 R. Prebisch, 'El desarrollo económico de la América Latina y algunos de sus principales problemas', reprint in *Desarrollo económico*, 26: 103 [1949] (1986), pp. 479–502.

15 C. Furtado, *Théorie du développement économique*, Trans. by A.B. Silva (Paris: PUF, 1970), on p. 30. Parts of that appendix were reproduced in C. Furtado 'Analyse économique et histoire quantitative', in *L'Histoire Quantitative du Brésil de 1800 a 1930* (Paris: Editions du Centre National de la Recherche Scientifique, Colloques Internationaux du Centre National de la Recherche Scientifique, # 543, 1973), pp. 23–26, and in C. Furtado, 'Underdevelopment: to conform or reform' in G.M. Meier (ed). *Pioneers in development – second series* (New York: Oxford University Press and the World Bank, 1987), pp. 205–27.

16 On the tension between the structural and historical approaches in French social sciences between the 1930s and 1960s see F. Dosse, *History of structuralism*, 2 vols. (Minneapolis: University of Minnesota Press, 1997).

17 See O. Rodríguez, *El estructuralismo latinoamericano*; R. Bielschowsky, 'Sixty years of ECLAC: structuralism and neo-structuralism', *CEPAl Review*, 97, (2009), pp. 171–92.

18 O. Sunkel, (with the assistance of P. Paz), *El subdesarrollo latinoamericano y la teoría del desarrollo*, (Mexico City: Siglo Ventiuno, 1970).

19 F.H. Cardoso and E. Faletto, *Dependencia y desarrollo en América Latina: ensayo de interpretación sociológica* (Mexico City: Siglo Ventiuno, 1969).

20 See M. Boianovsky, 'Between Lévi-Strauss and Braudel: Furtado and the historical-structural method in Latin American political economy' *Journal of Economic Methodology*. 22: 4, (2015), forthcoming.

21 See A. Saad-Filho,' The rise and decline of Latin American structuralism and dependency theory' in K.S. Jomo and E. Reinert (eds), *The origins of development economics* (London: Zed Books, 2005), pp. 128–45.

22 O. Sunkel, El subdesarrollo latinoamericano, p. 36.

23 See for example J. Cyr and L. Mahoney 'The enduring influence of historical-structural approaches' in P. Kingstone and D.J. Yashar (eds), *Routledge handbook of Latin American politics* (New York: Routledge, 2012), pp. 433–46.

24 F.H. Cardoso and E. Faletto, *Dependencia y desarrollo*, p. 18.

25 Ibid.

26 F.H. Cardoso and E. Faletto, *Dependency and development in Latin America*, trans. by M. Urquidi (Berkeley: University of California Press, 1979), on pp. ix–x.

27 C. Furtado, 'Dependencia externa y teoria económica', *El Trimestre Económico*, 38, (1971), pp. 335–49; C. Furtado, *Criatividade e dependência na civilização industrial* (Rio: Paz e Terra, 1978); C. Furtado, *Pequena introdução ao desenvolvimento: enfoque multidisciplinar* (S. Paulo: Cia Editora Nacional, 1980).

28 O. Rodríguez, *El estructuralismo latinoamericano*, ch. 9; A.M. Cunha and G. Britto, 'When development meets culture: Furtado in the1970s', Working paper # 429 (2011), CEDEPLAR/UFMG.

29 C. Furtado, *Accumulation and development: the logic of industrial civilization*, trans. by S. Macedo (Oxford: Martin Robertson [1978] 1983), on p. 183).

30 C. Furtado, *Introdução ao desenvolvimento: enfoque histórico-estrutural* (Rio: Paz e Terra, 2000), on pp. 41–42.

31 C. Furtado, *Accumulation and development*, pp. 182–83.

32 C. Furtado, *Introdução ao desenvolvimento: enfoque histórico-estrutural*, Preface.

33 A. Di Filippo, 'Latin American structuralism and economic theory', *CEPAL Review*, 98, (2009), pp. 175–96.
34 C. Furtado, *Introdução ao desenvolvimento: enfoque histórico-estrutural*.
35 C. Furtado, *Teoria e política do desenvolvimento econômico*, 5th edition (S. Paulo: Cia. Editora Nacional, 1975), on p. 83.
36 C. Furtado, *Théorie du développement*, pp. 28–29; C. Furtado, *Teoria e política do desenvolvimento*, pp. 80–81; italics in the original; partly reproduced in C. Furtado 'Analyse économique et histoire quantitative', p. 23.
37 T.N. Srinivasan, 'Introduction to part I', in H. Chenery and T.N. Srinivasan (eds), *Handbook of development economics*, vol. I (Amsterdam: North Holland, 1988), pp. 3–8, on p. 5.
38 See also C. Mallorquín, *Ideas e historia*; M. Boianovsky, 'A view from the tropics: Celso Furtado and the theory of economic development in the 1950s', *History of Political Economy*, 42, (2010), pp. 221–66; M. Boianovsky, 'Between Lévi-Strauss and Braudel'.
39 A. Marchal, *Systémes et structures économiques* (Paris: PUF, 1959), on pp. 71–72.
40 X. Ragot, 'L'économie est-elle structuraliste: un essai d'épistémologie', *L'année de la regulation*, 7, (2003), pp. 91–111, on p.107.
41 K.P. Jameson, 'Latin American structuralism'; S. Blackenburg, J.G. Palma and F. Tregenna 'Structuralism'.
42 M. Boianovsky and R. Solís 'The origins and development'.
43 L. Taylor, *Income distribution, inflation and growth: lectures on structuralist macroeconomic theory* (Cambridge MA: MIT Press, 1991).
44 See A.K. Dutt and J. Ros (eds), *Development economics and structuralist economics – essays in honor of Lance Taylor* (Cheltenham: Elgar, 2003).
45 See also B. Gibson, 'An essay on late structuralism', in A.K. Dutt and J. Ros (eds), *Development economics and structuralist macroeconomics: essays in honor of Lance Taylor* (Cheltenham: Elgar, 2003), pp. 52–76; R. Baghitathan, C. Rada and L. Taylor., 'Structuralist economics: worldly philosophers, models and methodology', *Social Research*, 71, (2004), pp. 305–26.
46 See chapter 3 above.
47 J. Flanders, 'Prebisch on protectionism: an evaluation', *Economic Journal*, 74, (1964), pp. 305–26.
48 United Nations, 'Growth, disequilibrium and disparities: interpretation of the process of economic development', in *Economic Survey of Latin America 1949* (New York: United Nations, [1950] 1951), E/CN.12/164, pp. 1–85; United Nations, 'Inflation in Chile, 1940 to 1953', in *World Economic Report 1953–54* (New York: United Nations, Department of Economic and Social Affairs, 1955), pp. 78–88, United Nations, *Analyses and projections of economic development – II. The economic development of Brazil* (New York: United Nations, 1956), E/CN.12/364; C. Furtado, *Development and underdevelopment*.
49 H.B. Chenery and M. Bruno 'Development alternatives in an open economy: the case of Israel' *Economic Journal*, 72, (1962), pp. 79–103; H.B. Chenery and A.M. Strout 'Foreign assistance and economic development', *American Economic Review*, 56, (1966), pp. 679–733; R.I. McKinnon, 'Foreign exchange constraints in economic development and efficient aid allocation', *Economic Journal*, 74, (1964), pp. 388–409.
50 L. Taylor, *Macro Models for Developing Countries* (New York: McGraw-Hill, 1979), on pp. 123, 127.
51 L. Taylor and P. Arida, 'Long-run income distribution and growth' in H. Chenery and T. Srinivasan (eds), *Handbook of development economics*, vol. I (Amsterdam: Elsevier, 1988), pp. 161–94, on p 172.
52 United Nations, *Theoretical and practical problems of economic growth*, Economic Commission for Latin America, fourth session (Mexico, 1951), D.F. E/CN.12/221, on ch. 2.

53 Ibid., p. 30.
54 Ibid., p. 32.
55 Ibid., p. 32, 35.
56 United Nations, *International co-operation in a Latin American development policy* (New York: United Nations, 1954), E/CN.12/359, on p. 63; R. Prebisch, 'Comments', in R. Lekachman (ed.), *National policy for economic welfare at home and abroad* (New York: Russell & Russell, 1955a), pp. 277–80, on p 278; R. Prebisch, 'Relações entre crescimento da população, formação de capital e as oportunidades de emprego nos países subdesenvolvidos', *Economica Brasileira*, 1, (1955b), pp. 135–43, on p. 136.
57 R. Prebisch, 'Commercial policy in the underdeveloped countries', *American Economic Review*, 49, (1959), pp. 251–73, on pp. 253–54.
58 R. Prebisch, 'Economic development or monetary stability: the false dilemma', *Economic Bulletin for Latin America*, 6, (1961), pp. 1–25, on pp. 3–4.
59 United Nations, *International co-operation*, p. 66; see also R. Prebisch, 'Commercial policy in the underdeveloped countries', p. 265.
60 J. Flanders, 'Prebisch on protectionism', pp. 306–07, 322.
61 United Nations, *International Co-operation*, p. 64.
62 United Nations, 'Growth, disequilibrium and disparities', p. 7; United Nations, 'Inflation in Chile', p. 4; C. Furtado, *Development and underdevelopment*, p. 150.
63 United Nations, *Analyses and projections of economic development*, p. 9.
64 H.B. Chenery and A.M. Strout 'Foreign assistance and economic development'.
65 C. Furtado, 'Capital formation and economic development', trans. by J. Cairncross, *International Economic Papers*, 4, ([1952] 1954), pp. 124–44, on p. 143; see also Id., *Development and underdevelopment*, p. 170; United Nations, 'Growth, disequilibrium and disparities, p. 10.
66 United Nations, *External disequilibrium in the economic development of Latin America: the case of Mexico*, 2 vols, Economic Commission for Latin America, seventh session (La Paz, 1957), E/CN.12/428, on p.131.
67 R. Findlay, *International trade and development theory* (New York: Columbia University Press, 1973), on chs. 10, 11.
68 P. Arida and E. Bacha, 'Balance of payments – a disequilibrium analysis for semi-industrialized economies', *Journal of Development Economics*, 27, (1987), pp. 85–108.
69 Ibid., section 6.
70 United Nations, 'Growth, disequilibrium and disparities', pp. 8–9.
71 C. Furtado, 'O desenvolvimento recente da economia venezuelana (exposição de alguns problemas)', in R.F. D'Aguiar Furtado (ed.), *Ensaios sobre a Venezuela: Subdesenvolvimento com Abundância de Divisas* (Rio: Contraponto and Centro Internacional Celso Furtado, [1957] 2008), pp. 35–135.
72 Ibid., pp. 35–36.
73 Ibid., p. 54.
74 W.M. Corden, 'Booming sector and Dutch disease economics: survey and consolidation', *Oxford Economic Papers*, 36, (1984), pp. 359–80.
75 C. Furtado, *A Fantasia Organizada* (Rio: Paz e Terra, 1985), on p. 195.
76 R.O. Campos, 'Two views on inflation in Latin America' in A. Hirschman (ed.), *Latin American Issues* (New York: Twentieth Century Fund, 1961), pp. 69–79, on p. 69.
77 R.O. Campos, 'Economic development and inflation, with special reference to Latin America' in Id. *Reflections on Latin American development* (Austin: University of Texas Press [1964] 1967), pp. 106–21, on p. 106.
78 K. Brunner, 'The role of money and monetary policy', *Federal Reserve Bank of St. Louis Review*, 50, (1968), pp. 8–24; N. Kaldor, 'The new monetarism', reprinted in Id. *Further essays on applied economics*, vol. VI (London: Duckworth [1970] 1978).
79 M. Bronfenbrenner and F.D. Holzman 'Survey of inflation theory', *American Economic Review*, 53, (1963), pp. 593–661, on p. 611.
80 O. Sunkel, 'Inflation in Chile: an unorthodox approach', *International Economic Papers*, 10, ([1958] 1960), pp. 107–31, on p. 111.

81 Ibid., p. 110.
82 J.H. Olivera, 'On structural inflation and Latin-American 'structuralism'', *Oxford Economic Papers*, 16, (1964), pp. 321–32, on pp. 331–32.
83 J.H. Olivera, 'La teoria no monetaria de la inflación', *El Trimestre Económico*, 27, (1960), pp. 616–28; Id. 'On structural inflation and Latin-American 'structuralism''; Id. 'Aspectos dinámicos de la inflación estrutural', *Desarrollo económico,* 7, (1967), pp. 261–66.
84 O. Sunkel, 'Um esquema geral para a analise da inflação', *Econômica brasileira*, 3, (1957), pp. 361–77, on p. 361; Id. 'El fracaso de las politicas de estabilización en el contexto del proceso de desarrollo latinoamericano', *El Trimestre Economico*, 30, (1963), pp. 620–40, on p. 623.
85 O. Sunkel, 'El fracaso de las politicas de estabilización', p. 624; see also A. Pinto, 'A analise da inflação – estruturalistas e monetaristas: Um inventario', in Id. *Inflação e desenvolvimento* (Petropolis: Vozes [1963] 1970), pp. 149–84, on p. 151.
86 J. Noyola, 'El desarrollo economico y la inflacion en Mexico y otros paises Latinoamericanos', *Investigacion Economica*, 16, (1956), pp. 603–48, on p. 646.
87 J.H. Olivera, 'On structural inflation and Latin-American "structuralism"', p. 322.
88 O. Sunkel, 'El fracaso de las politicas de estabilización', p. 622.
89 C. Furtado, *A economia brasileira* (Rio: A Noite, 1954), on p. 183; Id. C. Furtado, *The Economic Growth of Brazil – A Survey from Colonial to Modern Times* (Berkeley: University of California Press, 1963), trans. by R. Aguiar and E. Drysdale of *Formação Economica do Brazil* (Rio: Fundo de Cultura, [1959]), on p. 255; J. Noyola, 'El desarrollo economico y la inflacion', p. 610.
90 See J. Toye, *Dilemmas of development: reflections on the counter-revolution in development theory and policy* (Oxford: Basil & Blackwell, 1987).
91 I. Leiva, 'Toward a critique of Latin American neostructuralism', *Latin American politics and society*, 50, (2008a), pp. 1–25, on p. 2.
92 F. Fajnzylber, *Industrializacion en Latino America* (Santiago: CEPAL, 1989).
93 O.Sunkel, 'Introduction' in O. Sunkel (ed.), *Development from within: toward a neostructuralist approach for Latin America* (Boulder (Co.): L. Rienner, 1993), on p. 8.
94 See M. Boianovsky, 'A view from the tropics'.
95 A. Hounie, L. Pittaluga, G. Porcile and F. Scatolin, 'ECLAC and the new growth theories', *CEPAL Review*, 68, (1999), pp. 7–31.
96 J.L. Love, 'The rise and decline of economic structuralism', pp. 124–25.
97 See for example O. Rodríguez, *El estructuralismo latinoamericano*; R. Bielschowsky, 'Sixty years of ECLAC'.
98 I. Leiva, 'Toward a critique of Latin American neostructuralism'; Id., *Latin American neostructuralism: the contradictions of post-neoliberal development* (Minneapolis: University of Minnesota Press, 2008b).
99 M. Cimoli and G. Porcile 'Learning, technological capabilities and structural dynamics', in J.A. Ocampo and J. Ros (eds), *The Oxford handbook of Latin American economics* (Oxford: Oxford University Press, 2011), pp. 546–67, on p. 546.
100 A. Bárcena and A. Prado, *Neoestructuralismo y corrientes heterodoxas en América Latina y el Caribe a inicios del siglo XXI* (Santiago: CEPAL, 2015).
101 United Nations, *Changing production patters with social equity: the prime task of Latin American and Caribbean development in the 1990s* (Santiago, 1990), UN. E.90. II.G.6.
102 See R. Bielschowsky, 'Sixty years of ECLAC'.
103 C. Kay, 'Latin American structuralist school', in *International encyclopedia of human geography*, vol.6 (Oxford: Elsevier, 2009), pp. 159–64, on p. 163.
104 J.A. Ocampo, C. Rada and L. Taylor, *Growth and policy in developing countries: a structuralist approach* (New York: Columbia University Press, 2009).
105 J. Lin, *New structural economics: a framework for rethinking development and policy* (Washington, DC: World Bank, 2012).

6 The resurgence of dependency analysis

Nostalgia or renewed relevance?

Alan B. Cibils

6.1 Introduction

When it comes to development thinking, the post-WWII era was a fruitful one in Latin America. With epicentre in the Economic Commission for Latin America and the Caribbean (ECLAC, or CEPAL for its name in Spanish), first structuralism and then dependency analyses provided original theories on the development process.

Both theories had a significant impact and became widely accepted in Latin American academic and policy circles. The impact of these theories was also significant in other periphery countries, however, the impact on Northern academia was minimal in the case of structuralism,[1] and whatever impact dependency analysis had was mostly limited to sociological discussions with little or no impact on Northern development economics.[2]

Structuralism, and later dependency analysis, emerged as indigenous Latin American theories as a result of what was perceived as the inadequacy of 'one size fits all' Northern economic theories, especially neoclassical and Ricardian trade theories. Building on the works of Keynes, Kalecki and Marx, structuralists and dependency theorists built a significant theoretical corpus centred on the need to take the particular historical and structural realities of Latin America into account. A key component of these analyses was the centre-periphery paradigm, according to which countries in the periphery were not just backward, needing to 'catch up' to the centre. Rather, centre and periphery were part of a global capitalist system that in reproducing itself reproduced both centre and periphery. If theory was to be meaningful for policy purposes, then it needed to take these factors into account.

The rise of monetarism and the increasing deregulation and liberalization that resulted from the end of the Bretton Woods system in the early 1970s produced a sea change in economic theory in academic and policy circles. In Latin America, a series of bloody military coup d'état's did away with CEPAL-inspired developmentalist economic policies and with the advice of the 'Chicago Boys', implemented a broad range of 'market friendly' policies. With time, the theoretical framework became popularly known as 'neoliberalism' and the policies it promoted included trade and financial liberalization, privatizations, and labour market deregulation.

As neoliberal economics became mainstream world-wide, development thinking lost the richness and diversity of the decades prior to 1975. 'One size fits all' became the hallmark of economic theory, including development economics, and the Bretton Woods institutions became their main promoters and enforcers (through conditionality-based lending). Static, a-historical and heavily mathematical models became the tools of choice, leaving behind the holistic dynamic approaches of the Latin American theories.[3]

Four decades later, it is clear that neoliberalism has not delivered important results as promised by its promoters. Cyclical financial crises, erratic growth, rising inequality and social exclusion and very uneven development processes in the periphery have led many social scientists to 're-discover' the Latin American structuralist and dependency traditions and re-evaluate structuralist and dependency concepts on development.

In this chapter we review some of the recent developments in the application of dependency analysis to diverse situations hoping to contribute to the debate on its potential usefulness as an analytical tool. The chapter is structured as follows. In the following section (6.2) we discuss the roots of the dependency school in CEPAL's structuralism. There are very clear links to structuralism and many common threads, even if dependency eventually became a distinct set of theories. In section 6.3 we present the main currents of dependency analysis. For each current, the main authors and themes are discussed, as well as the specific views on the prospects of peripheral development. Section 6.4 briefly discusses some of the reasons why dependency analysis never became fully popular in the centre's economics academia. We consider this to be relevant to the possibilities of current renewed interest in dependency analysis moving beyond the periphery. Section 6.5 discusses many of the current applications of dependency analyses in the traditional periphery but also in the new peripheries in Europe and within centre countries. The chapter concludes with some general remarks about dependency's renewed relevance in the aftermath of neoliberal globalization.

6.2 The structuralist roots of dependency analysis

The main Latin American critical theories of development emerged mostly in the post WWII period. However, the Latin American debate on issues such as backwardness, industrialization, dualism and societal segmentation, and reform vs. revolution was rich and diverse and dates back at least to the late 1800s.[4] The most proximate roots probably lie in the debates between two Peruvian intellectuals, Victor Raúl Haya de la Torre and José Carlos Mariátegui, in the 1920s and 1930s. Each side of this debate contained the elements of what were eventually to become the structuralist (reformist) and the more radical dependency theories.

Both structuralism and dependency theories shared the view that neoclassical and modernization theories cannot fully account for underdevelopment in Latin America and much of the periphery (a term we owe to the Latin American school).[5] Rather, underdevelopment is the result of the process of capitalist accumulation in which the industrialized North (or centre) plays the leading role. In other words, the process of capitalist accumulation constantly reproduces development and underdevelopment. This means that underdevelopment is not just a problem of having arrived late, and therefore needing to 'catch-up'. Rather, it is a necessary by-product of world capitalist development.

The Latin American development theorists argued that underdeveloped countries have peculiarities and specificities of their own which neoclassical and modernization theories don't account for. Structuralists and dependency theorists also shared a holistic and historical approach to development thinking. Holistic because their analysis encompasses the interactions between social class, political and economic structures in the periphery and between the periphery and the centre. Historical because underdevelopment is the outcome of a specific historical process in which colonialism and Northern empires played a key role in shaping what were later to become independent peripheral nations.

Dependency thinking, evolved partly out of CEPAL's structuralist thinking on development, incorporating key elements of that analysis. In order to better understand dependency thinking, it is useful to briefly describe the key elements of structuralist theory.[6]

The starting point for CEPAL social scientists was the specific nature of Latin America's development history and problems. In this sense, their intention was not to develop a new, universal, development theory, but to think about the problems faced by Latin American countries from a development perspective. CEPAL thinking about the issues affecting Latin American development took into account the nature of the region's participation in the international division of labour and how this participation impacted development and the possibilities for development. As evidenced in Prebisch's much cited 1949 publication and the subsequent voluminous output of CEPAL thinkers, their theories resulted in a distinct outlook that challenged Northern development theories.

A second key aspect of CEPAL thinking was the centre-periphery paradigm, which was later also to be a central part of dependency thinking.[7] The centre-periphery paradigm was conceived as a way to depict the unequal nature of economic relations in the world system which originated with the industrial revolution in the centre when possibilities of increasing productivity rose dramatically. The centre countries developed capital goods sectors and internalized new technology by spreading the new technological developments to all sectors of their economies. This resulted in the development of a homogenous and integrated economy.

The diffusion of technical progress throughout the world, however, was highly uneven. In the periphery, new technologies were largely imported and were not the result of the needs of local economy development. As a result, the peripheral economy, unlike the economies of the centre, is both heterogeneous and disarticulated, with large productivity gaps between modern and backward sectors. The lack of autochthonous technological development means that peripheral capitalist formations are substantively different than those of the centre. All in all, development should not be viewed simply as an issue of having arrived late and needing to 'catch-up'. The problem of development in the periphery is unique and therefore requires unique theoretical and policy approaches.

A third key aspect of CEPAL thinking was the hypothesis that terms of trade for countries in the periphery experienced a sustained long-run tendency to deteriorate. This deterioration was due to unequal abilities of centre and periphery countries to retain the fruits of productivity gains resulting from technical progress. The existence of trade unions and oligopolies in the centre meant that prices would generally fall to a lesser extent than the increase in productivity, thus enabling workers and capitalists to retain part of the fruits of their technical progress via rises in wages and profits. The opposite is true for periphery exports as a result of weaker unions and competitive international export markets. Additionally, a large surplus labour force in the periphery exerted downward pressure on wages. As a result, the benefits of technical progress became increasingly unequally distributed between centre and periphery nations.[8]

The fourth distinct aspect of CEPAL thinking was their policy proposal for a way out of underdevelopment: import substituting industrialization (ISI). By pursuing ISI, the periphery would reduce its dependence on Northern imports and its vulnerability to international economic crises, leading to greater increases in productivity and incomes and reducing unemployment. In this way, one of sources of low wages in periphery would be eliminated, thus avoiding further deterioration of terms of trade. For industrialization to take off, protectionism was considered necessary as long as the productivity of the periphery's industry was below that of the centre countries and so long as productivity differentials were not compensated by wage differentials.

6.3 Dependency analysis: main currents

In many ways, at least initially, dependency analysis was an outgrowth of CEPAL structuralism. Like the structuralists, dependency theorists articulated their views through historical analysis. However, an important difference is that the latter generally focused more on politics and class struggle as an explanation of underdevelopment than the former. In this way, dependency analysis' contribution was 'to offer a new definition of underdevelopment combining the analysis of society with economy and politics, in specific historical situations'.[9]

Additionally, dependency analysis 'introduced some fundamental reconceptualizations. It opposed a universal theory of stages of growth; not all countries would go through the same stages'.[10] Furthermore, dependency analysis 'was the first major intellectual perspective that could be called truly Latin American and that urged people in Latin America to think about themselves regionally rather than nationally'.[11]

Dependency theory emerged in Santiago,[12] and later expanded around the world. 'Considered as a whole, the "dependentist group" consisted of about thirty social scientists' most of which were in their late twenties or early thirties during the most productive years of dependency analysis, i.e from 1964 to 1970. Half of them were economists and the other half were lawyers, sociologists and political scientists. A vast majority (90 per cent) were South Americans of which half were Brazilian.[13]

There were several think tanks and research institutes linked to CEPAL and various academic institutions that were key in the development of dependency analysis. The main research institutes were ILPES (Latin American Institute of Social and Economic Planning), linked to CEPAL; CESO (Centre for Social and Economic Studies), linked to the University of Chile; FLACSO (Latin American Social Science Faculty); and CEREN (Centre for the Study of the National Reality), linked to the Catholic University.

Before presenting our brief survey of the main currents within dependency analysis, a word of caution is in order. There is not an unequivocal demarcation between the different approaches to dependency analysis. Indeed, many authors are characterized as structuralists or dependency theorists depending on which of their publications one chooses (Celso Furtado and Osvaldo Sunkel are two of the authors in this category). Surveys of dependency analysis generally point this out, and the reader is encouraged to examine these potential tensions in the works of Cristóbal Kay, Joseph Love, and Gabriel Palma among others.[14]

What is commonly known as dependency theory is really a diverse literature that has been variously classified. For example, Palma classifies dependency theories into three major, not mutually exclusive groups. The first group views capitalist underdevelopment as inevitable (for example in the work of André Gunder Frank), with the only way out of underdevelopment being a socialist revolution. The second group proposes a reformulation and radicalization of CEPAL's development theory (for example, Celso Furtado, Aníbal Pinto and Osvaldo Sunkel). The third group uses the dependency concept as a method to understand specific situations of underdevelopment (the main proponents are Cardoso and Faletto).[15]

Cristóbal Kay, on the other hand, classifies dependency theories in two broad groups, namely reformist and Marxist, with each group having different currents within.[16] While both Kay's and Palma's classifications are valid, we will follow Kay's classification in this section as we believe it to be more nuanced.

Kay identifies three currents within the reformist dependency approach. The first reformist current is associated with the work of Osvaldo Sunkel who focuses on how the growth of transnational corporations (TNCs) has resulted in a new international division of labour.[17] The growing power of these corporations has led to a weakening of the State in the periphery, and could eventually lead to national disintegration in Latin America. For Sunkel, development without dependence and marginalization can take place only through a reform of the asymmetric international capitalist system and by hard bargaining and pragmatic negotiations.

The second reformist current is associated with the work of Celso Furtado, who maintained that technical progress through imported technology and the imposition of consumption patterns from the centre countries were key factors that explained the perpetuation of underdevelopment and dependence in the periphery.[18] The increasing diversification of consumption patterns, geared toward the high-income groups in the peripheral countries, structures an equally diversified industrial consumer-goods production pattern. The technology for producing these products comes from centre countries and largely from multinationals. This capital-intensive technology perpetuates the concentration of income and the surplus of labour thereby reproducing the vicious circle of underdevelopment and dependence.

The third current of the reformist dependency school is based on the work of Fernando Henrique Cardoso and Enzo Faletto who merge CEPAL's structuralism with dependency analysis.[19] Their economic analysis remains in line with structuralist theory, but they add a social and political analysis largely absent from structuralist writings. The originality of their analysis lies in how they link changing relationships between economic, social and political forces at key junctures in post-colonial Latin America to the changing relationships with the rest of the world. In this way, their analysis focuses on how the world system impinges differently on different Latin American countries. Dependence is not regarded simply as an external variable as they do not derive the internal national sociopolitical situation mechanically from external domination. Although the State's limits for manoeuvre are largely set by the world-system, the particular internal configuration of a country determines the specific response to particular external events. They conceive of the relations between internal and external forces as forming a complex whole.

A common point to the different reformist approaches is that some degree of development is possible, even if the world system exerts a heavy influence on the periphery. The Marxist dependency approaches generally disagree with this conclusion, holding that the only way to achieve development is through a socialist revolution and a break with the capitalist centre. The idea of a Marxist theory of dependency stems from the fact that Marx never fully addressed the colonial question. And, while the Marxist theories of imperialism tackled the different stages of capitalism, they were mostly concerned with the imperialist countries and had little to say about periphery countries, a gap which Marxist dependency theorists hoped to fill.[20]

For Marxist dependency theorists a key problem was how to explain the differences in the development trajectories of capitalism in the centre and in the periphery. Baran had a substantial influence on Marxist dependency theorists, who adopted his thesis that underdevelopment and development are the common results of the world-wide process of accumulation.[21] Baran and Sweezy's view that capitalism is no longer a progressive force in the stage of imperialism and monopoly capitalism also had a strong influence on the dependency school.[22]

Even though his work is little known in the English-speaking world, Ruy Mauro Marini is probably the most outstanding Marxist dependency theorist. Marini in 1973 made a systematic effort to determine the laws of underdevelopment, his central thesis being that dependency involves the super-exploitation of labour in the periphery. Super-exploitation arises partially from the need of capitalists to compensate for the fall in profit rates arising from unequal exchange. Unequal exchange results in falling profit rates in the periphery while they rise in the centre as value is transferred from the former to the latter.[23]

According to Marini the circuit of capital in dependent countries is different from that in centre countries as two key elements of the cycle (production and circulation) are separated as a result of the periphery being linked to the centre through unequal exchange. Production does not depend on internal capacity for consumption but on exports to centre countries. Wages are kept low in the dependent countries because the workers' consumption is not required for the realization of commodities. Thus, conditions are set for the super-exploitation of labour so long as a periphery surplus population exists. In centre countries, the two phases of the circulation of capital are completed internally, generating more propitious conditions for development.

Ironically, perhaps the best known dependency theorist outside Latin America, André Gunder Frank, is often classified as a Marxist dependency theorist (although Kay does not do so). Frank himself has said that that he is not a Marxist but a world-system theorist.[24] However, his use of certain Marxist categories and terminology has led many to assume he is a Marxist. Contrary to those who viewed Latin America as essentially dual societies, with modern capitalist and backward pre-capitalist segments, Frank contended that Latin America had been capitalist since the fifteenth century when it was included into the world economy dominated by Western Europe.[25] The European centre extracted surplus from the periphery, thus limiting its possibilities for development. In a world thus constituted, all Latin America only could aspire to the 'development of underdevelopment'.[26] The only way out for this dead-end was a socialist revolution.

From this brief survey we can conclude that despite differences there are some common threads to different approaches to dependency analysis, some of which show their debt to CEPAL structuralist thought as highlighted above. The focus on the unequal relations between centre and periphery countries, the impact of this relationship on the ability of periphery countries to develop and the different nature of centre and periphery social formations are common to all strands of dependency analysis. The biggest differences arise, perhaps, around the issues of whether development is or is not possible within the capitalist world economic order and if it is, to what extent.

6.4 Dependency analysis in centre countries: some issues

While dependency analysis became widespread in Latin America and other parts of the periphery, it was not able to attract a lot of attention in US academia, especially in economics departments.[27] Perhaps language was one significant barrier to dependency analysis diffusion in the North, since much published output was in Spanish and very few of the authors were translated into English. Further contributing to this problem, the author that was most widely translated into English was André Gunder Frank who, as we have said above, considered himself a world system theorist.[28]

A second factor possibly resulting in dependency analysis marginalization in centre countries was its more holistic approach to the study of underdevelopment. Indeed, to a much greater extent than had the structuralists before them, dependency theorists based their analysis of underdevelopment on more than economic factors, including social classes, political and historic factors as well. This resulted in a form of theorizing that was necessarily specific to the different peripheral social formations, to their history, and to their particular social class and political configurations. It was opposite to the 'one size fits all' economic modelling which became the norm in economics after the mid 1970s and certainly not a form of theorizing that easily fit into mathematical models.[29]

A third factor possibly resulting in the neglect of dependency theories in centre countries, even in the 1960s and 1970s, was related to the generally radical and anti capitalist ideological content. Dependency theories tended to be quite to the left of much of what was acceptable in centre academic departments, and especially so in economics departments.

Like Keynesian economics in centre countries, structuralism and dependency analysis were entirely displaced by neoclassical economics starting in the early 1970s. The transition from Keynesian, structuralist and dependency theory dominance to monetarism[30] and new classical economics dominance was not linear nor did it have a single cause. Falling profit rates in centre countries, and the push to transnationalize profit opportunities through trade and financial deregulation were a part of it. In South America, military dictatorships led the charge against structuralist-inspired welfare State and industrialization policies, implementing 'market friendly' policies while conducting fierce repression of leftist social movements and academics.

Academic economics also underwent substantial changes. Widespread use of increasingly complex individual agent maximizing mathematical models became the field's norm, effectively hiding from view and discussion the many questionable assumptions upon which neoclassical economics is built. Development economics and underdevelopment studies were not spared from this trend, replacing the more complex analyses of CEPAL and classical development economics with simpler concepts susceptible of being modelized.[31] This highly mathematized approach to economics, which emerged predominantly in the post-WWII US academia, eventually became the norm for the economics profession world-wide as a part of what Bourdieu would term the second 'imperialism of the universal'.[32]

All of this led to what Hernández López calls the death by decree and 'burying alive' of dependency analysis.[33] It was not a natural death, but a death at the hand of military dictatorships and a profound restructuring of international capitalism that lead to the temporary dominance of neoliberalism, including in academia and in the way economics was taught.

6.5 The rebirth of dependency: current views far and wide

After three decades of outward-oriented neoliberal policy regimes in Latin America there has been a rebirth of interest in the critical Latin American development theories, especially structuralist thought and dependency analysis.[34] This is not a coincidence, since neoliberalism has resulted in cyclical financial crises, a growing dependence on primary exports, growing inequality and erratic economic growth performance. Faith in free markets to produce development has all but disappeared in Latin America as a result of neoliberalism's dismal performance.[35]

Indeed, Kay and Gwynne provide important reasons on why structuralist and dependency theories should acquire renewed relevance when thinking about development in periphery countries.[36] In the first place, despite a profound globalization process by which countries are more deeply integrated into the capitalist world order, 'the economic divide and income gap between the centre or developed countries and the periphery or underdeveloped countries has widened continually'.[37] As the authors point out, this is a vindication of predictions of structuralist and dependency theorists against the predictions of convergence by neoclassical economists.[38]

Another key issue emphasized by structuralist and dependency analysis was technological dependence, which import substitution industrialization policies were supposed to address. Technological independence was never achieved, and the era of trade, financial and investment liberalization that followed the end of the Bretton Woods system, brought increasing transnational corporation presence in Latin America and throughout the periphery. This has not reversed the situation of technological dependence.

In addition to these global trends, Kay and Gwynne highlight that a process of differentiation has taken place within the periphery. On the one hand, the emergence of the South-East Asian NICs (newly industrialised countries – South Korea, Taiwan, Hong-Kong and Singapore) has resulted in formerly peripheral countries achieving – and sustaining – high levels of industrialization and development. It must be stressed that 'such a dramatic transformation was due to the role played by a national developmentalist state with a forceful industrial policy (imposed after sweeping land reform)'[39] confirming that the state is a fundamental player in the development process, as structuralists and dependency theorists maintained.

More recently, the emergence as a global political actor of the group of countries known as the BRICS (Brazil, Russia, India, China and South Africa) has led to a further differentiation within the periphery. Despite substantial heterogeneity within the BRICS (size of the economy, role of the state, macroeconomic policies, etc.), new discussions have arisen about the possibilities and paths to development in the periphery. Along these lines, Samir Amin distinguishes between dominant countries, first class peripheries and marginalised peripheries.[40] The distinction between periphery countries is not based exclusively on economic structure or productivity, it is also political. In other words, the differentiation is also centred on whether a periphery country can attempt to confront with centre imperialism.[41] Furthermore, confrontation takes place on any of what Amin labels the five central monopolies that benefit centre countries: control of technology, control of financial flows, access to natural resources, control over communications, and control over weapons of mass destruction. The US is clearly dominant in all of these monopolies, with the European Union and Japan disputing control of some of them.

According to Arceo, the centre-periphery paradigm and the concept of dependency are still relevant today after decades of neoliberal globalization.[42] Arceo centres his analysis on the distinction between the terms 'multinational' corporation and 'transnational' corporation. Multinational corporations located their entire production chain in periphery countries, where trade barriers enabled them to use older technologies no longer used in the centre and hiring locals for key management positions. Thus, while headquarters in centre countries imparted general directives, the day to day operation and production decisions were made in the countries where production was located.

With the advent of liberalization policies in the mid- to late-1970s, corporations changed their productions strategies, locating different parts of the production process in different countries. This new strategy transformed multinational into transnational corporations. Unlike multinational corporations, their transnational counterparts use the latest technology and production decisions are in real time. Production locations are generally decided based on relative local costs, which means that periphery countries compete based on cheap labour, generating a veritable race to the bottom.

Technology and production decisions are still made in the centre, where transnational corporations are headquartered. Given this situation, the conception-intensive part of the process still resides in centre countries, while the more labour intensive segments are located in the periphery. As a result, Arceo convincingly argues that the centre-periphery paradigm and dependency analysis are still valid analytical frameworks to analyse globalised production. Still, like Gwynne and Kay and Samin, Arceo argues that the periphery is not homogeneous as there is a growing differentiation within the periphery (BRICS, NICs, etc.).

Parallel to this global restructuring in manufacturing is a process of reprimarization that Pérez Caldentey and Vernengo ironically call a return to the future on Latin America's current development strategy.[43] Analyzing Latin America's performance during the first decade of the new century, the authors find that growth is explained mostly due to the external sector's growth, which is itself the result of primary exports and remittances. The authors conclude that Latin America's current development strategy is based on a variation of the agro–export model of the late nineteenth and early twentieth centuries, becoming once again dependent on primary commodity exports with all the risks that such a strategy entails.

Vernengo's analysis of the different dependency strains leads him to conclude that they would all:

> agree that at the core of the dependency relation between centre and periphery lies the inability of the periphery to develop an autonomous and dynamic process of technological innovation . . . Foreign capital did not solve this problem as it only led to a limited transmission of technology.[44]

In this sense, dependency analysis shares neoclassical economics's emphasis on the centrality of technical progress to growth and development. Based on the work a group of Brazilian dependency theorists,[45] Vernengo posits that international capital's domination of the periphery is centred on financial factors, 'international money', and not technical progress.[46]

According to Vernengo 'the existence of an international monetary hegemon that controls the international reserve currency implies that global dependency relations do not require international disparities in technology'.[47] In the case of periphery countries in Latin America, several decades of industrialization were not enough to break with financial dependency, as recurring balance-of-payments crises make agonizingly clear. Vernengo concludes that the financial dependency 'reflected in the inability of peripheral countries to borrow in international markets in their own currency, present since the first debt crisis in the late 1820s until the most recent Argentinean default in 2001, is the real obstacle to development'.[48]

Chick and Dow apply dependency analysis (together with Kaldor's cumulative causation) to the study of the impact of banking structure on regional development.[49] Based on their study of banking history, they develop a five stage approach to banking development, from the very early stages to the modern banking structures. They conclude that regional development in peripheral areas with banking structures in earlier stages of development will be negatively impacted when forced to interact with banking structures in later stages. In this way, it is possible to analyse the impact of post-Bretton Woods financial liberalization and deregulation policies on the development prospects of periphery regions. Chick and Dow's analysis has been applied to the case of regional development in Spain,[50] to the South American regional trading block MERCOSUR[51] and to transition economies.[52]

Structuralist and dependency theories were not only popular in Latin America; they were also quite popular in the European periphery of the post-war era, especially in Spain, Portugal and Romania. Theoretical developments in those countries already used terms as centre, periphery and underdevelopment, which later combined with the Latin American traditions to influence development policies locally.[53]

In recent years, financial dependence, as other dependency concepts have also been applied to two groups of European countries. On the one hand, the highly indebted group of Eurozone countries (Greece, Spain, Portugal, Italy and Ireland) are referred to as the European periphery. While the legitimacy and sustainability of these countries' public debt has come under strong inquiring by left-of-centre political parties and NGOs, questions are being raised about the viability of their continued participation in the Eurozone.[54] As a result, European periphery countries are being faced with the many of the same questions as other periphery countries regarding development, their place in the world economy, industrial policy, etc.[55]

A second application of the concept of dependency in Europe comes from the varieties of capitalism literature.[56] Indeed, some authors[57] suggest adding the 'dependent market economy' (DME) to the existing varieties of capitalism in order to explain economic behaviour in some of the formerly socialist countries of Eastern Europe, such as Romania.[58] According to Ban, the DME depends on multinational financial and FDI flows and uses both interventionism and liberalization to reinforce those flows. Its comparative advantage is not based on radical innovation or incremental innovation, but rather as an assembly platform for semi-standardised industrial goods.

Nölke and Vliegenthart identify four institutional characteristics of DMEs. First, TNCs operating in DMEs don't get finance from domestic banks or capital markets. Rather, TNCs headquarters in the centre control subsidiaries in a hierarchical fashion and get finance from the same sources as the TNCs headquarters.

In this way, both finance and governance highlight the dependence relationship. Second, TNCs push for low taxes, labour market deregulation and firm-level collective bargaining. Third, TNCs find it more efficient to transfer innovations to subsidiaries rather than invest in innovative relevant skills in DMEs. Fourth, and as a result of the previous characteristics, DMEs are more likely to remain assembly platforms for TNCs.[59]

In other words, the DME variety of capitalism shares some of the characteristics that dependency theorists have highlighted for many decades, including some of the more recent developments, even if dependency theory is not specifically acknowledged as a source. Financial and technological dependence in Eastern Europe, therefore, is not that unlike of what happens in Latin America, Africa and parts of Asia.

Beigel identifies several theoretical developments in recent years which call for a serious reconsideration of dependency categories.[60] John Saxe-Fernández *et al.* expose the ideological program behind the discourse of 'globalization' and 'interdependence' concepts that rest on the fuzzy notions of market forces and technological change where individual nation states cease to have a determining role.[61] The authors therefore propose reclaiming the notion of imperialism as a useful framework within which to analyze flows of capital, goods and services and technology in a setting of unequal power relations between states, markets and classes in conflict one with each other. The main forces behind these flows are transnational corporations, banks and imperial states.

By reclaiming the use of imperialism as a conceptual framework the authors are not ignoring the many substantial transformations in the world capitalist system. Rather, what they are noting is that there has been a deepening of dependency and that the distance between core and periphery countries has grown larger. According to Saxe-Fernández, the mechanisms through which this has happened are multiple and broader in scope than before. They include multiple exploitative and coercive mechanisms such as conditionality attached to World Bank, International Monetary Fund, and private creditor loans, bilateral investment treaties with imperial powers, and the still dominant presence of US capital in strategic areas such as natural resources, agriculture, and energy sectors. Imperialism, therefore, is the axis along which centre-periphery relations are ordered and dependent nations still transfer massive surpluses to the centre perpetuating underdevelopment in the periphery.

A further line of theoretical development came from the 'coloniality/modernity working group' (*Grupo colonialidad modernidad*), a group of prominent Latin American intellectuals, which included Aníbal Quijano, Enrique Dussell, Walter Mignolo, Arturo Escobar, Roberto Fernández Retamar and, from the US, Immanuel Wallerstein. According to these authors, it is necessary to interpret Latin America's current situation in the light of a long-run process that has marked the history of the region since the colonial era, namely the 'coloniality of power' that has generated a structural-historic dependence.[62]

For Quijano, dependence does not mean a mechanical causal relationship between a domestic and an external economy that exerts pressure on the former.

Rather, dependence is a more complex relation, a characteristic of the world-system since the emergence of capitalism. In the periods when centre countries were weaker (for example, during the great depression), periphery bourgeoisies implemented import substituting policies. However, these processes did not require a global capitalist restructuring; they were implemented within the existing structures.[63] For Quijano, this is a clear example of the coloniality of power and of how dependence is a structural-historic condition, even during times of apparent independence of periphery countries.

6.6 Concluding remarks

Dependency analysis played an important role in Latin America in the 1960s and 1970s, until it was displaced, together with other heterodox theories, by neo-liberalism. However, after four decades of neoliberal dominance in policy and academic spheres, and colossal policy failures, dependency analysis is making a comeback in both theoretical and applied work, making a clear statement of its renewed relevance as an analytical tool. It remains to be seen whether this comeback will have a substantial impact. We can make some observations as to what has happened so far and make a few suggestions for future research.

First, it is interesting to note that many of the authors currently writing on dependency analysis are from the periphery, many of whom write in Spanish. Additionally, many belong to branches of the social sciences other than economics. This has the advantage of enabling a broader analysis, compatible with the original dependency thinkers. However, it is at odds with the highly mathematized and a-historic tendencies in the centre's economics academia. In this sense, it may suffer the same fate as the original dependency analysis, even though current global circumstances are clearly different after decades of neoliberal globalization.

Second, it is interesting to note how current adaptations of dependency analysis have moved beyond Latin America to the European periphery and even to regions within centre countries. In a way this makes sense since, with increasing and widespread economic liberalization and deregulation, capitalism has become truly global. In this context, the periphery has also become global and many of the same phenomena are observed in parts of Asia, Africa, Latin America and centre countries.

Third, given some of the developments presented in the previous section, it is perhaps more fruitful to think of *dependencies* (plural), and not just dependency (singular). Neoliberal globalization has multiplied the channels through which dependency can manifest itself, with financial channels taking a leading role, as pointed out by Vernengo. It is therefore relevant and interesting to examine the ways in which these multiple channels interact and reinforce the different forms of dependency.

Fourth, dependency analysis is in line with the pluralistic approach advocated by many heterodox economists.[64] By approaching the analysis of specific situations from various disciplinary perspectives (economics, history, geography, sociology, international relations) and with various methodologies, dependency analysis embodies many of the principles of the pluralist approach.

Finally, if dependency analysis is to develop and grow as a viable framework within which to analyse the problems of development and underdevelopment, a greater effort needs to be made to define clearly and systematize concepts and methodologies. While rigid definitions should be avoided, it would be helpful to have a more clearly defined framework within which the various strains described above can interact and grow. This should enable and promote more fruitful work not only in the traditional periphery countries, but also in the new peripheries of Europe and even within centre countries.

Notes

1 Some key CEPAL documents were translated into English and the work of Lance Taylor helped to disseminate some of structuralism's ideas in mathematical form, see L. Taylor, *Macro Models for Developing Countries* (New York: McGraw-Hill, 1979); Id., *Structuralist Macroeconomics: Applicable Models for the Third World* (New York: Basic Books, 1983).
2 Seers observes that 'It is hard to resist the conclusion that most of us just do not care, assuming tacitly that nothing of intellectual significance is produced in the backward continents, a hangover from the colonial period', D. Seers (ed.), *Dependency Analysis: A Critical Reassessment* (UK: Short Run Press, 1981), on p. 13.
3 For a discussion of this process see D. Gualerzi and A. Cibils, 'High Development Theory, CEPAL, and Beyond' in J.L. Cardoso, M.C. Marcuzzo and M.E. Romero Sotelo (eds), *Economic Development and Global Crisis. The Latin American Economy in Historical Perspective* (Abingdon: Routledge, 2014), pp. 139–58.
4 For an account of these early debates see J.L. Love, 'The Origins of Dependency Analysis', *Journal of Latin American Studies*, 22: 1, (1990), pp. 143–68; Id. 'Economic ideas and ideologies in Latin America since 1930' in L. Behtell (ed.), *Latin America since 1930: Economy, Society and Politics* (Cambridge: Cambridge University Press, 1994), pp. 391–460.
5 See A. Saad-Filho, 'The Rise and Decline of Latin American Structuralism and Dependency Theory', in K.S. Jomo and E. Reinert (eds), *The Origins of Development Economics* (London: Zed Books, 2005), pp. 128–45.
6 For a more detailed discussion see J.L. Love, 'The Origins of Dependency Analysis'; M.G. Vázquez Olivera, 'Las fuentes teórico-metodológicas de la construcción del concepto de dependencia'. *Latinoamérica*, 38: 1, (2004), pp. 9–44.
7 See O. Rodríguez, 'Sobre la concepción del sistema centro-periferia', *Revista de la CEPAL*, 1st semester, (1977), pp. 203–48; A. Di Filippo, 'La visión centro-periferia hoy', *Revista de la CEPAL*, special issue, (1998), pp. 175–85.
8 On the issue of terms of trade see chapter 3 above.
9 F. Beigel, 'Dependency Analysis: The Creation of a New Social Theory in Latin America', in S. Patel (ed.), *The ISA Handbook of Diverse Sociological Traditions* (London: Sage, 2010), pp. 189–200, on p. 191.
10 S. Topik, 'Dependency Revisited: Saving the Baby from the Bathwater', *Latin American Perspectives*, 25: 6, (1998), pp. 95–9, on p. 95.
11 Ibid.
12 According to Beigel this was due in part to increased state funding during the first half of the twentieth century of the university system, with the University of Chile in Santiago becoming a central actor. The university movement 'played a central role in

the growth of intellectual activism' attracting intellectuals from other Latin American countries, many of whom were fleeing persecution from dictatorships at home, F. Beigel, 'Dependency Analysis, pp. 191–2.

13 Only André Gunder Frank, Franz Heinkelammert and Armand Mattelart were not Latin American, ibid., pp. 193–4.

14 C. Kay, *Latin American Theories of Development and Underdevelopment* (London: Routledge, 1989); Id., 'Reflections on the Latin American Contributions to Development Theory', *Development and Change*, 22: 1, (1991), pp. 31–68; J.L. Love, 'The Origins of Dependency Analysis'; Id., 'Economic Ideas and Ideologies in Latin America'; Id., 'The Rise and Decline of Economic Structuralism in Latin America', *Latin American Research Review*, 40: 3, (2005), pp 100–25; G. Palma, 'Dependency: A Formal Theory of Underdevelopment or a Methodology for the Analysis of Concrete Situations of Underdevelopment?', *World Development*, 6: 7–8, (1978), pp. 881–924; Id., 'Theories of Dependency', in A.K. Dutt and J. Ros (eds), *International Handbook of Development Economics*, Vol. 1 (Cheltenham, UK: Edward Elgar, 2008a), pp. 125–35; Id., 'Structuralism' in A.K. Dutt and J. Ros (eds.), *International Handbook of Development Economics*, Vol. 1 (Cheltenham, UK: Edward Elgar, 2008b), pp. 136–43.

15 G. Palma, 'Theories of Dependency'.

16 C. Kay, 'Reflections on the Latin American Contributions to Development'. Reformist authors include Fernando Henrique Cardoso, Celso Furtado, Osvaldo Sunkel, Helio Jaguaribe and Aníbal Pinto. Their ideas are best seen as a development of CEPAL structuralism as they attempt to reformulate the developmentalist position in the light of the crisis of import-substituting industrialization. Marxist authors include Ruy Mauro Marini, Theotônio dos Santos, Oscar Braun, Vania Bambirra, Aníbal Quijano, Edelbeto Torres Rivas, Tomás Amadeo Vasconi, Alonso Aguilar and Antonio García. According to Kay, this last group of authors are best classified as neo-Marxist as they question the progressive role of capitalism in the periphery. André Gunder Frank, perhaps the best known dependency theorist outside Latin America is an odd case. While many consider him a Marxist, he himself has disavowed such a classification, see A.G. Frank, 'Latin American Development Theories Revisited: A Participant Review', *Latin American Perspectives*, 19: 2, (1992), pp. 125–39.

17 See, for example, O. Sunkel, 'Big Business and "Dependencia:: A Latin American view', *Foreign Affairs*, 50: 3, (1972), pp. 517–31; Id., 'Transnational Capital and National Disintegration in Latin America', *Social and Economic Studies*, 22: 1, (1973), pp. 132–71.

18 See C. Furtado, *Development and Underdevelopment* (Berkeley: University of California Press, 1964); Id., 'Hacia una ideología del desarrollo', *El Trimestre Económico*, XXXIII: 3, (1966), pp. 379–91; C. Furtado, 'Dependencia externa y teoria económica', *El Trimestre Económico*, 38: 2, (1971), pp. 335–49. For a recent survey of Furtado's many contributions see M. Boianovsky, 'A View from the Tropics: Celso Furtado and the Theory of Economic Development in the 1950s', *History of Political Economy*, 42, (2010), pp. 221–66.

19 For the main exposition of this view see F.H. Cardoso and E. Faletto, *Dependencia y desarrollo en América Latina: ensayo de interpretación sociológica* (Mexico City: Siglo Ventiuno, 1969).

20 Indeed, dependency analysis came under substantial fire by some Marxists who considered that dependency was not faithful to Marx's interpretation of history and economic development. See, among many others, R. Brenner, 'The Origins of Capitalist Development: A Critique of Neo-Smithian Marxism', *New Left Review*, 104, (1977), pp. 25–92; H. Gülalp, 'Frank and Wallerstein Revisited: A Contribution to Brenner's Critique', *Journal of Contemporary Asia*, 11: 2, (1981), pp. 168–88.

21 P. Baran, *The Political Economy of Growth* (New York: Monthly Review Press, 1957).

22 P. Baran and P. Sweezy, *Monopoly Capital: An Essay on the American Economic and Social Order* (New York: Monthly Review Press, 1966).

23 R.M. Marini, 'Diaéctica de la dependencia', in Id., *América Latina: Dependencia y Globalización* (Buenos Aires: CLACSO and Prometeo Libros, [1973] 2007), pp. 99–136.

24 A.G. Frank, *Lumpenburgeoisie: Lumpendevelopment. Dependence, Class and Politics in Latin America* (New York: Monthly Review Press, 1972).

25 A.G. Frank, *Latin America: Underdevelopment or Revolution* (New York: Monthly Review Press, 1969).

26 Frank was criticized for his circulation-based definition of the capitalist mode of production and for the absence of a class-based analysis. He addressed these criticisms in A.G. Frank, *Lumpenburgeoisie*. Despite substantial criticisms to his deterministic views, he remained an influential writer for many years.

27 In the introduction to his edited volume, Dudley Seers reflects that 'it is hard to resist the conclusion that most of us just do not care, assuming tacitly that nothing of intellectual significance is produced in the backward continents, a hangover from the colonial period', D. Seers (ed.), *Dependency Analysis*, p. 13. This was not so in the field of sociology, where dependency generated a lot more interest, research and publications in Northern academia. The journal *Latin American Perspectives* is an example of this. It dedicated considerable space to the topic and published several books on related issues.

28 There were other dependency publications in English, as pointed out in D. Seers (ed.), *Dependency Analysis*. For example, an entire issue of the *Social and Economic Studies* journal was dedicated to dependency theory in 1973. Also, some of Celso Furtado's works were translated into English.

29 See D. Gualerzi and A. Cibils, 'High Development Theory'.

30 Monetarist ideas became quite widespread in Latin America in the 1970s and 1980s thanks to the 'Chicago boys', as University of Chicago economists – the most prominent of which was Milton Friedman – were known. These economists actively participated in many of the Latin American dictatorships as economics advisors, promoting economic policies which later became a part of the neoliberal Washington Consensus.

31 D. Gualerzi and A. Cibils, 'High Development Theory'.

32 Bourdieu's 'imperialism of the universal' refers to how ideas or theories that emerge in a particular context are eventually 'universalized'. The first of such an imperialism, according to Bourdieu, was the French imperialism, extending from the post French Revolution period until the end of WWII where the US ideas and epistemologies began their dominance, see P. Bourdieu, *Intelectuales, Política y Poder* (Buenos Aires: Eudeba, 1999).

33 R. Hernández López, 'La dependencia a debate', *Latinoamérica*, 40, (2005), pp. 11–54.

34 Andrés Velasco's poorly argued an obituary of dependency theory (published in the 'Dustbin of History' section of the journal at the very moment neoliberalism was crumbling down in Latin America) that turned out to be premature, see A. Velasco, 'Dependency Theory a Generation Later', *Foreign Policy*, 133, (2002), pp. 44–5.

35 Ironically, or perhaps depressingly, free market policies are being foisted upon members of the Eurozone by the so-called 'Troika' (the International Monetary Fund – IMF –, the European Central Bank and the European Commission). Clearly, the IMF has learned nothing from its multiple and repeated massive failures around the world.

36 C. Kay and R. Gwynne, 'Relevance of Structuralist and Dependency Theories in the Neoliberal Period: A Latin American Perspective', *Journal of developing societies*, 16: 1, (2000), pp. 49–69.

37 Ibid., p. 51.

38 Vernengo argues in a similar vein: 'The surge in academic work on globalization has . . . made several of the topics dear to the authors of the dependency school relevant once again. Therefore, a reconsideration of dependency theory seems to be appropriate', M. Vernengo, 'Technology, Finance and Dependency: Latin American Radical Political Economy in Retrospect', *Review of Radical Political Economics*, 38: 4, (2006), pp. 551–68, on p. 552.

39   C. Kay and R. Gwynne, 'Relevance of Structuralist and Dependency Theories', p. 52.
40   S. Amin, *Más allá del capitalismo senil: Por un Siglo XXI no norteamericano* (Buenos Aires: Paidós, 2003), Spanish trans. of *Au-delà du capitalisme senile* (Paris: Presses Universitaires de France, 2001).
41   Nef and Robles make a related point. For these authors, neoliberal globalization has resulted in the formation of a new centre and periphery not based exclusively on geographical location, but on social and economic conditions in both the North and the South, J. Nef and W. Robles, 'Globalization, Neoliberalism, and the State of Underdevelopment in the New Periphery', *Journal of Developing Societies*, 16: 1, (2000), pp. 27–48.
42   E. Arceo, 'El impacto de la globalización en la periferia y las nuevas y viejas formas de dependencia', *Cuadernos del CENDES*, 22: 50, (2005), pp. 22–61; Id., *El largo camino a la crisis: Centro, periferia y transformaciones en la economía social* (Buenos Aires: Cara o Ceca, 2011).
43   E. Pérez Caldentey and M. Vernengo, 'Back to the future: Latin America's current development strategy', *Journal of Post Keynesian Economics*, 32: 4, (2010), pp. 623–44.
44   M. Vernengo, 'Technology, Finance and Dependency', pp. 561–2. For Vernengo there are two main currents of dependency analysis. The first is the American-Marxist tradition developed by Paul Baran and André Gunder Frank, adopted and further developed in Latin America by Aníbal Quijano, Theotônio dos Santos, Vania Bambirra and Ruy Mauro Marini. The second dependency tradition is linked to the Latin American structuralists such as Raúl Prebisch and Celso Furtado. The main writers in this tradition are Cardoso, Faletto, Maria de Conceição Tavares, José Serra, Osvaldo Sunkel and Francisco Olivera.
45   These theorists were at the Universidade de Campinas and at the Universidade Federal do Rio de Janeiro, they worked under the leadership of Maria da Conceição Tavares. While originally linked to CEPAL, Tavares and the theorists working with her eventually developed a different interpretation of dependency.
46   Financial dependency is also pointed out as a form of dependency by P. Paz, 'Dependencia financiera y desnacionalización de la industria interna', *El Trimestre Económico*, 146, (1971), pp. 297–329; C. Kay and R. Gwynne, 'Relevance of Structuralist and Dependency Theories'; P. Salama, 'Deudas y dependencia financiera del Estado en América Latina', in A. Girón (ed.), *Confrontaciones Monetaria* (Buenos Aires: CLACSO, 2006), pp. 101–24; F. Beigel, 'Vida, muerte y resurrección de las "teorías de la dependencia"' in F. Beigel, et al (eds), *Crítica y teoría en el pensamiento social latinoamericano* (Buenos Aires: CLACSO, 2006), pp. 287–326; C. Aguiar de Medeiros, 'Financial Dependency and Growth Cycles in Latin American Countries', *Journal of Post Keynesian Economics*, 31: 1, (2008), pp. 79–99. However, they differ with Vernengo in that for the latter financial dependency is central whereas for the former it is one of several possible forms of dependency.
47   M. Vernengo, 'Technology, Finance and Dependency', pp. 561–2.
48   Ibid., p. 563.
49   V. Chick and S. Dow, 'A Post-Keynesian Perspective on the Relation between Banking and Regional Development', in P. Arestis (ed.), *Post-Keynesian Monetary Economics: New Approaches to Financial Modelling* (Cheltenham, UK: Edward Elgar. 1988), pp. 219–50.
50   C. Rodríguez Fuentes, 'El papel del sistema bancario en el desarrollo regional. ¿Reparto o creación de crédito?', *Estudios Regionales*, 47, (1997), pp. 117–39.
51   A.M. Amado, 'The Regional Impact of the Internationalisation of the Financial System: The Case of MERCOSUL' in P. Arestis, M. Desai and S. Dow (eds), *Methodology, Microeconomics and Keynes. Essays in Honour of Victoria Chick,* vol. 2 (London: Routledge, 2002), pp. 192–202.
52   S. Dow, D. Ghosh and R. Kobil, 'A Stages Approach to Banking Development in Transition Economies', *Journal of Post Keynesian Economics*, 31: 1, (2008), pp. 3–34.

53 J.L. Love provides an excellent account of the influence of structuralist and dependency ideas in the post-war European periphery, see J.L. Love, 'Structuralism and Dependency in Peripheral Europe: Latin American Ideas in Spain and Portugal', *Latin American Research Review*, 39: 2, (2004), pp. 114–39.

54 See, for example, C. Lapavitsas et al, 'Breaking Up? A Route Out of the Eurozone Crisis', *Research on Money and Finance*, Occasional Report 3, (2011).

55 An example of such analysis for Portugal is in A. Abreu et al., *A cries, a Troika e as alternativas urgentes* (Lisbon: Tinta da China, 2013).

56 See P. Hall and D. Soskice, 'An Introduction to Varieties of Capitalism' in P. Hall and D. Soskice (eds), *Varieties of Capitalism: The Institutional Foundations of Comparative Advantage* (Oxford: Oxford University Press, 2001), pp. 1–68.

57 See, for example, A. Nölke and A. Vliegenthart, 'Enlarging the Varieties of Capitalism: The Emergence of Dependent Market Economies in East Central Europe', *World Politics*, 61: 4, (2009), pp. 670–702; C. Ban, 'From Cocktail to Dependence: Revisiting the Foundations of Dependent Market Capitalism', *Boston University Global Economic Governance Initiative*, Working Paper n. 3, (2013). Interestingly, authors who write about dependent market economies don't use dependency analysis citations or references, although some of the concepts used bear a strong resemblance.

58 Formerly socialist Eastern European countries are generally classified as 'liberal market economies' (LME) and 'coordinated market economies' (CME). The LME, typical of Baltic countries, can be described as having financialized corporate sectors, deregulated industrial relations and thin safety nets. The CME, of which Slovenia is the best example, have a strong state that is active in coordinating capital-labour relations and providing a social democratic welfare safety net, see C. Ban, 'From Cocktail to Dependence', p. 3.

59 A. Nölke and A. Vliegenthart, 'Enlarging the Varieties of Capitalism', pp. 677–9.

60 F. Beigel, 'Vida, muerte y resurrección de las "teorías de la dependencia", p. 308.

61 J. Saxe-Fernández, J. Petras, H. Veltmeyer and O. Nuñez, *Globalización, Imperialismo y Clase Social* (Buenos Aires: Lumen Humanitas, 2001).

62 See F. Beigel, 'Vida, muerte y resurrección de las "teorías de la dependencia"'.

63 A. Quijano, 'Colonialidad del poder, eurocentrismo y América Latina', in E. Lander (ed.), *La colonialidad del saber: eurocentrismo y ciencias sociales. Perspectivas Latinoamericanas* (Habana: Editorial de la Habana, 2005), pp. 122–51.

64 See, for example, among many others, S. Dow, 'Methodology in a Pluralist Environment', *Journal of Economic Methodology*, 8: 1, (2001), pp. 33–40; Id., 'Structured Pluralism', *Journal of Economic Methodology*, 11: 3, (2004), pp. 275–90; E. Fullbrook, *Pluralist Economics* (London: Zed Books, 2008); R. Holcombe, 'Pluralism vs. Heterodoxy in Economics and the Social Sciences', *The Journal of Philosophical Economics*, 1: 2, (2008), pp. 51–72; J.E. King, 'Three Arguments for Pluralism in Economics', *Post Autistic Economic Review*, 23, (January 2004), at http://www.btinternet.com/~pae_news/review/issue23.htm [accessed 25 February 2015]; T. Lawson, 'The Nature of Heterodox Economics', *Cambridge Journal of Economics*, 30: 4, (2006), pp. 483–505. Interestingly, authors actively participating in the pluralism debates do not recognize the critical Latin American development theories as precursors to the current debate, despite clear evidence to that effect.

7 Development theory and poverty

Francesco Farina

7.1 Introduction

Poverty is the human condition that for centuries has deprived the large majority of world population of the freedom to build up a decent life. At the beginning of the nineteenth century, still 84 per cent of the world's population lived in extreme poverty.[1] The Industrial Revolution – the structural change vividly described in the works of Karl Marx and in masterpieces of the English literature – provided with an income previously unemployed males who had moved to metropolitan areas. Yet, in European regions involved in the industrial take-off, deprived people for instance those under the social protection of parishes in the countryside – were eradicated from their social environment. Fast-growing urbanization caused life conditions of the poor to worsen.[2] During the nineteenth century, institutions of impersonal charity dedicated to the relief of the poor were established in many European industrialized towns. Instead, in the rest of the known world the level of impersonal charity remained very low until the twentieth century.[3] An extreme case of absence of any kind of safety net was wife-selling, the survival strategy of many Chinese destitute husbands which lasted till Chinese Communist Party came to power in 1949.

In most western countries, the economic take-off was completed at the turn of the twentieth century. From the 1930s to the 1970s, due to high growth rates and the expansion of welfare institutions, within-country income inequality and poverty have shrunk.[4] Instead, between-country inequality kept increasing, mainly because in the second half of the century the process of development languished in many ex-colonial African countries, while in China and India – the two countries with the largest population worldwide – the production of industrial and service sectors has been rocketing. At the start of the new millennium, the per capita GDP of less developed countries (LDCs), in particular of poor economies with high fertility rates, exhibits an increasing gap with respect to emerging and advanced countries.[5]

7.2 The appraisal of poverty in the economics of development

The scope of development theory has progressively expanded from the investigation of overall inter-personal income disparities towards the evaluation of life conditions of specific groups, with a special focus on individuals at the bottom of the income distribution. Theoretical and empirical research has increasingly concentrated on the economic drivers of poverty and on the personal and social consequences of being poor. Differently from advanced countries, where the persistence of poverty is the distinctive outcome of a slow and non-inclusive growth process (and more recently also of the progressive expulsion from production of unskilled workers), in LDCs the intensity of poverty has been aggravated by very low pays and meagre labour conditions, due to a fragile industrialization process in densely urbanized areas.[6]

During the 1950s, at the dawn of the modern thought on economic development, a harmonious view on economic development prevailed. The constructive intellectual mood of the decade following World War II was nicely portrayed by the Rostovian hypothesis of five stages of development through which each economic system is bound to evolve: traditional society; preconditions for take-off; take-off; drive to maturity; age of high mass consumption.[7] Accordingly, the neo-classical theory of economic growth, formalized by Robert Solow in 1956, conveyed a confident message about a smooth convergence across per capita incomes.[8] In fact, the Solovian model describes an economic system in which labour productivity increases along with the rise in production of the capital-labour ratio, and the flow of savings efficiently finances investment projects. Developing countries, by starting from a capital/labour ratio lower than in the capital abundant industrialized countries, were supposed to attain higher returns on investment, thus expanding faster, and eventually catching-up the per capita income of advanced countries. According to this optimistic view, the continuous improvement of standard of living in advanced countries trickles down in increased demand of traditional goods produced by the LDCs, possibly benefitting also their poor. Provided that increasing fiscal revenues allow the reduction in the tax rate on the rich, thus fostering the incentive to invest, the faster growth rate of backward economies should become self-sustaining.

The analytical switch from the one-sector modelling to the dualistic model proposed by Lewis marked the start of the strand of literature accounting for the industrial take-off in western countries, with the corresponding decline in the population of the countryside.[9] Kuznets interpreted statistical evidence of a shrinking GDP share of the agricultural sector, along with the rise in industrial production, as a reflection of a rapidly rising productivity in manufacturing with respect to the constant productivity in agriculture.[10] The inverted-U 'Kuznets curve' was the first attempt to present a systematic appraisal of the dualistic process of economic growth in conjunction with income disparities. After that wider wage distances have brought income inequality to a climax, a downward path of the Gini coefficient sets off, with medium and high earnings accruing to the majority of urban workers; accordingly, poverty progressively falls.

In the mushrooming literature on development of the 1950s, this harmonious description of economic development was widely shared. Only a minority among the economists were afraid that the self-regulating market forces alone could not set up a process of development heading to the expansion of well-being for all sections of the population. In fact, many episodes in economic history highlight that a too low saving rate could impede the formation of the amount of resources needed for a country to get out of poverty, thus constraining the economy in a 'vicious circle of poverty'.[11] The hypothesis was also investigated that uneven growth paths across economic sectors could generate a disequilibrium dynamics. This impediment to a smooth accumulation of physical capital would have perpetuated backward social and economic conditions.[12]

Therefore, in the development theory of the decade, poverty was still not directly examined. The analytical framework interpreting the evolution of per capita income distances across countries was forecasting a smooth process of diffusion of higher standards of living, which would unavoidably have involved the poor of developing countries. The exception was represented by the structuralist and 'dependency theory', which posited themselves on the extreme side of the explanatory spectrum by denouncing the exploitation of the poor countries by the colonialist countries and by the United States. This approach, which was started by the Argentinean economist Prebisch has been proposing a gloomy appraisal of economic development.[13] The view propounded by neo-classical growth models of a well-balanced process through which poor countries would have exited poverty, is utterly turned down. All economies are regarded as strictly interconnected independently from their per capita GDP; unequal terms of trade in international markets harshly penalize backward economies where most of the world's poor was living. The main tenet is that the whole process of market integration works against enabling the LDCs to follow an autonomous path of growth, and in favour of the rich nations' accumulation of resources and wealth.

This theoretic vision has broken in the new millennium, by stressing that protectionism – in the form of tariff and non-tariff barriers – prevents the arrival in international markets of the LDCs' products of agriculture and traditional manufacturing. The economic take-off of backward countries, which would allow the poorest population of the world to overcome bleak deprivation, is also obstructed by the WTO negotiations, where blocking coalitions are organized against the LDCs' quest for agreements establishing fair trading conditions in truly free markets.[14]

Many studies were dedicated in the 'golden years' of development theory to the long-term economic planning of the exit from poverty. Two examples of two-sector models witness that this effort has been poorly performing. The Lewis two-sector model, that considered agriculture as the static sector where over-population is bound to be absorbed by a dynamic industrial sector, could not ponder the cost abatement of innovative production methods in agriculture and apparently ignored the complementarities ruling on the interaction among sectors during the take-off process.[15] The Mahalanobis' two-sector model of growth, by giving priority to the expansion of capital-goods production, was too strongly focused on capital accumulation to construct a large consumption goods sector, thus becoming responsible for the failure of India's Second Plan of economic development.[16]

The economic thought of the second half of the past century also largely overlooked heterogeneity across social groups and regions in developing countries.

New approaches have emerged to gauge why countries belonging to the same economic area, and even endowed with the same amount of resources, follow divergent growth paths and end up with a very different incidence of poverty.[17] In the mid-1980s, households living in poor rural areas were experiencing much lower prospects of progress in well-being than seemingly identical households living in the urban areas with a much higher per capita income.[18] In the subsequent tumultuous growth process, however, the attraction of affluent metropolitan areas fostered migration from agriculture, which led the contribution to national poverty reduction to be greater in rural than in urban areas.[19] While job creation is soaring in expanding towns, where innovative sectors are concentrated and high rates of total factor productivity can be obtained, the overwhelming flow of population moving towards metropolitan areas generates new agglomerations of destitute people.

A special case is India, where a cruel caste system, has been hampering the diffusion of the economic and social benefits stemming from liberalization. This system of social hierarchy is responsible for the enduring exploitation of the Dalit people, procrastinating deep inequalities and poverty especially in rural areas.[20] Poverty reduction is a much more complex endeavour than policy-oriented models could satisfactorily theorize. Many studies are putting in doubt the conjecture of the defeat of poverty through a progressive absorption of excess population in rural areas.[21]

The most relevant research lines at the inception of the twenty-first century definitely take distance from the harmonious view on economic development and directly focus on enduring poverty within countries. The approach in terms of 'poverty traps' emphasizes the strength of self-reinforcing mechanisms, which cause poverty to persist across time.[22] Many explanations for a society being kept in a 'poverty trap' have been put forward.[23] The various research lines are fastened together by sharing the analytical concepts of 'multiple equilibria' and 'path dependence'. As for the first, the underlying principle is that the given initial conditions will determine a particular equilibrium position: a too low index of life expectancy in the population of LDCs often discourages people to save, which makes it impossible that an initially low capital stock could reach the size to make the process of economic growth sustainable.[24] As for the second, history matters: whenever given initial conditions lead to an outcome which in turn reinforces the traditional factors of development, a steady-state equilibrium establishes in the economy.

7.3 Measures of absolute and relative poverty

Starting from the second half of the 1980s, development theory eventually turned to systematic analyses of the condition of the poor as a separate topic with respect to income inequality. In a path-breaking contribution, Atkinson warned governments about the need for an informed decision on the poverty line and the appropriate index of poverty to be used for policy aims.[25] The degree of poverty is defined according to two basic measurement concepts:

1   *Absolute poverty* is the income level insufficient to get the essential goods aimed at warranting sustenance (daily calories, safe shelter, decent clothes, etc.). The World Bank first introduced in 1990 the international poverty line, by the standards of the world's poorest countries, at $1 a day, then corrected to $1.25 a day for 2005 (equivalent to $1.00 a day in 1996 US prices) and recently updated to be $1.25 and $2.50 per day. However, the same level of welfare may depend on a different prices of goods and services, and different levels of consumption needs to be attained, in different countries. In some advanced countries, though the number of people in destitution is limited, an absolute threshold set at a too low level may result inadequate with regard to the standard of living. Developing countries use different absolute poverty threshold, depending on the country's endowments of factors and natural resources, and on the prevailing views on being poor. Since the absolute measure of poverty just points to the mere survival across space and time, in principle a variation of an index of income inequality has no bearing on this indicator of deprivation.

2   *Relative poverty* considers the poor as the share of population which is below a relative poverty threshold, defined as those individuals with an income which is lower than 50 per cent or 60 per cent of the mean or median income. This index then points to spot people characterized by a wide income distance from the per capita GDP of a country. We may follow Adam Smith in identifying the social cost of inclusion, which is the social value of the sentiment of comparing oneself with dignity with his neighbours.[26] Hence, the threshold of relative poverty can be regarded as the quantitative definition of social inclusion, whereby the relative poor vary at any place and in each time that people live.

The debate is very alive about which is today the appropriate measure of relative poverty in developing countries. To determine the appropriate relative threshold, in order to devise policies oriented to shield the poor and promote social inclusion, the rate of change of per capita GDP, and the internal dynamics of the growth process, are both crucial. In fact, despite the dropping numbers of the absolutely poor, the well-being of the poor may worsen during the economic take-off of a developing country. Regarding in particular the emerging economies, which are fully involved in international trade and in globalized financial markets, the need for the relative evaluation of poverty acquires a peculiar strength, as the poor are more harshly hit in case a deep economic crisis propagates across the world economy.[27]

One problem with this measure, which is common to most processes of development, arises when the rich increase their income while the earnings of the middle class and of the poor remain constant. The incidence of poverty could then be overestimated, as the rise in the mean income has the effect to posit too many poor individuals above the relative poverty threshold. The opposite problem arises whenever the choice of the relative threshold is influenced by the evolution of inequality within the income distribution. In fact. after any rise in per capita GDP growth, the relative poverty line may be set at a too 'high' level. By using the normalization with the median income, any rise in mean income results in a disproportional weight attributed to the relative income of the poor, so that the decline in the incidence of poverty could be underestimated. Moreover, the cost of living in developing and emerging countries tends to rise more proportionally than average income, so that for the very poor the cost of social inclusion is substantial.

An alternative method of measurement – the 'income standard approach', where the line is set at the mean income of the bottom 20 per cent of the population – is not advisable. This method is plagued by two faults: the arbitrariness of both a threshold set equal for all countries, and a cut-off that in a pro-poor growth process gives to those individuals above the threshold a weight equal to that of those below.

All in all, to be considered poor one has to be below two thresholds: an *absolute* one – related to consumption needs for physical survival – and a *relative* one – related to the objective distance from the mean income, which may reflect a bleak exposure to social exclusion.[28] Furthermore, the subjective perception of relative poorness, that is the sentiment of deprivation felt in the comparison with the other persons in the community, may aggravate the condition of the needy people.[29]

The indexes most used in the empirical literature are: (i) the *head-count*, computing the incidence of the poor in the population; (ii) the *poverty gap*, computing the intensity of poverty as the ratio with respect to the poverty threshold of the sum of the poor's income distances from the poverty threshold; (iii) *the Foster–Greer–Thorbecke generalized index of poverty*, assigning an increasing weight the more individuals earn incomes below the poverty threshold.[30] It is also important to determine whether the poor is a single individual, or he belongs to a household where individual welfare is equalized by means of intra-family redistribution. Due to a higher correlation across incomes of individuals belonging to the same family, the increases of the last decades in the index of income inequality, affecting both developing and advanced economies, probably contributed to the rise in polarization between rich and poor households.

In the perspective of development theory, it is worth noticing that many individuals, that are poor for the advanced countries' standards, constitute the 'middle class' of LDCs. Considering 70 countries belonging to the developing world, the 'middle class' of these LDCs can be assumed to range between their median poverty line ($2.00 per day at 2005 PPP) and the US poverty line ($13 a day at 2005 PPP).[31] An ibrid definition is used by Birdsall for the assessment of life conditions of the middle-income individuals in developing countries.[32] She considers poor those individuals of LDCs with income between $10 a day (in 2005 PPP) – a relatively high level if compared to the global poverty line of $1.25 a day, but fairly low by OECD standards – and at or below the 95th percentile of the income distribution.

7.4 The turn to multi-dimensional well-being and poverty

Development theory has gone through three succeeding appraisals of the 'content' of poverty conditions. The literature has initially focused on 'income', and then switched to the 'basic needs' perspective, as countries may differ a lot in terms of the cost of living even though they share the same mean (or median) income in the computation of relative poverty. Eventually, development theory has opened out to non-economic and non-social drivers of prosperity and poorness, namely culture and institutions. In presenting his 'capability approach', Amartya Sen advocates the freedom of every human being to achieve his well-being by autonomously choosing his preferred sets of functionings.[33] This liberty establish the right of any person to constitute his own capability to do and be what he/she has reason to value, reflecting the person's own conception of life. By embracing the 'capability' perspective, which is multidimensional by definition, many research lines started investigating poverty as a multi-dimensional phenomenon, pointing to the various life dimensions – in addition to income – through which social exclusion manifests.[34]

The fact that the process of economic development is fundamentally multidimensional,[35] has two important implications. First, it unavoidably exerts a heterogeneous impact across people, so that well-being achievements are unevenly distributed among the various groups of the population. Second, it causes the evolution of the various dimensions of well-being to follow uneven dynamic paths. These two main characteristics of development make it essential a careful evaluation of the progress of well-being – overall, and within each dimensions – in each country year by year.

In 1990 the United Nations have presented the Human Development Index (HDI), a composite index aggregating each country's achievements in income, health, and education. By characterizing human development as the sum of these three basic dimensions, the construction of the HDI aimed to counter the paradigm of development policy put forward by the 'Washington Consensus', where the sole diffusion of market relations is credited to trigger GDP growth, in turn defeating poverty and promoting the achievement of higher levels of well-being. Instead, the United Nations stresses the importance that governments set comprehensive guidelines for development, ranging from material to non-material goals.

The present HDI is the geometric average (replacing the arithmetic average in 2010) of three indices, one for each human dimension (H): health (life expectancy), education (mean years of schooling and expected years of schooling), and income (the per capita gross national income (GNI), the standard of living dimension is valued in PPP US$ and considered as an input into the formation of capabilities):

$$HDI = (H_{health}^{(1/3)} * H_{education}^{(1/3)} * H_{income}^{(1/3)}$$

This summary measure, though inelegantly combining inputs to well-being – income is a proxy for the person's command over resources to be used to acquire goods and services – and outcomes of well-being (health, schooling), represents the first important step towards the construction of a yardstick of capability achievements.[36] To allow each of the three sub-indices to vary between zero and one, they are normalized using given upper and lower bounds. From a theoretical perspective, these bounds correspond to a 'satiation' point, beyond which additional increments do not contribute to the expansion of capabilities, and to a subsistence minimum, respectively. The goalpost for the maximum income is $75,000 (PPP), and for the minimum is $100 (PPP). This very low minimum value for per capita GNI is explained by the considerable amount of unmeasured subsistence and nonmarket production in economies close to the minimum that is not captured in the official data. Setting aside the problem of data availability, many other relevant dimensions would of course be needed to fully assess human development as a function of capabilities' achievement. Sen deliberately leaves the selection of capabilities undetermined, as it pertains to the cultural values prevailing in each society at a certain time.[37]

The aggregation method of the HDI has been questioned on the ethical ground, as the marginal rate of substitution of any non-material well-being goes up with income. Moreover, the HDI has equal weights on each dimension. Obviously, weights are needed, as it is not always possible to identify who are the 'multidimensionally' poor. In the perspective to empower the individuals to be in control of their own conception of the good, a public discussion in each LDC, heading to a democratic deliberation about the choice of a different weight for each dimension, could be a wise solution.[38] How appropriate would be their choice in each context is highly questionable, as it entails to trade-off quite dissimilar indicators (e.g., cooking with wood and the risk of child death).[39] The task of the HDI just consists in exploiting the more comprehensive information delivered by a multidimensional index. The computed value should not be interpreted as a sort of social welfare function to be maximized, but only as an indicator of the achievement of capabilities.

A weakness of the HDI is its lack of consideration for cross-correlation among dimensions. Since higher levels of per capita GDP usually come together with high levels of health and education, the 'endogeneity problem' makes the causality links among these three dimensions of well-being hard to detect. While a lower income inequality has the likely effect to reduce the dispersion index of the other two dimensions, a substantial part of the impact of better health and education on the HDI is absorbed in the fall of the Gini index of income inequality, as improved skills and quality of life have the side-effect to boost the earnings particularly of the poor. The elasticity of a country's HDI to income inequality may then turn out to be much higher than the elasticity to the health and the education inequality. Which one out of the double direction of causality prevails across the three dimensions is central to the understanding of the many ways in which the attainments in terms of multidimensional well-being spread over in the relief of poverty conditions.

In his seminal 1976 paper, Amartya Sen objected to the uni-dimensional approach to the measurement of poverty. In proposing the ordinal measurement of poverty, he put forward the two main issues to be tackled by any index of poverty: (i) identification (i.e. a poverty line, so to answer the question: 'Who is poor?') for the purpose of targeting; (ii) aggregation (i.e. a poverty measure, so to answer the question: 'How much poverty?') for the purpose of evaluating and monitoring. Granted that poverty is tightly connected to multidimensional well-being, the United Nations has developed a Human Poverty Index (HPI), first published in the Human Development Report of 1997 as a composite indicator of the standard of living of a country, complementing the Human Development Index. The background paper for this Human Development Report was 'Concepts of Human Development and Poverty: A Multidimensional Perspective' by Anand and Sen.[40] They introduced non-material sources of deprivation in the construction of the HPI, but the 'multi-dimensionally' poor people could not be identified.

By positing the concept of poverty into the space of capabilities the 1998 Nobel Laureate wanted to signal that development is a crucial aspect of the interactions between the individual and society, and poor individuals are disproportionally present in backward economies.[41] On the one hand, society should feel committed to set up the appropriate conditions to warrant the person's right to 'being and doing'. The cost of social inclusion consists in overcoming not only limited consumption opportunities due to low income, but also precarious health, poor education, inadequate housing, insecure work, deprivation of social identity, and deficiency of political power.[42] On the other hand, this social responsibility does not freed, but on the contrary magnifies, the person's responsibility to pursuing his own substantive freedom.[43]

To establish a poverty line entails translating the *absolute* notion of capabilities in a *relative* approach in the spaces of income and commodities.[44] Empirical evidence supports this methodological approach. Research work conducted on data of developing countries found that a high percentage of people are deprived of essential capabilities while not being income-poor.[45] Objective non-income determinants of social exclusion are represented by the deprivation of the educational level needed to get a permanent job, as well as of some social rights – such as the lack of participation in the national system of health care, and/or of a public pension due to the failure in means-testing.[46] Subjective non-income determinants of social exclusion consist in the perception by the individual either of his lack of access to the community's functionings, or of his exclusion from fundamental aspects of social life[47].

The research line on multidimensional poverty has much contributed to the improvement of development theory, in particular by providing the basis for the design of anti-poverty policies. To identify the multi-dimensional poor two approaches have been proposed. At one extreme, the 'union approach' identifies the poor as the individuals who are deprived at least in one dimension.[48] At the other extreme, the 'intersection approach' identifies the poor as the deprived in every dimensions[49]. The arbitrary number of dimensions – as well as their quality – are decisive for the assessment of which between these two approaches leads to precisely detecting the poor. Cases of mismatch between uni-dimensional and multi-dimensional poverty manifest in the comparison between non-poor and poor countries. The failure in identifying the households below the multidimensional poverty line – known as the 'exclusion error', consisting in the percentage of people who are not income poor but 'multi-dimensionally' poor – is higher for poor countries. The same results apply with the wealth indicator.[50]

Alkire and Foster put forward the M_0 methodology, in order to generate more informative multi-dimensional indexes being mid-way between the union and the intersection approaches.[51] As a fall-out of this research work, in 2010 the UNDP Human Development Report Office and the Oxford Poverty and Human Development Initiative (OPHI) have released a Multidimensional Poverty Index (MPI) for developing countries. This index, covering 109 countries since 2011, combines the number and the intensity of overlapping human deprivations in health, education and standard of living. On the theoretical ground, this MPI is more informative than the HPI, as the M_0 allows the evaluation of multi-dimensional deprivation across dimensions for the same individual. The joint distribution of deprivations is a very relevant information, which is crucial to the assessment of the success of anti-poverty programmes.[52] The MPI indexes promise to become a valuable tool in devising special-purpose public policies to counteract a worsening quality of life caused by the cumulative cross-dimensional impact of multiple deprivations on poverty conditions.[53] All surveys show increasing shares of population enjoying a better health and a higher education the higher is per capita GDP in the country.

For the devising of development policies, the MPI has to abide by two important characteristics: (i) the computability of intensity of deprivation, as the poorest of the poor could be targeted; (ii) the decomposability by regions and population subgroups, as each dimension of poverty acquires a different weight in different socio-economic contexts and for each different aggregate of individuals, and also modifies across time as the process of economic development evolves. However, there is a trade-off between constructing a multidimensional measure sensitive to the distribution of deprivations and also allowing for decomposability by dimension; similarly, substitutability and complementarity between dimensions cannot be simultaneously taken into account.

The so-called 'welfarist approach' to relative poverty is conceived in the perspective to implement the social norm of a decorous life prompting the above mentioned sentiment of dignity of the person in society. The tenet is that the exit from relative poverty corresponds to rendering the social cost of inclusion negligible. A 'weakly relative poverty' threshold has also been proposed, where an objective appraisal of 'equal treatment in consumption' complements the varying measure of the minimum cost of social inclusion in different countries.[54]

Development theory has recently attempted to widen the temporal scope of poverty conditions. The recent research field on 'vulnerability to poverty' points to analysing – from the vantage point of human behaviour under uncertainty - how a hostile social and/or natural environment could activate impoverishment. The concept of vulnerability naturally refers to individuals suffering from exposure to macroeconomic and microeconomic risks to a much higher degree than the median individual – e.g., a remarkable probability to be hit by a negative shock heading to deprivation, the excessive length of spells of income deprivation, a high frequency of severe diseases and natural disasters, the everyday dramatic problems of living in areas with criminality and inadequate social capital in general. Hence, the measurement of vulnerability is at the cross-road of the contribution of a variety of research fields, ranging from biophysics, to epidemiology, anthropology, sociology, natural resources and environmental studies.

7.5 The theoretical debate on growth, inequality and poverty

A massive series of economic models strive to investigate the causality nexuses among the growth rate, per capita GDP growth, income inequality, and poverty, in order to identify which linkages prove to be robust. Further complications stem from the measurement of poverty reduction, as consumption from household surveys increases less rapidly than consumption computed in national accounts, particularly for large countries such as China and India.[55] However, the improvement in data availability (in particular, regarding national poverty lines, representative samples of household consumption and prices) indicates that the incidence of absolute poverty the developing world has fallen since the early 1980s.[56] International organizations fighting famine, diseases, under-nourishing, illiteracy, as well as governments and NGOs, are now endowed with sophisticated indicators, pointing to a global relative poverty measure for the less developed world, similarly to the '1 US dollar a day' absolute measure in the dimension of income.

Let us commence by analysing the relationship between GDP growth and poverty as mediated by an increase in per capita income. An influential 'free-market' view highlights that one-half of reductions in both absolute and relative poverty has to be traced back to a lift in the average income of a country. Since 'a rising tide lifts all boats', one should come to the conclusion that 'growth is good for the poor'.[57] Given that the free functioning of markets is credited to boost GDP growth, the deregulation of the economic system is considered the pre-condition for the result of a decrease in poverty. In this perspective, any pro-poor growth strategy should point to the protection of property rights and to liberalization reforms opening developing economies to international trade.[58]

A caveat to be moved towards this cavalier view is that the cross-correlation among the other drivers of well-being matters probably to a greater extent in the developing world: poor health, low education, lack of infrastructure and corrupted government are highly detrimental to work and investment, thus hindering growth. Also because of the ideological presumption of a positive influence of free market policies on poverty reduction, anti-poverty programmes have been exposed to many sources of failure ever since their inception. The tenet that the diffusion of market relations would have delivered a harmonious exit from underdevelopment, together with the 'catching-up' view of neo-classical growth models, led to an excessive emphasis on advancement of industrialization as such. The actual natural, social and political conditions in which the industrialization process was deployed were largely ignored. This flawed approach found its formalization in too narrowly-conceived development models. Economic history indicates that courageous agrarian reforms in developing countries, redistributing the land to peasants and agricultural workers, are effective in reducing also income inequality and poverty, thus constituting a growth-strengthening factor.[59] An important 'political economy' problem, underrated by the literature on 'poverty traps', is 'policy inconsistency'. Redistributive policies are badly needed in areas where the incidence of extreme poverty is high, and then wealth and income dispersion are high as well. Policy inconsistency stems from the high tax rate implied by the huge amount of the funding of redistributive programmes, which is harshly opposed by most powerful and well-off social groups.

The Dollar and Kraay interpretation, which is reminiscent of the 'trickle down' view of development mentioned in section 7.2, is still under scrutiny, as the empirical evidence on which it is built appears to be fuzzy. By proposing a new methodology to track low incomes, Foster and Székely find that the income of the poor does not increase one-for-one with the mean income, as the estimated growth elasticity is not significantly different from zero.[60] An initially low per capita income does not seem to entail an 'advantage of backwardness' for developing countries, as it may instead hold back the process of poverty reduction.[61] The other way round, due the low consumption of the poor weakening aggregate demand, a high initial poverty rate gravely dampens GDP growth, which in turn is bound to procrastinate a low level of per capita income, probably keeping acute the incidence of absolute poverty.

Therefore, the question is: why should a higher mean income, triggered by a raise in the growth rate, instead of a reduction in the index of income inequality, the most prominent tool to defeat poverty?

The answer of the 'free-market' view contends that a higher – and not a lower – income inequality is conducive to poverty reduction. Granted that the propensity to save of the rich is higher than that of the poor, the larger is the income share accruing to the rich, the higher the saving ratio and capital accumulation. Yet, this narrative is not confirmed by statistical estimates. The 'absolute' Gini index – which is based on absolute differences in incomes, not normalized by the mean – enlightens the presence of a trade-off between income inequality and poverty reduction.[62] Empirical evidence extensively confirms the hypothesis that the more right-skewed is the income distribution, the stronger will be the impact of a fall in income inequality in terms of poverty reduction.[63] For example, when the Gini falls from a value as high as 0.55 to the value of 0.45, a drop in poverty of more than 15 points in ten years ensues.[64] According to household surveys, whatever the impact of GDP growth on income disparities, the higher is the initial income inequality of a country, the lower the percentage of growth which trickles down to the poor.[65] In fact, at the turn of the millennium, the Chinese provinces with initial relatively high inequality have experienced a much slower increase in the incomes of the poor, due both to lower growth and a lower growth elasticity of poverty reduction.

Let us then turn to the relationship between GDP growth and poverty as mediated by income inequality. Since income inequality is very much correlated with essential drivers of economic growth – the incentives to trust and to cooperate – that are very weak in developing countries, a GDP expansion triggered by wide income disparities could not promote a decline in poverty conditions. Moreover, an initially high growth rate could not reduce income inequality, but provoke a higher Gini coefficient, due to widening absolute income distances at the two income tails (an upward hike in top incomes and/or a fall in the incomes of the poor) and some 'churning' in the middle of the income distribution. In fact, in spite of per capita income growing on average of 6,7 per cent per year, income inequality has risen in China between 1990 and 2009, due to the relative decline in the average income of the poor (the growth rate was only 5 per cent per year in the bottom 40 per cent of population, so that the income share of the bottom 40 per cent declined from 20.2 per cent to 14.4 per cent).

Therefore, poverty seem to be positively correlated to variations in income inequality, but the crucial role played by the level of income inequality makes the causality link going from growth to poverty difficult to assess. The main message conveyed by the literature is that the impact of growth on poverty reduction is severely hampered by a high level of income inequality. The empirical evidence showing that the initial level of income inequality is a good predictor of a low growth-elasticity of poverty reduction, gravely undermines the Dollar-Kraay interpretation. Due to the limited direct impact of growth on poverty, no 'trickled down' effect can be taken for granted. Economic growth is then not always 'good for the poor'.

Since any strategy aimed at lowering income inequality by targeting the purchasing power of a large number of deprived people should be effective in improving the standard of living, many schools of thought, both in economics and in social theory, advocate public policies directly orientated towards poverty reduction.[66]

Also the causality nexus going from income inequality to the growth rate could influence the exit from poverty. Regressions conducted on the cross-section data show a negative correlation between income inequality and growth, whereas the difference-based estimates conducted on time-series present a positive correlation.[67] These opposite results are mainly driven by the too many omitted variables which cannot find a place in the regressions, also because of the 'endogeneity problem'. Recent research work fruitfully puts forward the hypothesis of non-linearity in the nexus going from the income distribution to the growth rate. This important finding comes out both in cross-section and in within-country quantitative estimates. As for the first, Banerjee and Duflo found no relationship between inequality and growth for their whole bunch of countries, but broking up the sample a negative relationship emerged for the poor countries, and a positive relationship for the rich countries.[68] As for the second, empirical estimates investigating the impact on the growth across deciles rate (instead of just looking at the impact of the aggregate income distribution) indicate that the sign of the correlation depends on the decile of reference. The sign is positive for the top incomes – as a raise in 'high incomes' boosts the incentive to invest. The sign is negative for the 'low incomes' and the poor – as a falling low income tends to dampen consumption demand more than proportionally.[69]

The finding that each different portion of the income distribution exerts its own specific influence on GDP growth has been bonded with the timing of development policies.[70] A positive correlation between income inequality and growth points to the short or medium run, as income concentration boosts start-ups and innovation prompting the take-off of development. Instead, a negative correlation between income inequality and growth points to a long run development strategy aimed to overcome the negative influence on the growth rate of a high distance from the median income at the bottom-end of the distribution. The implication is that the design of anti-poverty policies has to cope with the presence of multiple equilibria along the development process: at every initial level of income dispersion seems to correspond a different impact of GDP growth on poverty.

The Welfare State typically represents the long-term economic institution which under appropriate conditions, by enhancing growth through the redistributive impact of public education and health care, can shield the middle and low income individuals – in particular in LDCs – from falling in poverty and deprivation. The message as for the influence of the bottom of the income distribution upon the growth rate is that in the long run a negative correlation between income inequality and growth prevails: the less distant is the income level at the bottom from the middle class, the higher GDP growth. The previous hint of a positive relationship between income inequality and poverty is then confirmed as for the bottom portion of the distribution: a higher income level of the poor is good for growth.

Another important aspect of the link between economic growth and poverty stems from empirical evidence showing the lack of further GDP expansion exhibited by the overwhelming majority of middle-income countries during the second half of the past century. The World Bank estimates that of 101 middle-income economies in 1960, only 13 became high income by 2008. Though this paradoxical finding is still to be fully understood, once the developing countries reach middle-income levels, in the light of the Lewis two-sector model the pool of rural workers drains, wages begin to rise, productivity growth from sectoral reallocation and technology catch-up reduces, and competitiveness is dampened. Therefore, the concept of vulnerability – that is a high exposure to job uncertainty and income volatility in case of negative macroeconomic shocks – looms crucial for the middle class of developing countries. When these economies come across the 'middle-income trap', income insecurity is bound to undermine well-being and aspirations of mean and low income individuals. Due to the mutual reinforcing among a series of factors of risk, these people suffer from a rising exposure to lowering multidimensional well-being.

The exposure to poverty of the middle class is then not only indicated by the increasing polarization in advanced countries, as manifested in the recent turn to bimodality of the kernel of income distribution for countries such as the United States and the United Kingdom, but is a severe problem also for developing countries. Since the income vulnerability of the middle class of these countries could easily turn out in episodes of poverty, eventually making more and more difficult to restore their previous stage of well-being, risk exposure is definitely a central component of poverty.[71] In the light of the 'fundamental laws of capitalism' put forward by Piketty, the trend of the last decades towards an increase of wealth inequality in advanced countries, even larger than the increase in income inequality, represents a gloomy signal for the future income convergence by developing countries.[72] The possible fall in income levels of the middle income people of developing countries could be also aggravated by the virtual absence of the safety net represented, for the middle class of advanced countries, by the stock – albeit declining – of real estate and financial wealth.

7.6 Recent views on institutions and poverty in developing countries

In 2012, considering an international poverty line of $1.25 a day (at 2005 PPP), still 1.2 billion people in the world live in poverty. The uni-dimensional and the multidimensional poverty indexes hand over similar results for the middle-income and the low-income countries. Though more poor people live in middle-income than in low-income countries, the incidence of both income poverty and multidimensional poverty is much higher in low-income countries.[73] Developing countries distinguish with respect to advanced countries for their much higher ratio between personalized and impersonal (market) transactions, where the former are less likely to be supported by the 'rule of law'.

A large strand of literature argues that the cultural heritage of the colonial period and the poor quality of present political institutions is the main obstacle to developing countries reducing poverty. However, this agreeable remark is hardly a blueprint for devising the most appropriate political organization to sustain a development process. In India, the largest democracy worldwide, poor peasants have been benefitting from limited programmes for insurance against disastrous shocks (famine, floods, etc.). In the authoritarian Cina, anti-poverty programmes and extensive market-oriented agrarian reforms, such as the decollectivization of agriculture since 1978, have been privileged by the Communist regime.[74] Therefore, empirical evidence is inconclusive about a democratic or an authoritarian regime being better in making fast poverty reduction in countries with a high percentage of poor. A sensible hypothesis is that in sustaining the catching-up by backward economies a democratic regime is more fitting to foster innovation, which is based on individual attitudes to risk and invest, while an authoritarian regime more fitting for the diffusion of technology, which requires a well-organized social environment.[75] However, it is wise to forecast that the advance of the poor's well-being in backward countries will depend upon the difficult task to improve the functioning of democratic political institutions. In many LDCs the representative roles are occupied by politicians who use political power for their self-interest (in particular, for the appropriation of foreign aid and the transfers of international charities), while it is small the size of the middle class committed to reforms, which is often also excluded from political power. Especially in former-colonial countries, the political institutions are not 'inclusive' (i.e., oriented to the upgrading of the population standard of living), but essentially 'extractive', as they are plagued by corruption.[76]

The fragility of governmental institutions in developing countries is detrimental to the industrial take-off, with the start-up of small and medium enterprises on which the growth process fundamentally relies. While an increase in the employment rate among the low-skill labour force is the most valuable policy to reduce the intensity and the ratio of poverty in LDCs, the missing or inefficient defence of property rights determines a low incentive for entrepreneurs to invest and risk.[77]

The neo-classical formula for economic development, that is the creation of a full-fledged market economy, has the limit of downplaying the need to set up an adequate system of social protection. Given that the interaction between the poor's low income and a low provision of *in-kind* benefits severely hinders economic development in poor countries, a 'pure' free-market economy is inadequate to guaranteeing that an autonomous process of development would start and acceler-ate the exit from poverty. The view is increasingly shared that the emergence of more sound social norms and cultural values is more effective in boosting socio-economic development of any creation of formal laws by top political leaders.[78] In non-poor countries, public institutions render the low incomes not deprived in some dimensions of well-being, so that the incidence of the multidimensional – but not income – poor is relatively lower than in poor countries. In developing countries, the lack of State provision of public and merit goods compels the poor to use their limited savings to cope with basic non-material needs, thus also hin-dering both the financing and the incentive to invest.

Which one between the two opposite development strategies aimed to the poor – 'perfect targeting' or 'basic income' – is the best? Should some kind of intermedi-ate solutions, for example 'conditional cash transfers', be preferred? Are special instruments needed to fight child poverty? The answer to these questions first of all depends on the expected effectiveness of monetary transfers to cope with the consumption needs of households, and with their ability to finance their children's health and schooling. Indeed, cross-country comparisons indicate that people with the same income achieve a lower well-being the more unequal is the income dis-tribution in their country.[79] The fact is that income inequality and the magnifying impact of inequality of opportunity on poverty reinforce each other. The higher is income inequality in a poor country, the more 'multi-dimensionally' deprived is the poor. A too unequal income distribution procrastinates inequality of opportu-nities, in turn impeding the improvement in capabilities by the poor.

The design and the implementation of development policies also depends on which equilibrium, among multiple social equilibria, society is stuck in.[80] The question is much debated about whether a sustainable development process could rely on domestic private and public sectors forces alone (Sachs, 2005).[81] The World Bank has recently underlined that economic and social development pro-gresses mainly through the evolution of mental models. Development policies should then take issue with the circumstance that backward societies are stuck mainly because the poor are too stressed people, who are short of the capacity to make correct and far-sighted decisions.[82]

It is now clear that the strategies build up by development theorists have to be implemented in tight connection with the real experience of the international agencies working on the territory. Provided that appropriate instruments are deployed in order to counteract corrupted governments in countries receiving the foreign aid, the role of international organizations emerges as decisive for the market economy in poor countries be backed by institutions of social protection fostering socio-economic development. A big-push centred on a huge increase in development aid to poor countries is certainly needed. The key question is that a clear method of governance is still lacking about the coordination of aid programmes of international organizations with the anti-poverty policies organized by the governments of backward economies. The proposal has been set off that in developing countries aid agencies should behave as venture capitalists and fund start-up companies progressively, in order not to jeopardize the incentive to the profitability of private investors.[83]

The World Bank approach to aid programmes promoting the poverty-reducing growth points to negotiations between advanced and developing countries in order to strengthen the participation of the latter to international markets and, more generally, to further the respect of the 'rule of law' as the inescapable condition for the implementation of investment projects.[84] In order to avoid that anti-poverty programs could be captured by the elite groups of the central government, the decentralized organization of aid may be preferred even at the cost of the efficiency of interregional resource allocation.[85] Aid programmes should aim at financing the poor countries' investment in human capital, so to help them accomplishing the achievements of a higher education among the young population, and of free health care to the poor.[86]

Many progresses have already been done. The Millennium Development Goals launched by the United Nations in 1990 have been the most successful global anti-poverty push in history. The world reached the poverty reduction target five years ahead of schedule. In developing regions, from 1990 to 2010 about 700 million fewer people lived in conditions of extreme poverty, and the proportion of people living on less than $1.25 a day fell from 47 per cent to 22 per cent. However, one in eight people worldwide remain hungry; too many women die in childbirth; more than 2.5 billion people lack improved sanitation facilities, of which one billion continue to practice open defecation, a major health and environmental hazard. Indeed, in fighting poverty the road ahead is still long and uncertain.

Notes

1 A. Maddison, *The World Economy. A Millennial Perspective* (Paris: OECD, 2001); F. Bourguignon and C. Morrison 'Income among world citizens: 1820–1992', *American Economic Review*, 92: 4, (2002), pp. 727–744.
2 M. Ravallion 'The Idea of Antipoverty Policy' (NBER Working Paper n. 19210, 2013).
3 A. Greif and G. Tabellini, *The Clan and the City: Sustaining Cooperation in China and Europe* (mimeo, Stanford, 2012).
4 T. Piketty, *Le capital au 21e siècle* (Paris: Seuil, 2013).
5 B. Milanovic, *Worlds Apart: Measuring International and Global Inequality* (Princeton: Princeton University Press, 2005).
6 E. Thorbecke, 'The Evolution of the Development Doctrine, 1950–2005' (UNU – WIDER, Research Paper No.155, 2006).
7 W.W. Rostow, *The Process of Economic Growth* (New York: Norton & Company, 1952), see Chapter 1 above.

8 R.M. Solow, 'A Contribution to the Theory of Economic Growth', *Quarterly Journal of Economics*, 70: 1, (1956), pp. 65–94.

9 W.A. Lewis, 'Economic Development with Unlimited Supplies of Labor', *Manchester School*, 22, (1954) pp. 139–191, see Chapter 4 above.

10 S. Kuznets, 'Economic Growth and Income Inequality', *American Economic Review*, 45, (1955), pp. 1–28.

11 R. Nurkse, *Problems of Capital Formation in Underdeveloped Countries* (Oxford: Oxford University Press, 1953).

12 G. Myrdal, Economic Theory and Under-Developed Regions (London: Duckworth, 1957).

13 R. Prebisch, 'The Economic Development of Latin America and its principal problems' (27 April 1950), New York: ECLA, at http://repositorio.cepal.org/bitstream/handle/11362/29973/002.df?sequence=1 [accessed 10 November 2014], see Chapters 5 and 6 above.

14 I.M. Wallerstein, *World-Systems Analysis: An Introduction*, (Durham N.C.: Duke University Press, 2004).

15 W.A. Lewis, 'Economic Development with Unlimited Supplies of Labor', *Manchester School*, 22, (1954) pp. 139–191.

16 P. Mahalanobis, 'Some Observations on the Process of the Growth of National Income', *Sankhrya. The Indian Journal of Statistics*, 12: 4, (1953), pp. 307–312.

17 D. Acemoglu and J.A. Robinson, *Why Nations Fail: The Origins of Power, Prosperity, and Poverty* (New York: Crown Publisher, 2012).

18 M. Ravallion, 'A Poverty-Inequality Trade-off?', (World Bank Policy Research Working Paper No. 3579, Washington DC: World Bank, 2005).

19 M. Ravallion and S. Chen, 'China's (Uneven) Progress Against Poverty', *Journal of Development Economics*, 82: 1, (2007), pp. 1–42.

20 J. Drèze and A. Sen, *An Uncertain Glory: India and its Contradictions* (Princeton: Princeton University Press, 2013).

21 P. Collier, *The Bottom Billion: Why the Poorest Countries are Failing and What Can Be Done About It* (Oxford: Oxford University Press, 2007).

22 C. Azariadis and J. Stachursky, 'Poverty Traps' in P. Aghion and S. Durlauf (eds), *Handbook of Economic Growth* (Amsterdam: North-Holland, 2005), pp. 295–384.

23 S.N. Durlauf, 'The Memberships Theory of Inequality: Ideas and Implications' in E.S. Brezis, P. Temin (eds), *Elites, Minorities, and Economic Growth* (Amsterdam: Elsevier, 1999), pp. 161–177; P. Collier, *The Bottom Billion*; S. Chantarat and C.B. Barrett, 'Social Network Capital, Economic Mobility and Poverty Traps', *Journal of Economic Inequality*, 10, (2012), pp. 299–342; S. Bowles, S. N. Durlauf and K. Hoff (eds), *Poverty Traps* (Princeton: Princeton University Press, 2006); in particular: C. Azariadis, 'The Theory of Poverty Traps. What Have We learned?', pp. 17–40; S. Bowles, 'Institutional Poverty Traps', pp. 116–138; S. N. Durlauf, 'Groups, Social Influences, and Inequality' pp. 141–175.

24 C. Azariadis, 'The Theory of Poverty Traps. What Have We learned?', in S. Bowles, S. N. Durlauf and K. Hoff (eds), *Poverty Traps* (Princeton: Princeton University Press, 2006), pp. 17–40.

25 A.B. Atkinson, 'On the Measurement of Poverty', *Econometrica*, 55, (1987), pp. 749–764.

26 A. Smith, *The Wealth of Nations*, A. Skinner (ed.), (Harmondsworth: Penguin [1776] 1974), Book V, ch.2.

27 S. Chen and M. Ravallion, 'More Relatively-Poor People in a Less Absolutely-Poor World', *Review of Income and Wealth*, 59: 1, (2013), pp. 1–28.

28 A.B. Atkinson and F. Bourguignon, 'Poverty and Inclusion from a World Perspective', in J. Stiglitz and P.A. Muet (eds) *Governance, Equity and Global Markets* (Oxford, Oxford University Press, 2001), pp. 151–164.

29 W.G. Runciman, *Relative Deprivation and Social Justice* (London: Routledge and Kegan Paul, 1966).

30 J. Foster, J. Greer and E. Thorbecke 'A Class of Decomposable Poverty Measures', *Econometrica*, 52, (1984), pp. 761–765.

31 M. Ravallion, 'The Developing World's Bulging (but Vulnerable) Middle Class', *World Development*, 38: 4, (2010a), pp. 445–454.

32 N. Birdsall, 'The (Indispensable) Middle Class in Developing Countries; or, The Rich and the Rest, Not the Poor and the Rest' (Center for Global Development, Working Paper n. 207: Washington (DC), 2010).

33 A.K. Sen, *Commodities and Capabilities* (Amsterdam: North Holland, 1985a).

34 S. Anand and A. Sen 'Concepts of Human Development and Poverty: A Multidimensional Perspective' (New York: UNDP, 1997).

35 B. Nolan and C. Whelan, 'On the Multi-dimensionality of Poverty and Social Exclusion', in J. Micklewright and S. Jenkins (eds), *Inequality and Poverty Reexamined* (Oxford: Oxford University Press, 2007), pp. 146–165.

36 UNDP, *Human Development Report. Sustainability and Equity: A Better Future for All* (New York: United Nations, 2011).

37 E. Chiappero-Martinetti and S. Moroni, 'An Analytical Framework for Conceptualizing Poverty and Re-examining the Capability Approach', *Journal of Socio-Economics*, 36, (2007), pp. 360–375.

38 A.K. Sen, 'Well-being, Agency and Freedom. The Dewey Lectures 1984', *Journal of Philosophy,* 82: 4, (1985b), pp. 169–221.

39 M. Ravallion, 'On Multidimensional Indices of Poverty', *Journal of Economic Inequality*, 9, (2011), pp. 235–248.

40 S. Anand and A. Sen, 'Concepts of Human Development and Poverty: A Multidimensional Perspective' (New York: UNDP, 1997).

41 A.K. Sen, *Commodities and Capabilities* (Amsterdam: North Holland, 1985a).

42 A.K. Sen, *Inequality Re-examined* (Oxford: Clarendon Press, 1992).

43 A.K. Sen, *Development as freedom* (New York: A.K. Knopf, 1999).

44 A.K. Sen, 'Poor, Relatively Speaking', *Oxford Economic Papers*, 35: 2, (1983), pp. 153–169.

45 S. Franco, 'Different Concepts of Poverty', in F. Stewart, R. Saith, B and Harris-White (eds), *Defining Poverty in the Developing World* (Basingtoke: Palgrave Macmillan, 2007), pp. 160–197.

46 S. Chakravarty and C. D'Ambrosio, 'Polarization Orderings of Income Distributions', *Review of Income and Wealth*, 56: 1, (2010), pp. 47–64.

47 F. Bourguignon and S. Chakravarty, 'The Measurement of Multidimensional Poverty' *Journal of Economic Inequality*, 1: 1, (2003), pp. 25–49.

48 A.B. Atkinson, 'Multidimensional deprivation: contrasting social welfare and counting approaches', *Journal of Economic Inequality*, 1, (2003), pp. 51–65; J.Y. Duclos, D. Sahn and S.D. Younger, 'Robust Multidimensional Spatial Poverty Comparisons in Ghana, Madagascar, and Uganda', *The World Bank Economic Review*, 20: 1, (2006), pp. 91–113.

49 S. Alkire and J. Foster, 'Counting and Multidimensional Poverty Measurement', *Journal of Public Economics*, 95: 7, (2011a), pp. 476–487.

50 S. Alkire and M.E. Santos, 'Acute Multidimensional Poverty: A New Index for Developing Countries' (OPHI Working. Paper Series N. 38, 2010).

51 S. Alkire and J. Foster, 'Counting and Multidimensional Poverty Measurement' (OPHI Working Paper N. 7, University of Oxford, 2007).

52 S. Alkire and J. Foster, 'Understandings and Misunderstandings of Multidimensional Poverty Measurement', *Journal of Economic Inequality*, 9, (2011b), pp. 289–314.

53 J. Stiglitz, A. Sen and J.P. Fitoussi, Report by the Commission on the Measurement of Economic Performance and Social Progress, (2009) in http://www.stiglitz-sen-fitoussi.fr/en/index.htm [accessed 12 September 2014].

54 M. Ravallion and S. Chen, 'Weakly Relative Poverty', *Review of Economics and Statistics*, 93:4, (2011), pp. 1251–61.

55 A.S. Deaton, 'Measuring Poverty in a Growing World (or Measuring Growth in a Poor World)', *Review of Economics and Statistics*, 87: 1, (2005), pp. 1–19.

56 S. Chen and M. Ravallion, 'The Developing World Is Poorer Than We Thought, but No Less Successful in the Fight Against Poverty' *Quarterly Journal of Economics*, 125: 4, (2010), pp. 1577–1625.

57 D. Dollar and A. Kraay, 'Growth Is Good for the Poor', *Journal of Economic Growth*, 7: 1, (2002), pp. 195–225.

58 A. Kraay, 'When Is Growth Pro-Poor? Evidence from a Panel of Countries', *Journal of Economic Development*, 80, (2006), pp. 198–227.

59 A. Alesina and D. Rodrik, 'Distributive Politics and Economic Growth', *Quarterly Journal of Economics*, 108, (1994), pp. 465–90.

60 J. Foster and M. Székely, 'Is Economic Growth Good for the Poor? Tracking Low Incomes Using General Means,', *International Economic Review*, 49: 4, (2008) pp. 1143–1172.

61 M. Ravallion 'Why Don't We See Poverty Convergence?', *American Economic Review*, 102: 1, (2012), pp. 504–523.

62 M. Ravallion, 'A Poverty-Inequality Trade-off?', (World Bank Policy Research Working Paper No. 3579, Washington DC: World Bank, 2005).

63 M. Ravallion and S. Chen, 'China's (Uneven) Progress Against Poverty', *Journal of Development Economics*, 82: 1, (2007), pp. 1–42.

64 F. Bourguignon, 'The Growth Elasticity of Poverty Reduction: Explaining Heterogeneity Across Countries and Time Periods', in T. Eicher and S. Turnovsky (eds), *Growth and Inequality*, (Cambridge, MA: MIT Press, 2003), pp. 3–27.

65 M. Ravallion, 'Can High Inequality Developing Countries Escape Absolute Poverty?', *Economics Letters*, 56, (1997), pp. 51–57; M. Ravallion, 'Inequality is Bad for the Poor', in S.P. Jenkins and J. Micklewright (eds), *Inequality and Poverty Re-examined* (Oxford: Oxford University Press, 2007), pp. 37–61.

66 P. Bardhan, S. Bowles and H. Gintis, 'Wealth Inequality, Credit Constraints, and Economic Performance' in A. Atkinson and F. Bourguignon (eds), *Handbook of Income Distribution* (Dortrecht: North-Holland 2000), pp. 541–603; A.V. Banerjee and E. Duflo 'Growth Theory through the Lens of Economic Development' in P. Aghion and S. Durlauf (eds), *Handbook of Economic Growth*, Vol. 1 (Amsterdam: North-Holland, 2005), pp. 473–552; R. Wilkinson and K. Pickett (2009), *The Spirit Level, Why Greater Equality makes Societies Stronger* (New York: Bloomsbury Press).

67 K. Forbes, 'A Reassessment of the Relationship between Inequality and Growth', *American Economic Review*, 90: 4, (2000), pp. 869–887.

68 A.V. Banerjee and E. Duflo 'Inequality and Growth: What Can the Data Say?', *Journal of Economic Growth*, 8: 3, (2003), pp. 267–299.

69 S. Voitchovsky, 'Does the Profile of Income Inequality Matter for Economic Growth? Between the Effects of Inequality on Different Parts of Income Distribution', *Journal of Economic Growth*, 10: 1, (2005), pp. 273–296.

70 D. Halter, M. Oechslin and J. Zweimüller, *Inequality and Growth: The Neglected Time Dimension* (Institute for Empirical Research in Economics: University of Zurich, Working Paper n. 507, 2011).

71 J. Morduch, 'Poverty and Vulnerabilty', *American Economic Review*, 84: 2, (1994), pp. 221–225.

72 T. Piketty, *Le capital au 21e siècle*.

73 S. Alkire, J.M. Roche and A. Sumner, 'Where Do the World's Multidimensionally Poor People Live?' (OPHI Working Paper 61, 2013).

74 M. Ravallion, 'Do Poorer Countries Have Less Capacity for Redistribution?', *Journal of Globalization and Development*, 1: 2, (2010b), pp. 1–29.

75 J.D. Sachs, *The End of Poverty* (London: Penguin Books, 2006).

76 D. Acemoglu, S. Johnson and J.A. Robinson 'Reversal of Fortune: Geography and Institutions in the Making of the Modern World Income Distribution', *Quarterly Journal of Economics*, 117: 4, (2002), pp. 1231–1294; D. Acemoglu and J. A. Robinson *Why Nations Fail*.

77 G. Abed and S. Gupta (eds), *Governance, Corruption, and Economic Performance*, (Washington DC: International Monetary Fund, 2002); R. Nallari and B. Griffith, *Understanding Growth and Poverty. Theory, Policy, and Empirics*, Washington: World Bank, 2011).

78 M. Ravallion, 'The Idea of Antipoverty Policy'.

79 R. Wilkinson and K. Pickett, *The Spirit Level*.

80 P. Dasgupta, *An Inquiry into Well-Being and Destitution* (Oxford: Clarendon Press, 1993).

81 J.D. Sachs, *Investing in Development: A Practical Plan to Achieve the Millennium Development Goals* (New York: United Nations, 2005).

82 World Bank, World Development Report. Mind, Society, and Behavior, 2015, at http://www.worldbank.org/en/publication/wdr2015 [accessed 5 March 2015].

83 J.D. Sachs, *The End of Poverty*.

84 P. Collier and D. Dollar, *Globalization, Growth, and Poverty. Building an Inclusive World Economy* (New York: World Bank, Oxford University Press, 2002).

85 P. Bardhan, 'Decentralization of Governance and Development', *Journal of Economic Perspectives*, 16: 4, (2002), pp. 185–205.

86 J. Klugman, F. Rodríguez and H.-J. Choi, 'The HDI 2010: new controversies, old critiques', *Journal of Economic Inequality*, 9, (2011), pp. 249–288.

8 Recovering macroeconomic policy for development

Alejandro Nadal

8.1 Introduction

Development theory as it evolved in the aftermath of World War II involved several very different (and even opposing) views. For example, Rosenstein-Rodan emphasized the crucial role of the State, Hirschman focused on backward linkages and Myrdal stressed the importance of circular causation processes.[1] In spite of their differences, these authors shared the view that development is a process of structural rupture that involves active State intervention and instability. Keynes's work on the relation between unemployment and aggregate demand greatly influenced, directly and indirectly, development theory.[2]

Krugman argues that the field of development economics 'no longer exists' and that a counterrevolution swept it away. He sees a lot of economists working on the economics of developing countries, but in a diffuse way: those who work on agriculture have no overlap with the ones working on the economics of manufacture or trade, and nobody talks to those focusing on macroeconomics.[3] If Krugman's assessment is accurate (and this involves a big 'if'), how did this come about? Our hypothesis is that right from the start, development economics harboured the seeds of this dispersion. From Rosenstein-Rodan's paper to Hirschman and Myrdal, key macroeconomic structures and processes, both in the real economy and in terms of banking and monetary creation, were either ignored or treated summarily. It may sound as an exaggeration, but macroeconomic theory *stricto sensu* was almost absent from the literature in the high years of development economics. In a way, especially in the case of Rosenstein-Rodan and Hirschman, development economics was more a set of real-world issues for practitioners than theoreticians. When the neoclassical counterrevolution came in the 1970s, development economics was caught empty-handed and had very little to offer in terms of a critique of the new turn in macroeconomic theory. Having discredited what had been the Keynesian paradigm of the fifties and sixties, the neoclassical 'counterrevolution' encountered little opposition to its macroeconomic policy package. The debt crisis in the 1980s played a key role in how this paradigm was imposed on most developing countries. But it remains a fact that development economics lacked the necessary elements to criticize the rationale and foundations of the new policy priorities. By the end of that decade macroeconomic policy in most developing economies was dominated by the key priorities of the neoliberal paradigm.

The rise of neoliberalism is associated with the re-emergence of what Keynes called the Classical school. This perspective of economics is based on the idea that markets are self-regulating entities that lead prices to equilibrium positions and efficient allocations. In macroeconomic terms, this means unemployment is a frictional problem and there is no room for endogenously generated crises. Investment and adequate growth rates will follow price stability. This macroeconomic posture resulted from the counterrevolution in macroeconomic theory that led from the monetarist critique and rational expectations critique of the post-WWII Keynesian paradigm to the view that government intervention is ineffective.

For developing countries this translates into a passive stance for monetary, credit, foreign exchange and fiscal policies. Most importantly, this also relegates the role of the State to a secondary position. Development would be the result of efficient resource allocation by market forces. The adoption of neoliberal policies by developing countries was justified on the grounds that this would lead to higher growth rates without inflation, equilibrium in external accounts, employment generation and the reduction of poverty. Although there is evidence that the control of inflation was achieved in many cases, this was attained through the repression of aggregate demand and with the help of overvalued exchange rates, all of this with a very high social cost. Economic performance remained mediocre in the global. South was the scene of a long string of financial crises since the mid-nineties. In many cases the crises were caused by the contradictions of the open macroeconomic model implemented in developing countries.[4] Today, in the midst of a protracted global recession, new threats appear in the horizon.

Redefining macroeconomic policy priorities in developing countries is crucial in order to attain development objectives and implement adequate sector level policies in agriculture and industrial development. Post-Keynesian macroeconomic theory offers a radical rupture with the highly unrealistic and logically flawed neoclassical world. From its vantage point it is possible to draw the lines for macroeconomic policy-making in the pursuit of sustainable development.

The structure of this chapter is as follows. Section 8.2 summarizes the key theoretical principles that need to be considered as the key reference in macroeconomic policy-making for development today. The vantage point of this section is post-Keynesian macroeconomic theory. Section 8.3 presents a series of criteria for policy-making that stem from this theoretical framework. The last section focuses on the redefinition of specific priorities for macro policies at the country level.

8.2 Post-Keynesian macroeconomic perspectives

An economic policy posture is strongly determined by the economist's theoretical perspectives. If he or she believes that market forces lead to efficient allocations, the policy stance calls for little intervention in economic life. But if one questions this theory, regulation and direct intervention in economic life will be accepted as normal. Since the early seventies the policy posture in most developing countries has been based on the first type of idea.

Ironically, it was in those years that neoclassical theory entered its deepest crisis. In the 1970s Sonnenschein, Mantel and Debreu showed that the Arrow–Debreu model, the main theoretical workhorse of neoclassical theory, always requires ad hoc assumptions in order to demonstrate that free markets lead to equilibrium prices.[5] The Sonnenschein–Mantel–Debreu theorem reveals that market excess demand functions are not restricted by the usual rationality conditions of individual demands in that economy: microeconomic rationality assumptions have no macroeconomic equivalent. A critical implication of this result is that the so-called representative agents of many mainstream macroeconomic models are fictions without any rational foundation.[6]

In spite of this devastating blow to neoclassical theory and the free market ideology, macroeconomic policy and theory proceeded *as if* general equilibrium theory had somehow demonstrated that free markets lead to optimum allocations and growth trajectories. This was translated into the following macroeconomic priorities: price stability, balanced budgets for fiscal policy, deregulation of the capital account, international trade liberalization and minimum state intervention in the economy. Today we know this policy mix did not lead to adequate growth rates, nor did it provide equilibrium of domestic aggregates and balanced external accounts.

Clearly there is need to move ahead and design and implement alternative development strategies. Post-Keynesian theory (PKT) provides a logically consistent alternative that is more realistic and closer to the needs of sustainable development strategies. In the next paragraphs we describe the fundamental characteristics of PKT and identify key implications for a more consistent and realistic macroeconomic policy for development.[7]

First, the economy is demand determined and not constrained by supply. According to the principle of effective demand, the production of goods adjusts itself to demand. This leads to a case of reverse causality: investment always causes saving (not the other way around). In other terms, investment is always independent of saving (investment and capital accumulation are not tied to inter-temporal decisions by households on saving and consumption). Investment depends on expectations and this is why capitalist economies are inherently unstable. For PKT unemployment is not caused by disequilibrium in the labour market but by inadequate levels of aggregate demand.

Second, post-Keynesian theory centres on the workings of a monetary economy. Money is not a neutral device that can be abstracted from because in capitalist economies contracts are denominated in money terms and production is organized in order to obtain money to pay debts. Everyone's ability to meet one's monetary contractual commitments is the foundation of a monetary economy. This is in stark contrast with neoclassical theory that reduces money to a transactions technology and carries out its analysis of markets and prices in real (non monetary) terms.

Third, the interest rate is not determined in a special market of loanable funds. It is not the price determined by the intersection of a downward sloping demand for funds and an upward sloping supply curve of (loanable) funds. Interest is the price for parting with liquidity. Interest is linked to the choice of assets in which an individual wants to place its savings and plays an important role in the economy, but not in the decision to save.

By turning his attention to money as a store of value and leaving momentarily aside its function as a means of exchange, Keynes integrated uncertainty and expectations into his analysis and revealed that the rate of interest is the driver, and not the passive result of the level of economic activity.[8] Authorities can have full control of the rate of interest through monetary and debt-management policies and this variable ceases to be an endogenous variable.

Fourth, there is no such thing as a labour market and wages are a distributional variable instead of a price that equilibrates the supply and demand for labour. It is not possible to aggregate the entire set of diverse transactions where labour is hired into a single market in which one price is determined, i.e. wages. The level of wages can be used to describe the evolution of aggregate demand, but it is not the price of a factor of production.

Fifth, monetary creation is carried out by private commercial banks that create money 'out of thin air', as Schumpeter pointed out.[9] Banks do not need deposits to carry out loans. In fact, loans create deposits, not the other way around. Thus, base money created exclusively by central banks typically amounts to less than five per cent of total money supply, while the rest corresponds to money created by the private banking system. A key implication is that there is no such thing as a money multiplier.[10] Central banks do not have control of money supply and behave in a more passive mode, delivering reserves in response to the requirements of the commercial banking system. Thus, banking is an inherently pro-cyclical activity: banks will expand credit in good times and contract it in bad times. Banks respond to a demand for loans by business firms that is not already satisfied by the existing stock of money. If the request for credit is deemed profitable and collateral is considered adequate, the loan is approved and a deposit is created.[11]

Sixth, investment is identical to savings. The identity is brought about because the development of the banking system brings about widespread acceptance of deposits as money for transactions. Because loans make deposits, investment is autonomous and depends only on (expectations concerning) aggregate demand, not on savings. The identity between investment and savings is supported by the analysis of the causal mechanisms that involve monetary creation by the banking system.[12] When credit is approved to meet the request of investors, a deposit is created for the same amount. Spending the deposit transforms it into somebody's income and these deposits become somebody's savings. Thus, savings are generated when credit is created.[13]

Seventh, price flexibility may have adverse or destabilizing effects. Post-Keynesian analysis rejects the notion that the workings of competitive forces lead to the formation of equilibrium prices. This applies to the analysis of all markets, but perhaps the most important case is provided by flexible wages. According to neoclassical theory, flexible wages are the key to stability, but for PKT the reduction of wages makes matters worse because it further depresses aggregate demand and increases the debt burden of firms, leading to bankruptcies and greater (not less) unemployment.

Eighth, capital flows pose serious risks because they have destabilizing potential. These pools of liquid assets seek to obtain higher rewards by arbitraging on real interest rates and exchange rate stability in various countries.[14] Capital flows involve portfolio investments that retain a high degree of liquidity and aim for speculative profits without making a positive contribution to growth or job creation.

Ninth, inflation is not always and everywhere the result of an excess supply of money. Causality in this relation between money and inflation operates in a different direction: the growth rate of prices and output bring about an increase in the stock of money.[15] Also, PKT disagrees with the notion that rising levels of capacity utilization lead to rising costs. Rising utilization rates and fast growth may be associated with increased productivity that compensates for rising wage costs. In addition, stability or high inflation periods are phenomena related to structural features of the economy, like income distribution. Inflation can be subdued not by a healthy monetary policy but through wage declines and falling import prices caused by increased international competition and exchange rate effects.[16]

Ten, post-Keynesian theory reserves a special place for uncertainty. PKT emphasizes the fact that the future is unknowable and very different from the past. Uncertainty is essentially different from risk because it is not amenable to any sort of calculation using probability distributions. The world is non-ergodic and averages and past fluctuations will not necessarily be observed in future time periods.[17]

8.3 Criteria for macroeconomic policy-making

The theoretical perspectives outlined above are in stark contrast with the standard models used in mainstream policy-making. For example, the open economy described by the Mundell–Fleming model is based on the assumption that the IS-LM framework can be adapted to an open economy through the addition of a new curve depicting the locus of equilibrium points of the balance of payments in the income-interest rate space. Adding aggregate supply (and allowing for flexible prices) results in the New Classical model in which adjustment is automatic. Interest and exchange rates play a key role in this adjustment, but at the cost of ignoring several crucial elements in the workings of the model, especially in the case of developing countries. In 2004 we show that the standard Mundell–Fleming model is marked by several fundamental contradictions that distort the role of interest and exchange rates and lead to the breakdown of the adjustment process.[18] The use of dynamic stochastic general equilibrium (DSGE) models is another important example of mainstream policy-making that needs to be abandoned. These models rely on representative agents and rational expectations in an inter-temporal optimization problem where no macroeconomic issues appear and policy becomes irrelevant.[19]

Typically the neoliberal open economy model as implemented in developing countries implies a restrictive posture in monetary and fiscal policies. This responds to several objectives. First, it aims at subduing inflationary pressures by contracting aggregate demand. Second, a restrictive monetary policy maintains high interest rates that reward capital inflows. Third, this restricts public expenditures and helps generate a primary surplus (to cover financial charges). The overarching priority of price stability is also achieved through an overvalued currency and wage controls in such a way that real wages deteriorate over time. This policy package leads to serious contradictions and needs to be radically reformed to achieve development goals.

The post-Keynesian theoretical perspectives we have outlined above have important implications for macroeconomic policy-making. The rest of this section translates this into guidelines for policy-making.

8.3.1 Counter-cyclicality

A critical issue that emerges from the previous section is that markets are not stable and do not lead to equilibrium allocations. Flexible prices in free markets should not be expected to generate the necessary conditions for development. In addition, if instability is an inherent characteristic of capitalist economies, cycles will also be one of their essential features. Clearly, in the downward phase of these cycles, macroeconomic policy has a role to play. It is urgent then to reassess the role of the state and the public sector in defining and guiding development strategies.

A pro-active macroeconomic policy posture for development involves a countercyclical stance and this implies reworking monetary and fiscal policies. This has to be accompanied by the re-regulation of the financial sector and some form of control over capital flows. Because the pro-cyclicality of financial markets has had disastrous consequences for developing countries, this needs to integrate the fact that in the boom phase of the cycle expectations by agents tend to favour increased risk adoption, the overestimation of assets' values, as well as high leveraging. A new approach must focus on discouraging speculative behaviour and on promoting productive investment.

8.3.2 Capital controls

Macroeconomic policy-making for development involves recovering the control over interest and exchange rates. Redefining priorities in monetary policy needs to be compatible with the capital account regime. There are two fundamental points here. The first concerns the need to recover control over the role of the interest rate as a reference for domestic monetary matters instead of a simple reward for external capital flows. The interest rate is related not to the decision on saving, but to decisions on the assets in which savings will be kept (i.e. the liquidity preference theory). But deregulating the capital account distorts the role of the interest rate. Clearly, mastery over the interest rate requires controls over capital flows. The second issue is that the exchange rate must recover its role as an adjustment variable for a country's external accounts. With a deregulated capital account, the exchange rate is affected by capital flows and tends to maintain an unhealthy overvaluation, even in the context of chronic trade deficits. This aspect of the neoliberal open economy model needs urgent attention. Capital controls contribute to re-align the interest and the exchange rate in accordance to long-term development objectives. They also reduce volatility and mitigate the intensity of the business cycle.[20]

8.3.3 Monetary and financial re-regulation

Private commercial banks are responsible for the creation of more than 90 per cent of total money supply in most capitalist economies today. The role of central banks is to provide adequate reserves (in the form of high power money) for the banking system. However, financial and credit policies continue to operate as if commercial banks required savings in order to make loans. This is why the notion of a money multiplier is misleading.[21] The capacity of private banks to emit debt money needs to be subjected to social and democratic controls through adequate public oversight. In addition, finance must be re-regulated in a truly meaningful way in order to reign in the excesses of the shadow banking sector and its amazing capacity to introduce financial innovations.

8.3.4 Macroeconomic aggregates, structures and institutions

Post-Keynesian theory has shown that macroeconomics must include institutions into the analysis. These institutions have a determinant effect in shaping individual conduct, collective behaviour and the design and implementation of economic regulations. They need to be accurately incorporated into the main theoretical macroeconomic model.[22]

Macroeconomics focuses on aggregates, but this does not mean that the *composition* of these aggregates is unimportant. In fact, macroeconomic policy for development only makes sense when the *structure* of these aggregates is taken into account. If the outstanding balance of the trade account shows a surplus, this is judged as a positive result by any macroeconomic standard. However, if exports are heavily biased towards goods that are natural resource-intensive, or if they are produced by cheap labour, that surplus may not be sustainable. Thus, the disaggregated components of macro accounts need to be taken into account.

Another example where structures and institutions are important is found in the struggle to control inflation. If this is attained through the containment of aggregate demand via a restrictive incomes' policy (i.e. wage controls), cuts in public spending, high interest rates and a tight monetary policy, or through an overvalued exchange rate, the costs will exceed the benefits. Stagnant real wages will intensify inequality and slower growth due to high interest rates will not help poverty. Reductions in public spending will affect social expenditures and will have a negative effect not only on social equity, but also on productivity. Typically, expenditures in items such as health, education, housing or the environment are the first to go. All of this will conspire against the social sustainability of an otherwise apparent good result. Thus, the structure or the composition of macroeconomic aggregates provides a relevant indicator for social and environmental sustainability.

The structural approach to macroeconomics recognizes the fact that an economy's institutions and distributional relationships across its productive sectors and social groups play essential roles in determining macro dynamics.[23] Macroeconomics should take into account causal and functional relations between aggregates, and this can only be approached with some sense of accuracy if the *structures* of these aggregates are taken in consideration.

8.4 Redefining policy priorities

The key priorities for neoliberal macroeconomic policy are price stability, balanced fiscal accounts and financial and trade liberalization. It is believed that these priorities can deliver growth and employment creation with control over inflation and equilibrium in the external accounts. Once these macroeconomic objectives are determined, every other policy target is defined in a subsidiary mode. Sector-level policies, whether for health, education, housing or the environment are disciplined by these macroeconomic priorities. The following paragraphs examine how the trajectory of macroeconomic policy-making can be redefined. The first group of priorities focuses on growth and full employment, while the second centres on banks and monetary policy objectives.

8.4.1. Growth and full employment

The main shift in priorities relates to the question of expansion and job creation. Development needs growth and economic expansion need not be associated with inflation. Unfortunately, the false dilemma of having to choose between price stability and full employment led to a passive posture in terms of public policy. In most developing countries price stability was pursued through the repression of aggregate demand via wage controls, high interest rates, the contraction of fiscal expenditures and overvalued exchange rates. Not surprisingly, these economies experienced mediocre growth rates, high unemployment rates, unsatisfactory fiscal revenues and the growth of public debt. In fact, price stability did not even bring about macroeconomic stability as can be seen in the long series of crises in the global south.

Inflation is not caused by the simple expansion of aggregate demand. It is not always a monetary phenomenon and it can be related to market structures and mark-up pricing. Capitalist economies do not possess an inherent tendency towards full employment. With Say's law jettisoned, the loanable funds theory and the notion of a labour market being discarded, the notion that a capitalist economy tends towards full employment if left undisturbed must likewise be abandoned. Unemployment is not caused by disequilibrium in the labour market but by inadequate levels of aggregate demand: it cannot be eliminated through adjustments in the wage rate and fiscal intervention may be required to restore employment.

8.4.1.1 Reducing inequality

Inequality is not the result of a bias in technological skills or of disparities in the contribution of each person or group to social production (the marginal productivity theory). Inequality is a political economy event driven by macroeconomic policies that can bring about unsustainable household indebtedness. A core objective of macroeconomic policies for development is the reduction of income disparities and social inequality.

A responsible macroeconomic policy stance involves parting with the notion that inequality will disappear through trickle down effects or limited anti-poverty programs. The experience of the past two decades shows these tools are not enough. Social and environmental objectives need to be put at the centre of macroeconomic policy-making right from the start. Together with this, we need to recover the redistributive role of fiscal policy, with a truly progressive tax reform and an intelligent structure for expenditures in key sustainability items. Also, incomes policy must cease to be an instrument to control aggregate demand by forcing negotiations to focus on expected instead of real inflation.

8.4.1.2 Fiscal consolidation versus fiscal policy for development

After the debt crisis in the eighties and the severe structural adjustment programs that were imposed on most developing countries, the golden rule in fiscal policy has been to maintain a fiscal balance. At first, fiscal retrenchment was imposed to cut down aggregate demand and suppress inflationary pressures. Once inflation was harnessed, fiscal balance was justified to prevent crowding out of private investment although there is no real theoretical basis for the crowding out hypothesis or its variants. In fact, the main reason behind the need to impose a fiscal balance is related to debt management. This is why fiscal balance is associated with the notion of a primary surplus (the result of subtracting expenditures net of financial charges from total fiscal revenues).

The primary surplus syndrome has been the dominant trait of fiscal policy in much of the global south. This posture implies transferring resources from the real sectors of the economy to the financial sphere (a primary surplus is typically generated by reducing per capita social expenditures, not by increasing fiscal revenues through progressive tax regimes). It undermines a country's capacity to attain sustainability objectives for the sake of satisfying short-term objectives related to the needs of the financial sector and debt management. The failure of this approach is revealed by the fact that the debt burden continues to weigh heavily over the developing world. Even though the debt of developing countries has been 'managed' through these policies for more than two decades, the problem has not been solved.[24]

Clearly, if sustainable development is to be attained debt management has to occupy a secondary position and cease to be the regulator of fiscal policy. A serious fiscal reform is required in order to raise fiscal revenues in a non-regressive tax system restoring the principle of tax equity. The notion that the wealthier groups in a society should receive tax breaks and support a low fiscal burden has been justified on the grounds that this promotes investment and creates favourable expectations. This is not supported by data on capital formation over the past decades; instead inequality increased in most OECD countries.[25]

To restore some equity into tax polices, governments have traditionally opted for a differentiated structure of tax rates, as a function of income. However, the progressiveness of this system has been severely curtailed as taxes for top income brackets have been significantly reduced. In the case of indirect or value added taxes, which have been promoted as an instrument that would increase everyone's fiscal contribution (including the so-called informal sector), the regressive effect is even stronger. Indirect or value added taxes should not be the centre of a strategy to increase tax revenues. Greater flexibility can be attained through different rates for dissimilar goods, exempting critical categories of goods (medicines and food) and by putting greater pressure on commodities that pose health hazards.

New programs to increase tax revenues have to be implemented by levying higher taxes on high-income brackets, capital gains and financial transactions. This has to be accompanied by a comprehensive tax reform that will eliminate incentives for evasion as well as elusion, especially in the corporate tax regime. Fiscal pressure need not discourage investment and capital formation. There is ample evidence that taxes on high-income groups are low and there is room to accommodate higher levels of taxation. Today's tax structure is the outcome of two decades of a fiscal policy based on a Laffer curve type of reasoning. It is also the result of the notion that taxes on capital gains and financial transactions were to be avoided lest capital flight take place or financial chaos ensue. But levies on financial transactions exist in places like the United Kingdom and they have not provoked capital flight.

Discriminating between sources of revenues is one way of introducing heterogeneity in fiscal policy. One important source of revenues can be found in financial transactions. Today the astronomical quantities of resources exchanged daily in the stock exchanges of the world, or in the global currency markets, offer a valuable opportunity for taxation. Even a modest tax on financial transactions can go a long way in generating an adequate flow of resources that can be used for development and social expenditures. These tools do not distort financial markets and introduce a more realistic approach to the role of finance in capitalist economies.

Expenditures in sectors such as health, education, housing and infrastructure have been lagging behind for many years in developing countries. It is urgent to restore them as key priorities if sustainable development is to be attained. In addition, the role of subsidies in developing economies needs to be seriously reassessed. There are many cases in which subsidies can correct problems that markets are incapable of redressing. In contrast, subsidies for activities in the financial sector or for energy companies have channelled billions of dollars for bailout schemes. In many cases, special interests and lobbyists have captured fiscal policy and misdirected public resources. These subsidies must be redirected to sustainability objectives.

8.4.2. Monetary policy and banking

The shift from full employment and growth to price stability during the seventies implied enormous changes. It brought about slower growth rates and important structural transformations both at the domestic and international levels. Today, when monetary policy is pursued in the context of an inflation-targeting regime, a deflationary bias is imposed on the economy. Typically, central banks are given a lot of recognition when their inflation targets are attained, while sluggish growth, sagging aggregate demand and unemployment are attributed to other factors. The capacity of monetary authorities to pursue expansionary policies is severely curtailed as inflation targeting induces higher interest rates and a depressing effect on growth and employment. Monetary policy may entail high interest rates for stabilization or to maintain a 'competitive' level and attract capital flows, but this imposes restrictions on rates of return and investment. A wise balance needs to be maintained between short-term rates and long-term interest rates that aim at fostering development. Clearly, *rentier* economics is not a healthy recipe for social and economic development.

In a world of endogenous money, the interest rate is an exogenous variable that can be manipulated by monetary authorities, with significant effects upon the entire spectrum of interest rates.[26] Lowering the key interest rate in an economy reduces the level at which investment projects become profitable and will also help reduce the differentials between active and passive interest rates, enabling large sectors of the economy to use financial services. Today central banks typically manipulate the overnight inter-bank lending rate in their attempts to achieve price stability.

Determining the interest rate also has implications for the exchange rate in the context of a deregulated capital account. Thus, determining an interest rate that is compatible with long-term priorities of sustainable development (and especially with growth and employment objectives) must work together with adequate controls over short-term capital flows.

Redefining priorities in monetary policy also needs to go hand in hand with re-regulating activities in the banking sector.[27] This is due to the role of private commercial banks in monetary creation and to the fact that in modern capitalist economies money supply is essentially controlled by private commercial banks, not by central banks. This means that the crucial function of monetary creation is carried out in the pursuit of private profitability by special firms called 'banks'. The creation of money by banks is debt-related and corresponds to credit demand by firms and households.[28] It is therefore a highly pro-cyclical activity that may lead to macroeconomic instability, especially in the context of extreme deregulation.[29]

Re-regulating the activities of the banking sector is a complex and multi-purpose task. There are at least four important aspects to this regulatory effort if banks are to make a positive contribution to a development strategy. First, re-regulating the banking system is required to dampen the pro-cyclical bias inherent to private banking. One way to do this is to impose strict capitalization requirements and reserve coefficients because banks will find in this an important moderator of their expectation-formation process. This will of course encounter objections from the banking sector as it reduces the amount of leverage with which banks can operate.

Reserve and capitalization requirements involve strict accounting, transparency and intense supervision by regulatory bodies.

A second round of regulatory measures concerns the set of activities in which banks can get involved. Separating conventional banking operations (the so-called 'boring' activities like mortgages and loans to small firms) from activities related to securities, the creation of investment vehicles and operations with higher risks that are the realm of investment banks is of course one of the first priorities in this context. In addition, banks need to be excluded from intervening in over the counter activities and operations with derivatives that are largely unregulated today.[30]

Third, regulating banking for sustainable development should also involve channelling credit into certain types of sectors or branches of the economy. Because credit will go to wherever the market calls for new loans, the activities that may be found profitable and worthy of credits may or may not be relevant for a long-term development strategy. Re-regulating banking activities may be needed to make sure that key sectors or branches in the economy have access to financial services. In development strategies this type of regulation has played an important role, allowing for the acquisition of endogenous technological capabilities that later became the foundation of competitive advantages in key industrial branches. Another consideration is that this may allow sectors like small-scale agriculture to have access to adequate financial services. This part of the regulatory agenda must be accompanied by active industrial and agricultural policies.

Fourth, regulations for the banking sector need to be based on the idea of differential treatment for various types of banks. This is a *de minimis* condition for an adequate regulatory framework. There is no reason why large banks that concentrate assets and equity need to be treated in the same manner as small banks or credit unions. Some big banks can generate instability and pose systemic risks, while others are socially useful institutions that may be discriminated against when faced with the same regulations imposed on large commercial banks.

None of the above regulatory steps will put under complete control of public policy the banking sector. From a more radical perspective, complete nationalization of banks may be considered the only rational manner through which monetary creation can be put at the service of social priorities. This would effectively place the volume of credit and the sectors to which loans would be channelled under public control. This approach to banking would return control of the money supply to banking authorities, something that does not happen today.[31]

8.4.2.1 Central banks

One of the most important aspects of macroeconomic policy calling for serious re-examination in the interest of sustainable development priorities is the question of central bank autonomy or independence (CBI). The idea that central banks should be institutionally separate from government institutions to prevent political interference in monetary policy-making gained predominance during the late 1980's.[32] Price stability was considered the key goal as it would bring about greater investment, growth and employment. However, there does not appear to be a strong association between CBI and lower inflation rates in developed countries.[33] Finally, the global financial crisis clearly shows that price stability is not equivalent to macroeconomic stability, so CBI does not seem to guarantee constancy and overall better performance.

The most important aspect of CBI is the notion that if governments have the capacity to run deficits in their own currency in cases where the treasury has control over the central bank, then it will force the monetary institute to monetize public debt. To counter this possibility, it was thought that independence of central bank authorities would lead to the formulation of ideology-free policies and that this would increase credibility and certainty for investors. The central idea here is that preventing the central bank from acting as the financial agent of the government would restrict the ability of politicians to monetize excessive fiscal deficits, reducing the risk of hyperinflationary events. In fact, what happened is that while governments lost their ability to finance long-term projects that are crucial in development strategies, central banks became subordinated to the priorities of finance capital. By the same token, governments had now to resort to private financial markets to obtain credit for their operations, just like any private entity. The justification here is that this imposes market discipline on public finance. The crisis in Europe exemplifies the absurdity of this situation, with governments of countries like Spain or Italy having to subordinate their macroeconomic policies for the sake of obtaining adequate ratings and credits from financial markets. Amputating the capacity of self-finance of modern states has brought about greater chaos and an intensification of the crisis. Countries like Spain have been forced to accept all the conditions imposed by private financial capital in order to finance their deficits, intensifying and extending the duration of the recession.

In trying to prevent political manipulation, CBI led to corporate capture of the central bank's regulatory and policy powers. Deregulating and getting rid of critical pieces of the regulatory framework that had kept the banking system in place for decades is just one example of this corporate capture.[34] In the specific case of developing countries, CBI is problematic because its capture by financial industry pressure groups is incompatible with long-term sustainable development objectives. On the other hand, it would be irresponsible to get rid of CBI and not impose democratic and political controls that can ensure the responsible management of this powerful financial instrument.

Central banks must expand the set of issues under their screening and regulatory powers. As core objectives, full employment, growth and achieving a healthy pattern of income distribution must be accompanied by other complementary goals. For example, monitoring the formation of asset bubbles and the evolution of the business cycle, especially if we take into consideration the role of private banks in the credit cycle, are factors that need to be integrated into the mission of central banks in any development strategy.

8.4.2.2 Development banks

Development banks were created to support long-term development strategies fulfilling roles that private banks cannot play. By providing long-term credit for infrastructure, key industrial projects or areas that were neglected by commercial banking systems (small scale agriculture, small and medium size firms) development banks performed a critical function during the period 1945-1975 in many developing countries. These banks can play an important countercyclical role, off-setting the contraction of credit from private banks during downturns. However, the neoliberal policy stance relegated development banks to a secondary position, a change that was consistent with the idea that the private sector and the market should be responsible for development. Development banks need to recover the active role they played in macroeconomic policies.

8.4.2.3 Capital account regulations

In order to recover control over interest rates, monetary policy and the exchange rate, it is essential to establish controls over capital flows. Recent studies have shown that countries that used capital controls performed better during the global financial crisis.[35] The main objective behind the deregulation of the capital account was to provide access to international capital sources (foreign savings) and thus supplement domestic savings. However, opening the capital account has led to capital flows that in the short run have strong destabilizing effects and in the long run are accompanied by critical structural distortions. These capital flows disturb development policies. First, in the case of countries that have a chronic current account deficit, capital flows artificially maintain a country's capacity to import goods, irrespective of its ability to maintain exports. As Bhaduri shows, this can have negative effects through the perverse application of the Kahn-Keynes multiplier where imports lead to reductions in aggregate income: the initial impulse towards contraction is provided by the substitution effect that replaces domestic production with imports in certain branches, the multiplier process leads to successive rounds of additional induced reductions.[36]

The second distortion is related to the interest rate and the money supply. As requirements for capital flows increase, the interest rate becomes the key instrument to attract these flows. In order to maintain the money supply stable, sterilization is used and this maintains the interest rate at an artificially high level, affecting the entire spectrum of interest rates in the economy. The third problem concerns the rigidities imposed on the exchange rate as a result of these capital flows. In the neoclassical open economy model, the exchange rate is a key adjustment variable that affects the set of relative prices with great informational efficiency. It is thus essential to maintain reasonable flexibility in the exchange rate. However, in the presence of capital flows the exchange rate loses its flexibility. For example, capital flows tend to appreciate the exchange rate and this prevents it from performing its role as an adjustment variable. If this happens when the recipient country suffers a trade deficit, the movement in the exchange rate will aggravate the external imbalance.

It is important to recognize the fact that capital controls can contribute to smooth cycles in the capital account and reduce overall economic vulnerability.[37] In Chile, unremunerated reserve requirements shielded the economy from overabundance of short-term capital at times of surges and helped attain higher growth rates.[38] They also protected the economy from contagion at a time of crisis and volatility. In Colombia, capital controls also allowed for better handling of maturity periods of external debt.[39] Capital controls allow policy makers to regain some autonomy for a countercyclical monetary policy. This is also consistent with the historical record of developed countries which shows long periods of capital controls and only gradual liberalization for capital flows.[40]

Capital controls can also enhance stability and allow for a greater degree of independence of monetary policy. But this objective can also be attained with the use of balance of payments provisions within the WTO framework. These provisions can offer a constructive response to external accounts' crises and should be reconsidered as an important tool in the intersection between trade and financial flows.[41] The world's trade regime needs to be revised in order to make it compatible with country-level counter-cyclical policies and with crisis-preventing regulations. In addition, trade agreements such as GATS need to be reviewed in terms of their balance of payments effects, their impacts on macroeconomic stability and the scope they provide for financial regulation.

8.5 Concluding remarks

After 30 years of having a single macroeconomic policy package imposed on most of the world's developing economies, the global crisis of 2008 sends a different message. The core lesson is that there is room for more than one set of policy priorities. This has been the main guidepost for this chapter, where we have attempted to lay down a set of general principles and guidelines that are useful while redefining and recovering macroeconomic policies for development.

Clearly macroeconomic policies in and by themselves cannot be the sole mechanism that leads to development. A key lesson from the recent experience with neoliberalism is that simple macroeconomic objectives, such as price stability, do not provide the necessary means to get on a development trajectory. Macroeconomic policy needs to be redesigned in order to become a faithful instrument for development objectives. For example, recovering the control over key macroeconomic policy parameters, such as interest and exchange rates, is crucial for the design and implementation of adequate macro policies. But it is also a *sine qua non* requisite for the implementation of good sector level policies, whether in the realms of agriculture and industry, or in the sphere of health, education, housing and environmental stewardship. Thus, implementing the policies that are required in response to the 'kicking away the ladder'[42] syndrome calls for this redefinition of macroeconomic priorities and policies.

The structural transformation involved in development needs an adequate macroeconomic framework, but it also requires active public agency at the sector level, in industry as well as in agriculture. In this sense, the macroeconomic framework outlined here should only be seen as a frame of reference for serious sector level policies for the acquisition of endogenous technological capabilities in industry and for the support of both small-scale and commercial scale agriculture that is both socially responsible and environmentally sustainable.

Notes

1 P.N. Rosenstein-Rodan, 'Problems of Industrialization of Eastern and South-Eastern Europe' in *The Economic Journal*, 53: 210/211, Jun–Sept, (1943), pp. 202–11; A.O. Hirschman, *The Strategy of Economic Development* (New Haven: Yale University Press, 1958); G. Myrdal, *Economic Theory and Under-developed Regions* (London: Duckworth, 1957).
2 J. Toye 'The Significance of Keynes for Development Economics' in K.S. Jomo (ed.), *The Pioneers of Development Economics. Great Economists on Development* (London: Zed Books, 2005), pp. 123–41.
3 P. Krugman, *Development, Geography and Economic Theory* (Cambridge, MA: The MIT Press, 1998).
4 A. Nadal, 'Contradictions of the Open Economy Model as Applied in Mexico', in F. Ackerman and A. Nadal, *The Flawed Foundations of General Equilibrium. Critical Essays in Economic Theory* (London: Routledge, 2004), pp. 132–48.
5 H. Sonnenschein, 'Market Excess Demand Functions', *Econometrica*, 40: 3, (1972), pp. 549–63; R. Mantel, 'On the Characterization of Aggregate Excess Demand', *Journal of Economic Theory*, 7, (1974), pp. 348–53; G. Debreu, 'Excess Demand Functions', *Journal of Mathematical Economics*, 1, (1974), pp. 15–23.
6 A.P. Kirman, 'Whom or What Does the Representative Individual Represent?', *Journal of Economic Perspectives*, 6: 2, (1992), pp. 117–36.
7 The term post-Keynesian theory (PKT) is applied to theoretical work that developed Keynes's theses as presented and developed in his *General Theory* and other essays, see for example P. Davidson, 'Reviving Keynes's Revolution', *Journal of Post-Keynesian Economics*, 6: 4, (1984), pp. 561–75. PKT authors and their followers rejected the standard mainstream view that the IS-LM model, brought forward by John Hicks in 1937, represented Keynes' theoretical developments. In fact, for post-Keynesians, the IS-LM model as a description of how shifts in the IS and/or LM curves could restore full employment has almost nothing to do with Keynes' theory and actually betrays his most important insights, see M. Lavoie, *Introduction to Post-Keynesian Economics* (Basingstoke, Hampshire and New York: Palgrave MacMillan, 2006).
8 G. Tily, *Keynes's General Theory, the Rate of Interest and 'Keynesian' Economics* (Basingstoke, Hampshire and New York: Palgrave Macmillan, 2007).
9 J.A. Schumpeter, *The Theory of Economic Development* (Cambridge, MA: Harvard University Press, 1934), on p. 73.
10 S.B. Carpenter and S. Demiralp, 'Money, Reserves, and the Transmission of Monetary Policy: Does the Money Multiplier Exist?', *Finance and Economics Discussion Series*, Divisions of Research & Statistics and Monetary Affairs, Federal Reserve Board, Washington, DC (2010).
11 H. Minsky, *Stabilizing an Unstable Economy* (New York: McGraw Hill, 2008).
12 According to Tily, Keynes did not provide sufficient justification for his appeal and use of the identity between savings and investment. He reasoned in terms of macroeconomic equations but did not discuss the underlying mechanisms that are microeconomic and monetary in nature, G. Tily, *Keynes's General Theory*, p. 153.
13 Ibid., pp. 154–5.
14 These arbitraging operations curtail the policy space for countries that would like to receive capital inflows. Their capacity to embark in expansionary policies is severely restricted.

15 M. Lavoie, *Introduction to Post-Keynesian Economics*, p. 58.
16 N. Perry and N. Cline 'Wages, Exchange Rates and the Great Inflation Moderation: A Post-Keynesian View', Working Paper N. 759, Levy Economics Institute, (2013).
17 M. Lavoie, *Introduction to Post-Keynesian Economics*, p. 17.
18 A. Nadal, 'Contradictions of the Open Economy Model'.
19 In the realm of rational expectations and mainstream classical macroeconomics, macroeconomic policies have no role to play, even in the short run. This was translated into specific policy goals through the Washington Consensus, where fiscal balance, a tight money supply, and a balanced set of external accounts (with a surplus in the capital account) became the core components of the macroeconomic policy posture in both developed and developing countries. The importance of these balanced accounts implied the extinction of countercyclical policies and an almost complete disregard for what happened in the real sectors of the economy.
20 See J.A. Ocampo, 'Capital Account and Counter-cyclical Prudential Regulations in Developing Countries', *Serie Informes y Estudios Especiales*, CEPAL 6, February (2003); R. Ffrench-Davis and H. Tapia, 'The Chilean Style of Capital Controls: An Empirical Assessment', ECLAC Project on Management of Volatility, Financial Liberalization and Growth. Econometric Society Latin American Meetings, (2004).
21 S.B. Carpenter and S. Demiralp, 'Money, Reserves, and the Transmission of Monetary Policy'.
22 L. Taylor, *Reconstructing Macroeconomics. Structuralist Proposals and Critiques of the Mainstream* (Cambridge MA and London: Harvard University Press, 2004).
23 Ibid.
24 Using World Bank data, the Committee for the Abolition of Third World Debt (CADTM) reveals that the internal public debt of all developing countries rose from $1,300 to $3,500 billion between 1997 and 2005, see www.cadtm.org.
25 J.K. Galbraith, *Inequality and Instability: A Study of the World Economy Just Before the Crisis* (New York: Oxford University Press, 2012).
26 It is clear that the interest rate is not determined by a so-called market of loanable funds and is, instead, an exogenous variable with critical distributional implications. *Rentier* economics is incompatible with development strategies.
27 Monetary policy cannot be redirected towards the objectives of development and sustainability without taking into account the fact that private commercial banks create money 'out of thin air', in the words of Schumpeter. One interpretation of this is that once the fractional reserve banking system was introduced, private banks were endowed with the power to create money, although there was a restriction as deposits and reserves were a *sine qua non* condition for monetary creation. But this later evolved and led to the situation in which banks can create credit in excess of savings, see V. Chick, *Macroeconomics After Keynes* (Cambridge, MA: The MIT Press, 1991), on p. 190. In the context of endogenous money this does not mean that central banks have no role to play, but the ability of banks (private agents with a profit-making motive) to create money through credit means that central banks do not control the money supply. Today's crisis is related to this privatization of monetary creation.
28 H. Minsky, *Stabilizing an Unstable Economy*.
29 In times of favourable expectations banks may look at market demand in an equally positive outlook. But market sentiment may feed on exaggerated news concerning future benefits and may lead to the creation of bubbles in asset prices, intensifying the severity of cycles. Under these circumstances banks will be inclined to approve new loans because their profitability depends on the willingness of business to engage in greater indebtedness. When expectations are unfavourable, banks will normally put a brake on their lending activities and will further contribute to decelerating economic activity, deteriorating unemployment and affecting prospects for long-term development.
30 All off-balance-sheet transactions must be outlawed. In 2007 and 2008, Lehman Brothers Holdings, Inc. used these off-book operations to understate its leverage and

deceived shareholders about its ability to withstand losses. The complex financial operations that took place were compatible with the Generally Accepted Accounting Principles and, from this perspective, were not illegal. But these practices are on the fringes of deception and speculation. They allow agents to escape regulations and constitute a negative incentive to engage in fraudulent operations that can lead to the collapse of the entire financial system. Clearly, stealthy operations are incompatible with healthy regulation.

31 An alternative approach to re-regulating banking operations was the so-called Chicago Plan presented in the 1930s by Henry Simons and Irving Fisher of the University of Chicago and Yale respectively, J. Benes and M. Kumhof, 'The Chicago Plan Revisited', *IMF Working Paper* n. WP/12/202, (2012). It aimed at separating the monetary and credit functions of the banking system by requiring 100 per cent backing of deposits by government-issued money and by ensuring that the financing of new bank credit only takes place through earnings retained in the form of government-issued money (or through borrowing of government-issued money from non-banks, but not through the creation of new deposits ex nihilo by banks). This means that banks would not be able to make loans by creating new deposits: their loan portfolio has to be backed by a combination of their own equity and non-monetary liabilities. Under these circumstances there would be better control of credit cycles and bank runs would be almost eliminated.

32 J. Bibow, 'A Post-Keynesian Perspective on the Rise of Central Bank Independence: A Dubious Success Story in Monetary Economics', *Working paper 625*, Levy Economics Institute of Bard College, (2010).

33 C. Crowe and E.E. Meade, 'The Evolution of Central Bank Governance around the World', *Journal of Economic Perspectives*, 21: 4, (2007), pp. 69–90; J. Bibow, 'A Post-Keynesian Perspective'.

34 See T. Palley, 'Monetary Policy and Central Banking after the Crisis: The Implications of Rethinking Macroeconomic Theory', IMK Working Paper 8/2011, (2011).

35 K. Gallagher, S. Griffith-Jones and J.A. Ocampo, 'Regulating Global Capital Flows for Long Run Development' Boston University, Frederick S. Pardee Centre for the Study of the Longer Range Future, (2012), at http://www.bu.edu/pardee/files/2012/03/RegulatingCapitalTF-March2012.pdf [accessed 12 January 2015].

36 A. Bhaduri, 'Implications of Globalization for Macroeconomic Theory and Policy in Developing Countries', in D. Baker, G. Epstein and R. Pollin (eds.), *Globalization and Progressive Economic Policy* (Cambridge: Cambridge University Press, 1998), pp. 149–59.

37 J. Furman and J. Stiglitz, 'Economic Crises: Evidence and Insights from East Asia', Brookings Papers on Economic Activity, N. 2. Washington, DC: Brookings Institution (1998); J.A. Ocampo, 'Capital Account'.

38 R. Ffrench-Davis and H. Tapia 'The Chilean Style of Capital Controls'.

39 J.A. Ocampo and C.E. Tovar, 'La experiencia colombiana con los encajes a los flujos de capital', *Revista de la CEPAL*, 81, (2003), pp. 7–32.

40 B. Eichengreen, *Globalizing Capital. A History of the International Monetary System* (Princeton, NJ: Princeton University Press, 1996).

41 A. Nadal, *Rethinking Macroeconomics for Sustainability* (London and New York: Zed Books, 2011).

42 As in H.J. Chang's masterpiece, see H.J Chang, *Kicking Away the Ladder: Development Strategy in Historical Perspective* (London: Anthem Press, 2003).

References

G. Abed and S. Gupta (eds), *Governance, Corruption, and Economic Performance* (Washington DC: International Monetary Fund, 2002).

A. Abreu et al, *A cries, a Troika e as alternativas urgentes* (Lisbon: Tinta da China, 2013).

D. Acemoglu, S. Johnson and J.A. Robinson, 'Reversal of Fortune: Geography and Institutions in the Making of the Modern World Income Distribution', *Quarterly Journal of Economics*, 117: 4, (2002), pp. 1231–94.

D. Acemouglu, S. Johnson and J.A. Robinson, 'Institutions as a Fundamental Cause of Long-Run Growth' in P. Aghion and S.N. Durlauf (eds), *Handbook of Economic Growth*, vol. 1 (Amsterdam: North Holland, 2005), pp. 385–372.

D. Acemoglu and J.A. Robinson, *Why Nations Fail: The Origins of Power, Prosperity, and Poverty* (New York: Crown Publisher, 2012).

J. Adelman, *Worldly Philosopher: The Odyssey of Albert Hirschman* (Princeton: Princeton University Press, 2013).

C. Aguiar de Medeiros, 'Financial Dependency and Growth Cycles in Latin American Countries', *Journal of Post Keynesian Economics*, 31: 1, (2008), pp. 79–99.

A. Alesina and D. Rodrik, 'Distributive Politics and Economic Growth', *Quarterly Journal of Economics*, 108, (1994), pp. 465–90.

S. Alkire and J. Foster, 'Counting and Multidimensional Poverty Measurement' (OPHI Working Paper N. 7, University of Oxford, 2007).

—— 'Counting and Multidimensional Poverty Measurement', *Journal of Public Economics*, 95: 7, (2011a), pp. 476–87.

—— 'Understandings and Misunderstandings of Multidimensional Poverty Measurement', *Journal of Economic Inequality*, 9, (2011b), pp. 289–314.

S. Alkire and M.E. Santos, 'Acute Multidimensional Poverty: A New Index for Developing Countries' (OPHI Working. Paper Series No. 38, 2010).

S. Alkire, J.M. Roche and A. Sumner, 'Where Do the World's Multidimensionally Poor People Live?' (OPHI Working Paper 61, 2013).

M. Alacevich, *Le origini della Banca Mondiale* (Milano: Bruno Mondadori, 2007).

A.M. Amado, 'The Regional Impact of the Internationalisation of the Financial System: The Case of MERCOSUL', in P. Arestis, M. Desai and S. Dow (eds), *Methodology, Microeconomics and Keynes. Essays in Honour of Victoria Chick,* vol. 2 (London: Routledge, 2002), pp. 192–202.

S. Amin, 'The End of a Debate', re-published as Part IV of *Imperialism and Unequal Development* (English trans., Hassocks: Harvester, 1977).

—— *Capitalism in the Age of Globalization* (London: Zed Books, 1997).

—— *Más allá del capitalismo senil: Por un Siglo XXI no norteamericano* (Buenos Aires: Paidós, 2003, Spanish trans. of *Au-delà du capitalisme senile*, Paris: Presses Universitaires de France, 2001).

A. Amsden, *Asia's Next Giant: South-Korea and Late Industrialization* (Oxford: Oxford University Press, 1989).

—— *The Rise of the 'Rest': Challenges to the West from Late-Industrializing Economies* (Oxford: Oxford University Press, 2001).

S. Anand and A. Sen, 'Concepts of Human Development and Poverty: A Multidimensional Perspective' (New York: UNDP, 1997).

E. Arceo, 'El impacto de la globalización en la periferia y las nuevas y viejas formas de dependencia', *Cuadernos del CENDES*, 22: 50, (2005), pp. 22–61.

—— *El largo camino a la crisis: Centro, periferia y transformaciones en la economía social* (Buenos Aires: Cara o Ceca, 2011).

P. Arida and E. Bacha, 'Balance of Payments – a Disequilibrium Analysis for Semi-industrialized Economies', *Journal of Development Economics*, 27, (1987), pp. 85–108.

H.W. Arndt, 'The Origins of Structuralism', *World Development*, 13, (1985), pp. 151–59.

—— *Economic Development. The History of an Idea* (London: The University of Chicago Press, 1987).

W. Ascher, 'The Evolution of Postwar Doctrines in Development Economics' in A.W. Coats (ed), *The Post-1945 Internationalization of Economics*, annual supplement to *History of Political Economy* (Durham: Duke University Press, 1996), pp. 312–36.

A.B. Atkinson, 'On the Measurement of Poverty', *Econometrica*, 55, (1987), pp. 749–64.

—— 'Multidimensional Deprivation: Contrasting Social Welfare and Counting Approaches', *Journal of Economic Inequality*, 1, (2003), pp. 51–65.

A.B. Atkinson and F. Bourguignon, 'Poverty and Inclusion from a World Perspective', in J. Stiglitz and P.A. Muet (eds), *Governance, Equity and Global Markets* (Oxford, Oxford University Press, 2001), pp. 151–64.

C. Azariadis, 'The Theory of Poverty Traps. What Have We learned?', in S. Bowles, S.N. Durlauf and K. Hoff (eds), *Poverty Traps* (Princeton: Princeton University Press, 2006), pp. 17–40.

C. Azariadis and J. Stachursky, 'Poverty Traps' in P. Aghion and S. Durlauf (eds), *Handbook of Economic Growth*, vol.1a, (Amsterdam: North-Holland, 2005), pp. 295–384.

R. Baghitathan, C. Rada and L. Taylor, 'Structuralist Economics: Worldly Philosophers, Models and Methodology', *Social Research*, 71, (2004), pp. 305–26.

T. Balogh, 'Modelli statici e problemi attuali', in T. Balogh *Unequal Partners* (Italian trans. *Una società di ineguali*, Torino: Einaudi, [1949] 1967), pp. 210–19.

—— 'Investimenti all'interno e investimenti all'estero', in T. Balogh *Unequal Partners* (Italian trans. *Una società di ineguali*, Torino: Einaudi, [1960] 1967), pp. 220–35.

C. Ban, 'From Cocktail to Dependence: Revisiting the Foundations of Dependent Market Capitalism', *Boston University Global Economic Governance Initiative* (Working Paper N. 3, 2013).

A.V. Banerjee and E. Duflo, 'Inequality and Growth: What Can the Data Say?', *Journal of Economic Growth*, 8: 3, (2003), pp. 267–99.

—— 'Growth Theory through the Lens of Economic Development', in P. Aghion and S. Durlauf (eds), *Handbook of Economic Growth*, vol. 1a (Amsterdam: North-Holland, 2005), pp. 473–552.

M. Banik, 'Dualism, Structural Change and the Development Experience of Brazil', working paper, *Economic Development, INTS*, (2011).

P.A. Baran, 'Review of *The Process of Economic Growth* by W.W. Rostow', *American Economic Review*, 42: 5, (1952), pp. 921–23.

—— *The Political Economy of Growth* (New York: Monthly Review Press, 1957).

P.A. Baran and E.J. Hobsbawm, 'Review of *Stages of Economic Growth* by W.W. Rostow', *Kyklos*, 14: 2, (1961), pp. 234–42.

P. Baran and P. Sweezy, *Monopoly Capital: An Essay on the American Economic and Social Order* (New York: Monthly Review Press, 1966).

P. Bardhan, 'Decentralization of Governance and Development', *Journal of Economic Perspectives*, 16: 4, (2002), pp. 185–205.

P. Bardhan, S. Bowles and H. Gintis, 'Wealth Inequality, Credit Constraints, and Economic Performance', in A. Atkinson, F. Bourguignon (eds), *Handbook of Income Distribution* (Dortrecht: North-Holland 2000), pp. 541–603.

P.T. Bauer, 'Lewis' Theory of Economic Growth', *The American Economic Review*, 46: 4, (1956), pp. 632–41.

—— 'The Spurious Consensus and its Background' in P.T. Bauer, *Dissent on Development. Studies and Debates in Development Economics* (Cambridge, MA: Harvard University Press, [1969] 1972), pp. 306–42.

F. Beigel, 'Vida, muerte y resurrección de las "teorías de la dependencia"' in F. Beigel, et al. (eds), *Crítica y teoría en el pensamiento social latinoamericano* (Buenos Aires: CLACSO, 2006), pp. 287–326.

—— 'Dependency Analysis: The Creation of a New Social Theory in Latin America', in S. Patel (ed.), *The ISA Handbook of Diverse Sociological Traditions* (London: Sage, 2010), pp. 189–200.

J. Benes and M. Kumhof, 'The Chicago Plan Revisited', *IMF Working Paper* n. WP/12/202, (2012).

C. Bettelheim, 'Remarques théoriques', in A. Emmanuel (ed.), *L'Échange inégal* (Paris: Maspero [1969] 1979), pp. 297–341.

A. Bhaduri, 'Disguised Unemployment', in J. Eatwell, M. Milgate and P. Newman (eds), *The New Palgrave – Economic Development* (New York–London: Macmillan, 1987), pp. 109–13.

—— 'Implications of Globalization for Macroeconomic Theory and Policy in Developing Countries', in D. Baker, G. Epstein and R. Pollin (eds), *Globalization and Progressive Economic Policy* (Cambridge: Cambridge University Press, 1998), pp. 149–59.

J. Bibow, 'A Post-Keynesian Perspective on the Rise of Central bank Independence: A Dubious Success Story in Monetary Economics', *Working paper 625* (Levy Economics Institute of Bard College, 2010).

R. Bielschowsky, 'Sixty Years of ECLAC: Structuralism and Neo-structuralism', *CEPAl Review*, 97, (2009), pp. 171–92.

N. Birdsall, 'The (Indispensable) Middle Class in Developing Countries; or, The Rich and the Rest, Not the Poor and the Rest' (Center for Global Development, Working Paper n. 207: Washington DC, 2010).

S. Blackenburg, J.G. Palma and F. Tregenna, 'Structuralism', in S. Durlauf and L. Blume (eds), *The New Palgrave Dictionary of Economics*, 2nd edition (London: Macmillan, 2008) pp 69–74.

J.H. Boeke, *Economics and Economic Policy of Dual Societies as Exemplified by Indonesia* (New York: Institute of Pacific Relations, 1953).

M. Boianovsky, 'A View from the Tropics: Celso Furtado and the Theory of Economic Development in the 1950s', *History of Political Economy*, 42: 2, (2010), pp. 221–66.

—— 'Friedrich List and the Economic Fate of Tropical Countries', *History of Political Economy*, 45: 4 (2013), pp. 647–91.

—— 'Between Lévi-Strauss and Braudel: Furtado and the Historical–Structural Method in Latin American Political Economy', *Journal of Economic Methodology*. 22: 4, (2015), forthcoming.

M. Boianovsky and R. Solís, 'The Origins and Development of the Latin American Structuralist Approach to the Balance of Payments, 1944–1964', *Review of Political Economy*, 26, (2014), pp. 23–59.

M. Boianovsky and K.D. Hoover, 'In the Kingdom of Solovia: the Rise of Growth Economics at MIT, 1956–1970', *History of Political Economy*, Annual supplement, 46, (2014), pp. 198–228.

P. Bourdieu, *Intelectuales, Política y Poder* (Buenos Aires: Eudeba, 1999).

F. Bourguignon, 'The Growth Elasticity of Poverty Reduction: Explaining Heterogeneity across Countries and Time Periods', in T. Eicher and S. Turnovsky (eds), *Growth and Inequality*, (Cambridge, MA: MIT Press, 2003), pp. 3–27.

F. Bourguignon and S. Chakravarty, 'The Measurement of Multidimensional Poverty', *Journal of Economic Inequality*, 1: 1, (2003), pp. 25–49.

F. Bourguignon and C. Morrison, 'Income among World Citizens: 1820–1992', *American Economic Review*, 92: 4, (2002), pp. 727–44.

S. Bowles, S. N. Durlauf and K. Hoff (eds), *Poverty Traps* (Princeton: Princeton University Press, 2006).

S. Bowles, 'Institutional Poverty Traps', in S. Bowles, S. N. Durlauf and K. Hoff (eds), *Poverty Traps* (Princeton: Princeton University Press, 2006), pp. 116–38.

S. Brankovic, *Il problema dei paesi sottosviluppati* (Milano: Feltrinelli, 1959).

R. Brenner, 'The Origins of Capitalist Development: A Critique of Neo-Smithian Marxism', *New Left Review*, 104, (1977), pp. 25–92.

M. Bronfenbrenner and F.D. Holzman, 'Survey of Inflation Theory', *American Economic Review*, 53, (1963), pp. 593–661.

K. Brunner, 'The Role of Money and Monetary Policy', *Federal Reserve Bank of St. Louis Review*, 50, (1968), pp. 8–24.

R. Cantillon, *Essai sur la nature du commerce en général* (London: Macmillan, [1730] 1931).

R.O Campos, 'Two Views on Inflation in Latin America' in A. Hirschman (ed.), *Latin American Issues* (New York: Twentieth Century Fund, 1961), pp. 69–79.

—— 'Economic development and inflation, with special reference to Latin America' in Id. *Reflections on Latin American development* (Austin: University of Texas Press [1964] 1967), pp. 106–1.

F.H. Cardoso and E. Faletto, *Dependencia y desarrollo en América Latina: ensayo de interpretación sociológica* (Mexico City: Siglo Ventiuno, 1969).

—— *Dependency and development in Latin America*, trans. by M. Urquidi (Berkeley: University of California Press, 1979).

S.B. Carpenter and S. Demiralp 'Money, Reserves, and the Transmission of Monetary Policy: Does the Money Multiplier Exist?', *Finance and Economics Discussion Series*, Divisions of Research & Statistics and Monetary Affairs, Federal Reserve Board, Washington, DC (2010).

S. Chakravarty and C. D'Ambrosio, 'Polarization Orderings of Income Distributions', *Review of Income and Wealth*, 56: 1, (2010), pp. 47–64.

H.J. Chang, *Kicking Away the Ladder: Development Strategy in Historical Perspective* (London: Anthem Press, 2003).

—— *Institutional Change and Economic Development* (London: Anthem Press, 2007).

—— *Bad Samaritans. The Myth of Free Trade and the Secret History of Capitalism* (New York–Berlin–London: Bloomsbury, 2008).

H.J. Chang (ed.), *Rethinking Development Economics* (London: Anthem Press, 2003).

S. Chantarat and C.B. Barrett, 'Social Network Capital, Economic Mobility and Poverty Traps', *Journal of Economic Inequality* , 10, (2012), pp. 299–342.

S. Chen and M. Ravallion, 'The Developing World Is Poorer Than We Thought, but No Less Successful in the Fight Against Poverty', *Quarterly Journal of Economics*, 125: 4, (2010), pp. 1577–625.

—— 'More Relatively-Poor People in a Less Absolutely-Poor World', *Review of Income and Wealth*, 59: 1, (2013), pp. 1–28.

H.B. Chenery, 'Comparative Advantages and Development Policy', in B. Jossa (ed.), *Economia del sottosviluppo* (Bologna: il Mulino [1961] 1973), pp. 295–333.

—— 'Development Policies for Southern Italy', *The Quarterly Journal of Economics*, 76: 4, (1962), pp. 512–47.

—— 'The Structuralist Approach to Development Policy', *American Economic Review*, 65, (1975), pp. 310–16.

—— 'Introduction to Part II', in H.B. Chenery and T.N. Srinivasan (eds), *Handbook of Development Economics*, vol. 1 (Amsterdam: North Holland, 1988), pp. 197–202.

H.B. Chenery and M. Bruno, 'Development Alternatives in an Open Economy: The Case of Israel', *Economic Journal*, 72, (1962), pp. 79–103.

H.B. Chenery and A.M. Strout, 'Foreign Assistance and Economic Development', *American Economic Review*, 56, (1966), pp. 679–733.

H.B. Chenery and M. Syrquin, *Patterns of Development 1950–1970* (London: Oxford University Press, 1975).

E. Chiappero-Martinetti and S. Moroni, 'An Analytical Framework for Conceptualizing Poverty and Re-examining the Capability Approach', *Journal of Socio-Economics*, 36, (2007), pp. 360–75.

V. Chick, *Macroeconomics After Keynes* (Cambridge, MA: The MIT Press, 1991).

V. Chick and S. Dow, 'A Post-Keynesian Perspective on the Relation between Banking and Regional Development', in P. Arestis (ed.), *Post-Keynesian Monetary Economics: New Approaches to Financial Modelling* (Cheltenham, UK: Edward Elgar. 1988), pp. 219–50.

M. Cimoli and G. Porcile, 'Learning, Technological Capabilities and Structural Dynamics', in J.A. Ocampo and J. Ros (eds.), *The Oxford Handbook of Latin American Economics* (Oxford: Oxford University Press, 2011), pp. 546–67.

P. Collier, *The Bottom Billion: Why the Poorest Countries are Failing and What Can Be Done About It* (Oxford: Oxford University Press, 2007).

P. Collier and D. Dollar, *Globalization, Growth, and Poverty. Building an Inclusive World Economy* (New York: World Bank, Oxford University Press, 2002).

W.M. Corden, 'Booming Sector and Dutch Disease Economics: Survey and Consolidation', *Oxford Economic Papers*, 36, (1984), pp. 359–80.

C. Crowe and E.E. Meade, 'The Evolution of Central Bank Governance around the World', *Journal of Economic Perspectives*, 21: 4, (2007), pp. 69–90.

A.M. Cunha and G. Britto, 'When Development Meets Culture: Furtado in the1970s', Working paper no. 429 (2011), CEDEPLAR/UFMG.

J. Cyr and L. Mahoney, 'The Enduring Influence of Historical–Structural Approaches', in P. Kingstone and D.J. Yashar (eds), *Routledge Handbook of Latin American Politics* (New York: Routledge, 2012), pp. 433–46.

M. Damian and J.C. Graz (eds), *Commerce international et développement soutenable* (Paris: Economica, 2001).

P. Dasgupta, *An Inquiry into Well-Being and Destitution* (Oxford: Clarendon Press, 1993).

P. Davidson, 'Reviving Keynes's Revolution', *Journal of Post-Keynesian Economics*, 6: 4, (1984), pp. 561–75.

A.S. Deaton, 'Measuring Poverty in a Growing World (or Measuring Growth in a Poor World)', *Review of Economics and Statistics*, 87: 1, (2005), pp. 1–19.

G. Debreu, 'Excess Demand Functions', *Journal of Mathematical Economics*, 1, (1974), pp. 15–23.

D. Defoe, *Plan of the English Commerce* (New York: Kelley [1728] 1967).

A. Di Filippo, 'La visión centro-periferia hoy', *Revista de la CEPAL*, special issue, (1998), pp. 175–85.

—— 'Latin American Structuralism and Economic Theory', *CEPAL Review*, 98, (2009), pp. 175–96.

A. Dixit, 'Optimal Development in the Labour-Surplus Economy', *Review of Economic Studies*, 35, (1968), pp. 23–34.

—— 'Models of Dual Economies', in J. Mirrlees and N.H. Stern (eds), *Models of Economic Growth* (London: MacMillan, 1973), pp. 325–52.

D. Dollar and A. Kraay, 'Growth Is Good for the Poor', *Journal of Economic Growth*, 7: 1, (2002), pp. 195–225.

F. Dosse, *History of Structuralism*, 2 vols (Minneapolis: University of Minnesota Press, 1997).

S. Dow, 'Methodology in a Pluralist Environment', *Journal of Economic Methodology*, 8: 1, (2001), pp. 33–40.

—— 'Structured Pluralism', *Journal of Economic Methodology*, 11: 3, (2004), pp. 275–90.

S. Dow, D. Ghosh and R. Kobil, 'A Stages Approach to Banking Development in Transition Economies', *Journal of Post Keynesian Economics*, 31: 1, (2008), pp. 3–34.

J. Drèze and A. Sen, *An Uncertain Glory: India and its Contradictions* (Princeton: Princeton University Press, 2013).

J.Y. Duclos, D. Sahn and S.D. Younger, 'Robust Multidimensional Spatial Poverty Comparisons in Ghana, Madagascar, and Uganda', *The World Bank Economic Review*, 20: 1, (2006), pp. 91–113.

S.N. Durlauf, 'The Memberships Theory of Inequality: Ideas and Implications', in E. S. Brezis, P. Temin (eds), *Elites, Minorities, and Economic Growth* (Amsterdam: Elsevier, 1999), pp. 161–77.

S.N. Durlauf, 'Groups, Social Influences, and Inequality', in S. Bowles, S.N. Durlauf and K. Hoff (eds), *Poverty Traps* (Princeton: Princeton University Press, 2006), pp. 141–75.

A.K. Dutt and J. Ros (eds), *Development Economics and Structuralist Economics – Essays in Honor of Lance Taylor* (Cheltenham: Elgar, 2003).

R.S. Eckaus, 'The Factor Proportion Problem in Underdeveloped Areas', *The American Economic Review*, 45: 4, (1955), pp. 539–65.

B. Eichengreen, *Globalizing Capital. A History of the International Monetary System*, Princeton, NJ: Princeton University Press, 1996).

A. Emmanuel (ed.), *L'Échange inégal* (Paris: Maspero [1969] 1979).

F. Fajnzylber, *Industrializacion en Latino America* (Santiago: CEPAL, 1989).

J.C.H. Fei and G. Ranis, *Development of the Labour Surplus Economy: Theory and Practice* (Homewood, IL: Irwing, 1964).

R. Ffrench-Davis and H. Tapia, 'The Chilean Style of Capital Controls: An Empirical Assessment', ECLAC Project on Management of Volatility, Financial Liberalization and Growth. Econometric Society Latin American Meetings, (2004).

M. Figueroa, 'W. Arthur Lewis versus the Lewis Model. Agricultural or Industrial Development?', *Manchester School*, 72: 6, (2004), pp. 736–50.

R. Findlay, *International Trade and Development Theory* (New York: Columbia University Press, 1973).

—— 'On W. Arthur Lewis' Contribution to Economics', *The Scandinavian Journal of Economics*, 82: 1, (1980), pp. 62–79.

B. Fine, C. Lapavitsas and J. Pincus (eds), *Development Economics in the Twentieth-first Century. Beyond the Post-Washington Consensus* (London: Routledge, 2001).

J. Flanders, 'Prebisch on Protectionism: An Evaluation', *Economic Journal*, 74, (1964), pp. 30–26.

K. Forbes, 'A Reassessment of the Relationship between Inequality and Growth', *American Economic Review*, 90: 4, (2000), pp. 869–87.

J. Foster, J. Greer and E. Thorbecke, 'A Class of Decomposable Poverty Measures', *Econometrica*, 52, (1984), pp. 761–65.

J. Foster and M. Székely, 'Is Economic Growth Good for the Poor? Tracking low incomes using general means', *International Economic Review*, 49: 4, (2008), pp. 1143–72.

S. Franco, 'Different Concepts of Poverty', in F. Stewart, R. Saith and B. Harris-White (eds), *Defining Poverty in the Developing World* (Basingtoke: Palgrave Macmillan, 2007), pp. 160–97.

A.G. Frank, *Latin America: Underdevelopment or Revolution* (New York: Monthly Review Press, 1969).

—— *Lumpenburgeoisie: Lumpendevelopment. Dependence, Class and Politics in Latin America* (New York: Monthly Review Press, 1972).

—— 'Latin American Development Theories Revisited: A Participant Review', *Latin American Perspectives*, 19: 2, (1992), pp. 125–39.

E. Fullbrook, *Pluralist Economics* (London: Zed Books, 2008).

J. Furman and J. Stiglitz, 'Economic Crises: Evidence and Insights from East Asia', Brookings Papers on Economic Activity, N. 2. Washington, DC: Brookings Institution (1998).

C. Furtado, 'Capital Formation and Economic Development', trans. by J. Cairncross, *International Economic Papers*, 4, ([1952] 1954), pp. 124–44; also in A.N. Agarwala and S.P. Singh, (eds), *The Economics of Underdevelopment* (Oxford: Oxford University Press, [1952] 1958), pp. 309–37.

—— *A economia brasileira* (Rio: A Noite, 1954).

—— 'O desenvolvimento recente da economia venezuelana (exposição de alguns problemas)', in R.F. D'Aguiar Furtado (ed), *Ensaios sobre a Venezuela: Subdesenvolvimento com Abundância de Divisas* (Rio: Contraponto and Centro Internacional Celso Furtado, [1957] 2008), pp. 35–135.

—— *The Economic Growth of Brazil – A Survey from Colonial to Modern Times* (Berkeley: University of California Press, 1963), trans. by R. Aguiar and E. Drysdale of *Formação Economica do Brasil* (Rio: Fundo de Cultura, [1959]).

—— *Development and Underdevelopment* (Berkeley: University of California Press, 1964), translation by R. Aguiar and E. Drysdale of *Desenvolvimento e Subdesenvolvimento* (Rio: Fundo de Cultura [1961]), partly included in *Théorie du développement* économique (Italian trans. Bari: Laterza, [1961] 1972).

—— *Théorie du développement économique*, trans. by A.B. Silva (Paris: PUF, 1970).

—— 'Dependencia externa y teoria económica', *El Trimestre Económico*, 38: 2, (1971), pp. 335–49.

—— *Teoria e política do desenvolvimento econômico*, 5th edition (S. Paulo: Cia. Editora Nacional, 1975).

—— 'Analyse économique et histoire quantitative', in *L'Histoire Quantitative du Brésil de 1800 a 1930* (Paris: Editions du Centre National de la Recherche Scientifique,

Colloques Internationaux du Centre National de la Recherche Scientifique, # 543, 1973), pp. 23–26.

—— *Criatividade e dependência na civilização industrial* (Rio: Paz e Terra, 1978).

—— *Pequena introdução ao desenvolvimento: enfoque multidisciplinar* (S. Paulo: Cia Editora Nacional, 1980).

—— *Accumulation and Development: The Logic of Industrial Civilization*, trans. by S. Macedo (Oxford: Martin Robertson [1978] 1983).

—— *A Fantasia Organizada* (Rio: Paz e Terra, 1985).

—— 'Underdevelopment: to Conform or Reform' in G.M. Meier (ed). *Pioneers in Development – Second Series* (New York: Oxford University Press and the World Bank, 1987), pp. 205–27.

—— *Introdução ao desenvolvimento: enfoque histórico-estrutural* (Rio: Paz e Terra, 2000) (revised edition of Furtado 1980 with a new preface and title).

—— 'Hacia una ideología del desarrollo', *El Trimestre Económico*, XXXIII:3, (1966), pp. 379–91.

J.K. Galbraith, *Inequality and Instability: A Study of the World Economy Just Before the Crisis* (New York: Oxford University Press, 2012).

K. Gallagher, S. Griffith-Jones and J.A. Ocampo, 'Regulating Global Capital Flows for Long Run Development' Boston University, Frederick S. Pardee Centre for the Study of the Longer Range Future, (2012), at http://www.bu.edu/pardee/files/2012/03/RegulatingCapitalTF-March2012.pdf [accessed 12 January 2015].

P. Garegnani, 'Heterogeneous Capital, the Production Function and the Theory of Distribution', *Review of Economic Studies*, 37: 3, (1970), pp. 407–36.

—— 'Value and Distribution in the Classical Economists and Marx', *Oxford Economic Papers*, 36: 2, (1984), pp. 291–325.

—— 'Quantity of Capital', in J.L. Eatwell, M. Milgate and P. Newman (eds), *Capital Theory: The New Palgrave* (London: MacMillan, 1990a), pp. 1–78.

—— 'Sraffa: Classical Versus Marginal Analysis', in K. Bharadwaj and B. Schefold (eds), *Essays on Piero Sraffa: Critical Perspectives on the Revival of Classical Theory* (London: Unwin Hyman, 1990b), pp. 112–40.

B. Gibson, 'An Essay on Late Structuralism', in A.K. Dutt and J. Ros (eds), *Development Economics and Structuralist Macroeconomics: Essays in Honor of Lance Taylor* (Cheltenham: Elgar, 2003), pp. 52–76.

A. Greif and G. Tabellini, *The Clan and the City: Sustaining Cooperation in China and Europe*, (mimeo, Stanford, 2012).

D. Gualerzi, *The Coming of Age of Information Technologies and the Path of Transformational Growth* (London: Routledge, 2010).

—— 'Towards a Theory of the Consumption-Growth Relationship', *Review of Political Economy*, 24: 1, (2012), pp. 15–32.

D. Gualerzi and A. Cibils, 'High Development Theory, CEPAL, and Beyond', in J.L. Cardoso, M.C. Marcuzzo and M.E. Romero Sotelo (eds), *Economic Development and Global Crisis. The Latin American Economy in Historical Perspective* (Abingdon: Routledge, 2014), pp. 139–58.

H. Gülalp, 'Frank and Wallerstein Revisited: A Contribution to Brenner's Critique', *Journal of Contemporary Asia*, 11: 2, (1981), pp. 168–88.

H. Hagemann, 'Dismissal, Expulsion, and Emigration of German-speaking Economists after 1933', *Journal of the History of Economic Thought*, 27: 4, (2005), pp. 405–20.

—— 'German-speaking Economists in British Exile 1933–1945', *Banca Nazionale del Lavoro Quartely Review*, LX: 242, (2007), pp. 323–63.

P. Hall and D. Soskice, 'An Introduction to Varieties of Capitalism', in P. Hall and D. Soskice (eds), *Varieties of Capitalism: The Institutional Foundations of Comparative Advantage* (Oxford: Oxford University Press, 2001), pp. 1–68.

D. Halter, M. Oechslin and J. Zweimüller, 'Inequality and Growth: The Neglected Time Dimension' (Institute for Empirical Research in Economics: University of Zurich, Working Paper n. 507, 2011).

J.R. Harris and M.P. Todaro, 'Migration, Unemployment and Development: A Two-Sector Analysis', *The American Economic Review*, 40: 1, (1970), pp. 126–42.

R. Hernández López, 'La dependencia a debate', *Latinoamérica*, 40, (2005), pp. 11–54.

J.R. Hicks, 'Review of *The Process of Economic Growth* by W.W. Rostow', *Journal of Political Economy*, 61: 2, (1953), pp. 173–74.

B. Higgins, 'The "Dualistic Theory" of Underdeveloped Areas', *Economic Development and Cultural Change*, 4: 2, (1956), pp. 99–115.

A.O. Hirschman, *National Power and the Structure of Foreign Trade* (Italian trans. Bologna: il Mulino, [1945] 1987).

—— 'Investment Policies and "Dualism" in Underdeveloped Countries', *The American Economic Review*, 47: 5, (1957), pp. 550–70.

—— *The Strategy of Economic Development* (New Haven: Yale University Press, 1958).

—— *Journeys Toward Progress. Studies of Economic Policy-Making in Latin America* (New York: The Twentieth Century Fund, 1963).

—— *Development Projects Observed* (Washington DC: The Brookings Institution [1967] 1995).

—— *Exit, Voice, and Loyalty: Responses to Decline in Firms, Organizations, and States* (Cambridge MA: Harvard University Press, 1970).

—— 'The Rise and Decline of Development Economics', *Essays in Trespassing, Economics to Politics and Beyond* (Cambridge: Cambridge University Press, 1981), pp. 1–24.

—— *Shifting Involvements* (Princeton: Princeton University Press,1982).

R. Holcombe, 'Pluralism vs. Heterodoxy in Economics and the Social Sciences', *The Journal of Philosophical Economics*, 1: 2, (2008), pp. 51–72.

A. Hounie, L. Pittaluga, G. Porcile and F. Scatolin, 'ECLAC and the new growth theories', *CEPAL Review*, 68, (1999), pp. 7–31.

D. Hunt, *Economic Theories of Development: An Analysis of Competing Paradigms* (New York: Harvester Wheatsheaf, 1989).

N. Islam and K. Yokoda, 'An Initial Look at China's Industrialization in Light of the Lewis Growth Model, *East Asia Economic* Perspectives, 17: 2, (2006), pp. 103–32.

K.P. Jameson, 'Latin American Structuralism: a Methodological Perspective', *World Development*, 14, (1986), pp. 223–32.

K.S. Jomo (ed.), *Pioneers of Development Economics: Great Economists on Development* (London, Zed Books, 2005).

N. Kaldor, *Causes of the Slow Rate of Economic Growth in the United Kingdom* (Cambridge: Cambridge University Press, 1966).

—— 'The Problem of Intersectoral Balance', in N. Kaldor, *Causes of Growth and Stagnation in the World Economy* (Cambridge: Cambridge University Press, 1996), pp. 39–54.

—— 'The New Monetarism', reprinted in Id. *Further essays on applied economics*, vol. VI (London: Duckworth [1970] 1978).

R. Kanbur and J. McIntosh, 'Dual Economies', in J. Eatwell, M. Milgate and P. Newman (eds), *The New Palgrave – Economic Development* (New York–London: Macmillan, 1987), pp. 114–21.

C. Kay, *Latin American Theories of Development and Underdevelopment* (London: Routledge, 1989).

―― 'Reflections on the Latin American Contributions to Development Theory', *Development and Change*, 22: 1, (1991), pp. 31–68.

―― 'Structuralism', in R.J. Barry Jones (ed.), *Routledge Encyclopedia of International Political Economy* (London: Routledge, 2001), pp. 1502–11.

―― 'Latin American Structuralist School', in *International Encyclopedia of human geography*, vol.6 (Oxford: Elsevier, 2009), pp. 159–64.

C. Kay and R. Gwynne, 'Relevance of Structuralist and Dependency Theories in theNeo-liberal Period: A Latin American Perspective', *Journal of developing societies*, 16: 1, (2000), pp. 49–69.

A.C. Kelly, J.G. Williamson and R.J. Cheetham, *Dualistic Economic Development: Theories and History* (Chicago: University of Chicago Press, 1972).

C.P. Kindleberger, *Europe's Postwar Growth: The Role of the Labor Supply (Cambridge, MA: Harvard University Press, 1967).*

―― *Economic Laws and Economic History* (Cambridge: Cambridge University Press, 1989), pp. 21–42.

J.E. King, 'Three Arguments for Pluralism in Economics', *Post Autistic Economic Review*, 23, (January 2004), at http://www.btinternet.com/~pae_news/review/issue23.htm [accessed 25 February 2015].

K. Kirkpatrick and A. Barrientos, 'The Lewis Model after 50 Years', *Manchester School*, 72: 6, (2004), pp. 679–90.

A.P. Kirman, 'Whom or What Does the Representative Individual Represent?', *Journal of Economic Perspectives*, 6:2, (1992), pp. 117–36.

J. Klugman, F. Rodríguez and H.-J. Choi, 'The HDI 2010: New Controversies, Old Critiques', *Journal of Economic Inequality*, 9, (2011), pp. 249–88.

A. Kraay, 'When Is Growth Pro-Poor? Evidence from a Panel of Countries', *Journal of Economic Development*, 80, (2006), pp. 198–227.

P. Krugman, 'Toward a Counter-Revolution in Development Theory', *Proceedings of the World Bank Annual Conference on Development Economics* (Washington DC: World Bank, 1993), pp. 15–38.

―― *Development, Geography and Economic Theory* (Cambridge, MA: The MIT Press, 1998).

―― 'The Fall and Rise of Development Economics' (2005), at http://web.mit.edu/krugman/www/dishpan.html, [accessed 20 January 2015].

H.D. Kurz and N. Salvadori, *Theory of Production*: *A Long Period Analysis* (Cambridge: Cambridge University Press, 1995).

S.S. Kuznets, 'Economic Growth and Income Inequality', *American Economic Review*, 45, (1955), pp. 1–28.

―― 'Notes on the Take-off', in W.W. Rostow, (ed.), *The Economics of Take-off into Sustained Growth: Proceedings of a Conference held by the International Economic Association* (London: St Martin's Press, 1963), ch. 2, pp. 22–43.

D. Lal, *The Poverty of 'Development Economics* (London: Institute of Economic Affairs, 1983).

S. Lall, 'World Trade and Development', in R.Beynon (ed.), *The Routledge Companion to Global Economics* (London–New York: Routledge, 2001), pp. 21–46.

C. Lapavitsas, et al., 'Breaking Up? A Route Out of the Eurozone Crisis', *Research on Money and Finance*, Occasional Report 3, (2011).

R. La Porta and A. Shleifer, 'The Unofficial Economy and Economic Development', *Brookings Papers on Economic Activity*, (2008), pp. 275–352.

M. Lavoie, *Introduction to Post-Keynesian Economics* (Basingstoke, Hampshire and New York: Palgrave MacMillan, 2006).

T. Lawson, 'The Nature of Heterodox Economics', *Cambridge Journal of Economics*, 30: 4, (2006), pp. 483–505.

P. Leeson, 'The Lewis Model and Development Theory', *Manchester School*, 47: 3, (1979), pp. 196–209.

I. Leiva, 'Toward a Critique of Latin American Neostructuralism', *Latin American Politics and Society*, 50, (2008a), pp. 1–25.

—— *Latin American Neostructuralism: The Contradictions of Post-neoliberal Development* (Minneapolis: University of Minnesota Press, 2008b).

W.A. Lewis, 'Economic Development with Unlimited Supply of Labour' in *Manchester School*, 22, (1954), pp 139–91; also in in A.N. Agarwala and S.P. Singh, (eds) *The Economics of Underdevelopment* (Oxford: Oxford University Press, [1954] 1958), pp. 400–49.

—— *The Theory of Economic Growth*, Italian trans., *Teoria dello sviluppo economico* (Milano: Feltrinelli, [1955] 1963).

—— 'Unlimited Labour: Further Notes', *Manchester School*, 26: 1, (1958), pp. 1–32.

—— 'A Review of Economic Development', *The American Economic Review*, 55: 1–2, (1965), pp. 1–16.

—— *Development Planning* (Italian trans., Milano: Feltrinelli, [1966] 1968).

—— 'Reflections on Unlimited Labour' in L.E. Di Marco (ed.), *International Economics and Development. Essays in Honour of Raul Prebisch* (New York: Academic Press, 1972), pp. 75–96.

—— 'The Dual Economy Revisited', *Manchester School*, 47: 3, (1979), pp. 211–29.

—— 'Development Economics in the 1950s', in G.M. Meier and D. Seers (eds), *Pioneers in Development* (New York–Oxford: Oxford University Press, 1984a), pp. 121–37.

—— 'The State of Development Theory', *The American Economic Review*, 74: 1, (1984b), pp. 1–10.

J. Lin, *New Structural Economics: A Framework for Rethinking Development and Policy* (Washington, DC: World Bank, 2012).

I.M.D. Little, *Economic Development: Theory, Policy and International Relations* (New York: Basic Books, 1982).

F. López Castellano (ed.), *Desarrollo: Crónica de un desafío permanente* (Granada: Editorial Universidad de Granada, 2007).

J.L. Love, 'The Origins of Dependency Analysis', *Journal of Latin American Studies*, 22: 1, (1990), pp. 143–68.

—— 'Economic Ideas and Ideologies in Latin America since 1930', in L. Behtell (ed), *Latin America since 1930: Economy, Society and Politics* (Cambridge: Cambridge University Press, 1994), pp. 391–460.

—— 'Structuralism and Dependency in Peripheral Europe: Latin American Ideas in Spain and Portugal', *Latin American Research Review*, 39: 2, (2004), pp. 114–39.

—— 'The Rise and Decline of Economic Structuralism in Latin America', *Latin American Research Review*, 40: 3, (2005), pp. 100–25.

A. Maddison, *The World Economy. A Millennial Perspective* (Paris, OECD, 2001).

P. Mahalanobis, 'Some Observations on the Process of the Growth of National Income', *Sankhrya. The Indian Journal of Statistics*, 12: 4, (1953), pp. 307–12.

C. Mallorquín, *Ideas e historia en torno al pensamiento económico latinoamericano* (Mexico City: Plaza y Valdés, 1999).

A. Maneschi, *Comparative Advantage in International Trade. A Historical Perspective* (Cheltenham UK–Northampton USA: Elgar, 1998).

R. Mantel, 'On the Characterization of Aggregate Excess Demand', *Journal of Economic Theory*, 7, (1974), pp. 348–53.

A. Marchal, *Systémes et structures économiques* (Paris: PUF, 1959).

R.M. Marini, 'Diaéctica de la dependencia, in R.M. Marini, *América Latina: Dependencia y Globalización*, Buenos Aires: CLACSO and Prometeo Libros, [1973] 2007), pp. 99–136.

V. Marrama, *Saggio sullo sviluppo economico dei paesi arretrati* (Torino: Boringhieri [1958] 1963).

K. Marx, *Il Capitale*, vol. 3 (Italian trans., Roma: Editori Riuniti [1864-65]1972).

——— *Il Capitale,* vol. 1, (Italian trans., Roma: Editori Riuniti, [1867] 1964).

J. Mattar, 'Panorama de la gestión pública en América Latina. En la Hora de la Higualdad', Santiago, CEPAL, (2011).

R.I. McKinnon, 'Foreign Exchange Constraints in Economic Development and Efficient Aid Allocation', *Economic Journal*, 74, (1964), pp. 388–409.

G.M. Meier, 'The Old Generation of Development Economists and the New', in G.M. Meier and J.E. Stiglitz (eds), *Frontiers of Development Economics. The Future in Perspective* (Oxford: Oxford University Press, 2001), pp. 13–48.

——— *Biography of a Subject. An Evolution of Development Economics* (Oxford: Oxford University Press, 2005).

G.M. Meier and R. Baldwin, *Economic Development. Theory, History, Policy* (New York: John Wiley and Sons, 1957).

B. Milanovic, *Worlds Apart: Measuring International and Global Inequality* (Princeton: Princeton University Press, 2005).

H. Minsky, *Stabilizing an Unstable Economy* (New York: McGraw Hill, 2008).

J.U. Melville, 'Autonomous and Induced Investment', *The American Economic Review*, 42: 4, (1952), pp. 587-89.

J. Morduch, 'Poverty and Vulnerabilty', *American Economic Review*, 84: 2, (1994), pp. 221–25.

H. Myint, 'An Interpretation of Economic Backwardness', in A.N. Agarwala and S.P. Singh, (eds), *The Economics of Underdevelopment* (Oxford: Oxford University Press, [1954] 1958), pp. 93–132.

——— 'The Classical Theory of International Trade and the Underdeveloped Countries' in B. Jossa (ed), *Economia del sottosviluppo* (Bologna: il Mulino [1958] 1973), pp. 353–77.

——— H. Myint, 'Economic Theroy and the Underdeveloped Countries', *The Journal of Political Economy*, 73: 5, (1965), pp. 477–91.

G. Myrdal, *Economic Theory and Under-developed Regions* (London: Duckworth, 1957), Italian trans. *Teoria economica e paesi* sottosviluppati, Milano: Feltrinelli, 1966).

——— *Beyond the Welfare State* (New Haven–London: Yale University Press, [1960] 1965).

——— *Asian Drama. An Inquiry into the Poverty of Nations* (Allen Lane: The Penguin Press, 1968).

——— 'The World Poverty Problem', in G. Myrdal, *Against the Stream. Critical Essays in Economics* (New York: Vintage Books [1968] 1975), pp. 65–100.

——— 'Place of Values in Social Policy', in G. Myrdal, *Against the Stream. Critical Essays in Economics*, (New York: Vintage Books, 1975), pp. 33–51.

A. Nadal, 'Contradictions of the Open Economy Model as Applied in Mexico', in F. Ackerman and A. Nadal, *The Flawed Foundations of General Equilibrium. Critical Essays in Economic Theory* (London: Routledge, 2004), pp. 132–48.

——— *Rethinking Macroeconomics for Sustainability* (London and New York: Zed Books, 2011).

R. Nallari and B. Griffith, *Understanding Growth and Poverty. Theory, Policy, and Empirics*, Washington: World Bank, 2011).

S.K. Nath, 'The Theory of Balanced Growth', *Oxford Economic Papers*, 14: 2 (1962), pp. 138–53.

A.J. Navarrete and I. Navarrete, 'Underemployment in Underdeveloped Economies' in A.N. Agarwala and S.P. Singh, (eds), *The Economics of Underdevelopment* (Oxford: Oxford University Press, [1953] 1958), pp. 341–47.

J. Nef and W. Robles, 'Globalization, Neoliberalism, and the State of Underdevelopment in the New Periphery', *Journal of Developing Societies*, 16: 1, (2000), pp. 27–48.

E.J. Nell, *The General Theory of Transformational Growth* (Cambridge: Cambridge University Press, 1998).

B. Nolan and C. Whelan, 'On the Multi-dimensionality of Poverty and Social Exclusion', in J. Micklewright and S. Jenkins (eds), *Inequality and Poverty Reexamined* (Oxford: Oxford University Press, 2007), pp. 146–65.

A. Nölke and A. Vliegenthart, 'Enlarging the Varieties of Capitalism: The Emergence of Dependent Market Economies in East Central Europe', *World Politics*, 61: 4, (2009), pp. 670–702.

D.C. North, *Institutions, Institutional Change, and Economic performance* (Cambridge: Cambridge University Press, 1990).

J. Noyola, 'El desarrollo economico y la inflacion en Mexico y otros paises Latinoamericanos', *Investigacion Economica*, 16, (1956), pp. 603–48.

R. Nurkse, *Problems of Capital Formation in Underdeveloped Countries* (Oxford: Oxford University Press, 1953); Italian trans. (Torino: Einaudi, 1965).

—— 'Some International Aspects of the Problem of Economic Development', in A.N. Agarwala and S.P. Singh, (eds), *The Economics of Underdevelopment* (Oxford: Oxford University Press, [1952] 1958), pp. 256–71.

—— *Patterns of Trade and Development*, (Italian trans., Milano: Etas Kompass, [1959] 1970).

—— 'Notes on "Unbalanced Growth"', *Oxford Economic Papers*, 11: 3, (1959), pp. 295–97.

—— 'Further Comments on Professor Rosenstein-Rodan's Paper', in H.S. Ellis and H.C. Wallich (eds), *Economic Development for Latin America, Proceedings of a Conference held by the International Economic Association* (London: MacMillan, 1961), pp. 74–78.

J.A. Ocampo, 'Capital Account and Counter-cyclical Prudential Regulations in Developing Countries', *Serie Informes y Estudios Especiales*, CEPAL 6, February (2003).

J.A. Ocampo and C.E. Tovar, 'La experiencia colombiana con los encajes a los flujos de capital', *Revista de la CEPAL*, 81, (2003), pp. 7–32.

J.A. Ocampo, C. Rada and L. Taylor, *Growth and Policy in Developing Countries: A Structuralist Approach* (New York: Columbia University Press, 2009).

J.H. Olivera, 'La teoria no monetaria de la inflación', *El Trimestre Económico*, 27, (1960), pp. 616–28.

—— 'On Structural Inflation and Latin-American "structuralism"', *Oxford Economic Papers*, 16, (1964), pp. 321–32.

—— 'Aspectos dinámicos de la inflación estrutural', *Desarrollo económico,*7, (1967), pp. 261–66.

C. Oman and G. Wignaraja, *The Postwar Evolution of Development Thinking*, Italian trans., *Le teorie dello sviluppo economico dal dopoguerra a oggi* (Milano: LED, [1991] 2005).

L. Ortiz, *Memorial a Felipe II*, in *Anales de Economia*, 63, [1558] (1957), pp. 117–200.

T. Palley, 'Monetary Policy and Central Banking after the Crisis: The Implications of Rethinking Macroeconomic Theory', IMK Working Paper 8/2011, (2011).

C. Palloix, 'The Internationalization of Capital and the Circuit of Social Capital' in H. Radice (ed), *International Firms and Modern Capitalism* (Harmondsworth: Penguin, 1975), pp. 63–88.

G. Palma, 'Dependency: A Formal Theory of Underdevelopment or a Methodology for the Analysis of Concrete Situations of Underdevelopment?', *World Development*, 6: 7–8, (1978), pp. 881–924.

—— 'Theories of dependency', in A. K. Dutt and J. Ros (eds), *International Handbook of Development Economics*, vol. 1 (Cheltenham, UK: Edward Elgar, 2008a), pp. 125–35.

—— 'Structuralism', in A. K. Dutt and J. Ros (eds), *International Handbook of Development Economics*, vol. 1 (Cheltenham, UK: Edward Elgar, 2008b), pp. 136–43.

L.L. Pasinetti, *Structural Economic Dynamics* (Cambridge, Cambridge University Press, 1993).

P. Paz, 'Dependencia financiera y desnacionalización de la industria interna', *El Trimestre Económico*, 146, (1971), pp. 297–329.

E. Pérez Caldentey and M. Vernengo, 'Back to the Future: Latin America's Current Development Strategy', *Journal of Post Keynesian Economics*, 32: 4, (2010), pp. 623–44.

J. Perkins, *Confessions of an Economic Hit Man* (Italian trans. Roma: Minimum fax, 2004).

N. Perry and N. Cline, 'Wages, Exchange Rates and the Great Inflation Moderation: A post-Keynesian View', Working Paper N. 759, Levy Economics Institute, (2013).

C. Perrotta, *Consumption as an Investment* (New York–London: Routledge 2004).

—— 'Economic Development. Past and Present', in J.L. Cardoso, M.C. Marcuzzo and M.E. Romero (eds), *Economic Development and Global Crisis* (New York–Abingdon: Routledge, 2014), pp. 15–33.

F. Perroux, *L'économie du 20.me siècle*, (Italian trans. Milano: Comunità, [1948–1959] (1966).

F. Petri, *General Equilibrium, Capital and Macroeconomics, A Key to Recent Controversies in Equilibrium Theory* (Cheltenham, UK: Edward Elgar, 2004).

A. Pinto, 'A analise da inflação – estruturalistas e monetaristas: Um inventario', in Id. *Inflação e desenvolvimento* (Petropolis: Vozes [1963] 1970), pp. 149–84.

T. Piketty, *Le capital au 21e siècle* (Paris, Seuil, 2013).

S. Pollard, *The International Economy since 1945* (Italian trans., Roma-Bari: Laterza [1997] 1999).

A. Portes, M. Castells and L.A. Benton (eds), *The Informal Economy. Studies in Advanced and Less Developed Countries* (Baltimore–London: The Johns Hopkins University Press, 1989).

L. Pradella, *Globalisation and the Critique of Political Economy. New insights from Marx's writings* (Abingdon–New York: Routledge, 2015).

R. Prebisch, 'El desarrollo económico de la América Latina y algunos de sus principales problemas', reprint in *Desarrollo económico*, 26: 103 [1949] (1986), pp. 479–502, English trans. 'The Economic Development of Latin America and its principal problems' (27 April 1950), New York: ECLA, at http://repositorio.cepal.org/bitstream/handle/11362/29973/002.df?sequence=1 [accessed 10 November 2014].

—— 'Comments', in R. Lekachman (ed.), *National Policy for Economic Welfare at Home and Abroad* (New York: Russell & Russell, 1955a), pp. 277–80.

—— 'Relações entre crescimento da população, formação de capital e as oportunidades de emprego nos paises subdesenvolvidos', *Economica Brasileira*, 1, (1955b), pp. 135–43.

—— 'Commercial Policy in the Underdeveloped Countries', *American Economic Review*, 49, (1959), pp. 251–73.

—— 'Economic Development or Monetary Stability: The False Dilemma', *Economic Bulletin for Latin America*, 6, (1961), pp. 1–25.

A. Quijano, 'Colonialidad del poder, eurocentrismo y América Latina', in E. Lander (ed.), *La colonialidad del saber: eurocentrismo y ciencias sociales. Perspectivas Latinoamericanas* (Habana: Editorial de la Habana, 2005), pp. 122–51.

X. Ragot, 'L'économie est-elle structuraliste: un essai d'épistémologie', *L'année de la regulation*, 7, (2003), pp. 91–111.

G. Ranis, 'Labour Surplus Economies', in J. Eatwell, M. Milgate and P. Newman (eds), *The New Palgrave – Economic Development* (New York–London: Macmillan, 1987), pp. 191–98.

—— 'Analytics of Development: Dualism', in H.B. Chenery and T.N. Srinivasan (eds), *Handbook of Development Economics*, vol. 1 (Amsterdam: North Holland, 1988), pp. 73–92.

—— 'Arthur Lewis' Contribution to Development Thinking and Policy', *Manchester School,* 72: 6, (2004), pp. 712–23.

G. Ranis and J.C.H. Fei, 'A Theory of Economic Development', *The American Economic Review*, 51: 4, (1961), pp. 533–65.

M. Ravallion, 'Can High Inequality Developing Countries Escape Absolute Poverty?', *Economics Letters*, 56, (1997), pp. 51–57.

—— 'A Poverty-Inequality Trade-off?', (World Bank Policy Research Working Paper No. 3579, Washington DC: World Bank, 2005).

—— 'Inequality is Bad for the Poor', in S.P. Jenkins and J. Micklewright (eds), *Inequality and Poverty Re-examined* (Oxford: Oxford University Press, 2007), pp. 37–61.

—— 'The Developing World's Bulging (but Vulnerable) Middle Class', *World Development*, 38: 4, (2010a), pp. 445–54.

—— 'Do Poorer Countries Have Less Capacity for Redistribution?', *Journal of Globalization and Development*, 1: 2, (2010b), pp. 1–29.

—— 'On Multidimensional Indices of Poverty', *Journal of Economic Inequality*, 9, (2011), pp. 235–48.

—— 'Why Don't We See Poverty Convergence?', *American Economic Review*, 102: 1, (2012), pp. 504–23.

—— 'The Idea of Antipoverty Policy', (NBER Working Paper n. 19210, 2013).

M. Ravallion and S. Chen, 'China's (Uneven) Progress Against Poverty', *Journal of Development Economics*, 82: 1, (2007), pp. 1–42.

—— 'Weakly Relative Poverty', *Review of Economics and Statistics*, 93: 4, (2011), pp. 1251–61.

D. Ricardo, *The Principles of Political Economy and Taxation* (New York: Dutton, [1821] 1973).

J. Robinson, 'Disguised Unemployment', *The Economic Journal*, 46: 182, (1936), pp. 225–37.

—— *Aspects of Development and Underdevelopment* (Cambridge: Cambridge University Press, 1979).

W.C. Robinson, 'Types of Disguised Rural Unemployment and Some Policy Implications', *Oxford Economic Papers*, 21: 3, (1969), pp. 373–86.

O. Rodríguez, 'Sobre la concepción del sistema centro-periferia', *Revista de la CEPAL*, 1st semester, (1977), pp. 203–48.

—— *El estructuralismo latinoamericano* (Mexico City: Siglo XXI and CEPAL, 2006).

C. Rodríguez Fuentes, 'El papel del sistema bancario en el desarrollo regional. ¿Reparto o creación de crédito?', *Estudios Regionales*, 47, (1997), pp. 117–39.

P.N. Rosenstein-Rodan, 'Problems of Industrialization of Eastern and South-Eastern Europe' *The Economic Journal*, 53: 210/211, Jun–Sept, (1943), pp. 202–11; also in A.N. Agarwala and S.P. Singh (eds), *The Economics of Underdevelopment* (Oxford: Oxford University Press, [1943] 1958), pp. 245–55.

—— 'Disguised Unemployment and Underemployment in Agriculture' in *Monthly Bulletin of Agricultural Economics and Statistics*, 6: 7-8, (1956), pp. 1–7.

—— 'Notes on the Theory of the "Big Push"', in H.S. Ellis and H.C. Wallich (eds), *Economic Development for Latin America, Proceedings of a Conference held by the International Economic Association* (London: MacMillan, 1961), pp. 57–73.

—— 'Natura Facit Saltum: Analysis of the Disequilibrium Growth Process', in G.M. Meier and D. Dudley (eds), *Pioneers in Development* (New York–Oxford: Oxford University Press, 1984), pp. 207–21.

W.W. Rostow, 'The Terms of Trade in Theory and Practice', *Economic History Review*, 1, (1950), pp. 1–20.

—— *The Process of Economic Growth* (New York: Norton & Company, 1952).

—— 'The Take-off into Sustained Growth', *Economic Journal*, 66: 261 (1956), pp. 25–48.

—— 'The Stages of Economic Growth', *The Economic History Review*, NS 12: 1, (1959), pp. 1–16.

—— *The Stages of Economic Growth: A Non-Communist Manifesto* (Cambridge: Cambridge University Press, 1961).

—— (ed.), *The Economics of Take-off into Sustained Growth: Proceedings of a Conference held by the International Economic Association* (London: St Martin's Press, 1963).

W.G. Runciman, *Relative Deprivation and Social Justice* (London: Routledge and Kegan Paul, 1966).

A. Saad-Filho, 'The Rise and Decline of Latin American Structuralism and Dependency Theory', in K.S. Jomo and E. Reinert (eds), *The Origins of Development Economics* (London: Zed Books, 2005), pp. 128–45.

J.D. Sachs, *Investing in Development: A Practical Plan to Achieve the Millennium Development Goals* (New York: United Nations, 2005).

—— *The End of Poverty* (London: Penguin Books, 2006).

P. Salama, 'Deudas y dependencia financiera del Estado en América Latina', in A. Girón (ed.), *Confrontaciones Monetaria* (Buenos Aires: CLACSO, 2006), pp. 101–24.

P.A. Samuelson, 'International Trade and the Equalisation of Factor Prices', *The Economic Journal*, 58: 230, (1948), pp. 163–84.

—— 'International Factor-Price Equalisation Once Again', *The Economic Journal*, 59: 234 (1949), pp. 181–97.

—— 'Illogic of Neo-Marxian Doctrine of Unequal Exchange', in D.A. Belsley, E.J. Kane, P.A. Samuelson (eds), *Inflation, Trade and Taxes* (Columbus: Ohio State University Press, 1976), pp 96–107.

J. Saxe-Fernández, J. Petras, H. Veltmeyer and O. Nuñez, *Globalización, Imperialismo y Clase Social* (Buenos Aires: Lumen Humanitas, 2001).

F. Schneider (ed.), *Handbook on the Shadow Economy* (Cheltenham: Edward Elgar, 2011).

F. Schneider and D.H. Enste, *The Shadow Economy. An International Survey* (Cambridge: Cambridge University Press, 2004).

T.W. Schultz, 'Investment in Man: An Economist's View', *The Social Service Review*, 32: 2, (1959), pp. 109–17.

—— 'Capital Formation by Education', *Journal of Political Economy*, 68: 6, (1960), pp. 571–83.

—— 'Investment in Human Capital', *The American Economic Review*, 51: 1, (1961), pp. 1–17.

—— *Transforming Traditional Agriculture* (New Haven: Yale University Press, 1964).

J.A. Schumpeter, *The Theory of Economic Development* (Cambridge, MA: Harvard University Press, 1934).

T. Scitovsky, *Welfare and Competition. The Economics of a Fully Employed Economy* (Chicago: R.D. Irving, 1951).

—— 'Two concepts of external economies', *Journal of Political Economy*, 62: 2 (1954), pp. 143–51.

—— 'Growth – Balanced or Unbalanced?', in T. Scitovsky, *Papers on Welfare and Growth* (London: Allen and Unwin Ltd. [1959] 1964), pp. 97–110.

—— 'Balanced Growth', in J. Eatwell, M. Milgate and P. Newman (eds), *The New Palgrave – Economic Development* (New York–London: W.W. Norton, 1987), pp. 55–58.

D. Seers (ed.), *Dependency Analysis: A Critical Reassessment* (UK: Short Run Press, 1981).

A.K. Sen, 'Poor, Relatively Speaking', *Oxford Economic Papers*, 35: 2, (1983), pp. 153–69.

—— *Commodities and Capabilities* (Amsterdam, North Holland, 1985a).

—— 'Well-being, Agency and Freedom. The Dewey Lectures 1984', *Journal of Philosophy,* 82: 4, (1985b), pp. 169–221.

—— *Inequality Re-examined* (Oxford: Clarendon Press, 1992).

—— *Development as freedom* (New York: A.K. Knopf, 1999).

F. Serrano, 'Long Period Effective Demand and the Sraffian Supermultiplier', *Contributions to Political Economy*, 14, (1995), pp. 67–90.

H.W. Singer 'Economic Progress in Underdeveloped Countries', *Social Research*, 16, 1949, pp. 1–11.

—— 'The Distribution of Gains between Investing and Borrowing Countries', *American Economic Review*, 40: 2, (1950), pp. 473–85.

—— 'Editorial: The Golden Age of the Keynesian Consensus – The Pendulum Swings Back', *World Development*, 25: 3, (1997), pp. 293–95.

—— 'The Terms of Trade Fifty Years Later. Convergence and Divergence', *Zagreb International Review of Economics and Business*, 1: 1 (1998), at http://gesi.soz-phil.uni-leipzig.de/fileadmin/media/Global_Studies/Download_Content_EMGS/Preparatory_readings/Singer_-_The_Terms_of_Trade_Fifty_Years_Later_-_Convergence_and_Divergence. pdf, [accessed 15 October 2014].

A. Smith, *The Wealth of Nations,* A. Skinner (ed.), (Harmondsworth: Penguin [1776] 1974).

M. Smith, 'Demand-Led Growth Theory: An Historical Approach', *Review of Political Economy*, 24: 4, (2012), pp. 543–73.

R.M. Solow, 'A Contribution to the Theory of Economic Growth', *Quarterly Journal of Economics*, 70: 1, (1956), pp. 65–94.

H. Sonnenschein, 'Market Excess Demand Functions', *Econometrica*, 40: 3, (1972), pp. 549–63.

L. Spaventa, 'Dualism in Economic Growth', *Banca Nazionale del Lavoro Quarterly Review*, 12: 51, (1959), pp. 386–434.

P. Sraffa, *Production of Commodities by Means of Commodities: Prelude to a Critique of Economic Theory* (Cambridge: Cambridge University Press, 1960).

T.N. Srinivasan, 'Introduction to Part I', in H.B. Chenery and T.N. Srinivasan (eds), *Handbook of Development Economics*, vol. I (Amsterdam: North Holland, 1988), pp. 3–8.

J. Stanovnik, *I paesi in via di sviluppo nell'economia mondiale* (Italian trans., Milano: Feltrinelli, 1965).

T. Starkey, *A Dialogue between Pole and Lupset*, (London: Royal Historical Society, University College, [1529-32] 1989).

J. Stiglitz, Comment on 'Toward a Counter-Revolution in Development Theory', in P. Krugman, *Proceedings of the World Bank Annual Conference on Development Economics* (Washington DC: World Bank, 1993), pp. 39–50.

—— *Globalization and its Discontents* (New York–London: Norton, 2002).

J. Stiglitz, A. Sen and J.P. Fitoussi, Report by the Commission on the Measurement of Economic Performance and Social Progress, (2009) in http://www.stiglitz-sen-fitoussi.fr/en/index.htm [accessed 12 September 2014].

J. Steuart, *Principles of Political Oeconomy* (Chicago: Chicago University Press, [1767] 1966).

P. Streeten, 'Unbalanced Growth', *Oxford Economic Papers. New Series*, 11: 2, (1959), pp.167–90.

—— 'Unbalanced Growth: A Reply', *Oxford Economic Papers*, 15: 1, (1963), pp. 66–73.

—— 'Disguised Unemployment and Underemployment', in G.R. Feiwel (ed.), *Joan Robinson and Modern Economic Theory* (New York: New York University Press, 1985), pp. 723–26.

O. Sunkel, 'Um esquema geral para a analise da inflação', *Econômica brasileira*, 3, (1957), pp. 361–77.

—— 'Inflation in Chile: An Unorthodox Approach', *International Economic Papers*, 10, ([1958] 1960), pp. 107–31.

—— 'El fracaso de las politicas de estabilización en el contexto del proceso de desarrollo latinoamericano', *El Trimestre Economico*, 30, (1963), pp. 620–40.

—— (with the assistance of P. Paz), *El subdesarrollo latinoamericano y la teoría del desarrollo*, Mexico City: Siglo Ventiuno, 1970).

—— 'Big Business and "Dependencia": A Latin American View', *Foreign Affairs*, 50: 3, (1972), pp. 517–31.

—— 'Transnational Capital and National Disintegration in Latin America', *Social and Economic Studies*, 22: 1, (1973), pp. 132–71.

—— 'Introduction', in O. Sunkel (ed), *Development from within: toward a Neostructuralist Approach for Latin America* (Boulder (Co.): L. Rienner, 1993).

L. Taylor, *Macro Models for Developing Countries* (New York: McGraw–Hill, 1979).

—— *Structuralist Macroeconomics: Applicable Models for the Third World* (New York: Basic Books, 1983).

—— *Income Distribution, Inflation and Growth: Lectures on Structuralist Macroeconomic Theory* (Cambridge MA: MIT Press, 1991).

—— *Reconstructing Macroeconomics. Structuralist Proposals and Critiques of the Mainstream* (Cambridge, MA–London: Harvard University Press, 2004).

L. Taylor and P. Arida, 'Long-run Income Distribution and Growth', in H.B. Chenery and T.N. Srinivasan (eds), *Handbook of Development Economics*, vol. I (Amsterdam: North Holland, 1988), pp. 161–94.

A.P. Thirlwall, *The Nature of Economic Growth* (Cheltenham: Edward Elgar, 2002).

E. Thorbecke, 'The Evolution of the Development Doctrine, 1950–2005', (UNU – WIDER, Research Paper No.155, 2006).

R.L. Tignor, *W. Arthur Lewis and the Birth of Development Economics*, Princeton, NJ: Princeton University Press, 2006).

G. Tily, *Keynes's General Theory, the Rate of Interest and 'Keynesian' Economics* (Basingstoke, Hampshire and New York: Palgrave Macmillan, 2007).

J. Tinbergen, 'Optimanl Development Policies: Lessons from Experience', *World Economy*, 7: 1, (1984), pp. 112–17.

M.P. Todaro, 'A Model of Labor Migration and Urban Unemployment in Less Developed Countries', *The American Economic Review*, 59: 1, (1969), pp. 138–48.

S. Topik, 'Dependency Revisited: Saving the Baby from the Bathwater', *Latin American Perspectives*, 25: 6, (1998), pp. 95–99.

J. Toye, *Dilemmas of Development: Reflections on the Counter-revolution in Development Theory and Policy* (Oxford: Basil & Blackwell, 1987).

—— 'The Significance of Keynes for Development Economics', in K.S. Jomo (ed.), *The Pioneers of Development Economics. Great Economists on Development* (London: Zed Books, 2005), pp. 123–41.

UNDP, *Human Development Report. Sustainability and Equity: A Better Future for All* (New York: United Nations, 2011).

United Nations, 'Growth, Disequilibrium and Disparities: Interpretation of the Process of Economic Development', in *Economic Survey of Latin America 1949* (New York: United Nations, [1950] 1951), E/CN.12/164, pp. 1–85.

—— *Theoretical and Practical Problems of Economic Growth*, Economic Commission for Latin America, fourth session (Mexico, 1951), D.F. E/CN.12/221.

—— *International Co-operation in a Latin American Development Policy* (New York: United Nations, 1954), E/CN.12/359.

—— 'Inflation in Chile, 1940 to 1953', in *World Economic Report 1953–54* (New York: United Nations, Department of Economic and Social Affairs, 1955), pp. 78–88.

—— *Analyses and Projections of Economic Development – II. The Economic Development of Brazil* (New York: United Nations, 1956), E/CN.12/364.

—— *External Disequilibrium in the Economic Development of Latin America: The Case of Mexico*, 2 vols, Economic Commission for Latin America, seventh session (La Paz, 1957), E/CN.12/428.

—— *Changing Production Patters with Social Equity: The Prime Task of Latin American and Caribbean Development in the 1990s* (Santiago, 1990), UN. E.90.II.G.6.

M.G. Vázquez Olivera, 'Las fuentes teórico-metodológicas de la construcción del concepto de dependencia'. *Latinoamérica*, 38: 1, (2004), pp. 9–44.

A. Velasco, 'Dependency Theory a Generation Later', *Foreign Policy*, 133, (2002), pp. 44–45.

M. Vernengo, 'Technology, Finance and Dependency: Latin American Radical Political Economy in Retrospect', *Review of Radical Political Economics*, 38: 4, (2006), pp. 551–68.

J. Viner, 'The Economics of Development', in A.N. Agarwala and S.P.Singh (eds), *The Economics of Underdevelopment* (Oxford: Oxford University Press, [1953] 1958), pp. 9–31.

S. Voitchovsky, 'Does the Profile of Income Inequality Matter for Economic Growth? Between the Effects of Inequality on Different Parts of Income Distribution', *Journal of Economic Growth*, 10: 1, (2005), pp. 273–96.

I.M. Wallerstein, *World-Systems Analysis: An Introduction*, (Durham NC: Duke University Press, 2004).

A.N. Whitehead, *Process and Reality* (New York: Macmillan, 1930).

R. Wilkinson and K. Pickett, *The Spirit Level, Why Greater Equality makes Societies Stronger* (New York: Bloomsbury Press, 2009).

J.G. Williamson, 'Migration and Urbanization', in H.B. Chenery and T.N. Srinivasan (eds), *Handbook of Development Economics*, vol. 1 (Amsterdam: North Holland, 1988), pp. 425–65.

World Bank, World Development Report. Mind, Society, and Behavior, 2015, at http://www.worldbank.org/en/publication/wdr2015 [accessed 5 March 2015].

A.A. Young, 'Increasing Returns and Economic Progress', *The Economic Journal*, 38: 152, (1928), pp. 527–42.

Index

For Product Safety Concerns and Information please contact our EU
representative GPSR@taylorandfrancis.com
Taylor & Francis Verlag GmbH, Kaufingerstraße 24, 80331 München, Germany